KU-504-807

Cross-Cultural Business Behavior

To Hopi:
This is *our* book. As with the previous editions, I couldn't have done it without you.

Richard R. Gesteland

Cross-Cultural Business Behavior

Marketing, Negotiating, Sourcing
and Managing Across Cultures

Copenhagen Business School Press

UNIVERSITY OF
LIBRARY
SERVICES
CENTRAL ENGLAND

Cross-Cultural Business Behavior
Marketing, Negotiating, Sourcing
and Managing Across Cultures

© *Copenhagen Business School Press*, 2002
Cover design by Jur-sats
Set in Plantin and printed by Narayana Press, Gylling

Printed in Denmark
3. edition 2002

ISBN 87-630-0093-8

Distribution:

Scandinavia
Djoef/DBK, Siljangade 2-8, P.O. Box 1731
DK-2300 Copenhagen S, Denmark
phone: +45 3269 7788, fax: +45 3269 7789

North America
Copenhagen Business School Press
Books International Inc.
P.O. Box 605
Hendon, VA 20172-0605, USA
phone: +1 703 661 1500, fax: +1 703 661 1501

Rest of the World
Marston Book Services, P.O. Box 269
Abingdon, Oxfordshire, OX14 4YN, UK
phone: +44 (0) 1235 465500, fax: +44 (0) 1235 465555
E-mail Direct Customers: direct.order@marston.co.uk
E-mail Booksellers: trade.order@marston.co.uk

BIRMINGHAM CITY
UNIVERSITY
DISCARDED

Book no. 324599
Subject no. 658.049 Ges

All rights reserved.
No part of this publication may be reproduced or used in any form or by any means – graphic, electronic or mechanical including photocopying, recording, taping or information storage or retrieval systems – without permission in writing from Copenhagen Business School Press at www.cbspress.dk

Table of Contents

6

Foreword to the Third Edition

My sincere thanks to the alert readers who have suggested corrections and improvements to the second edition. One of the most helpful was Janusz Jacewicz of the Gdansk Foundation for Management Development in Poland.

Since 1999 many readers have requested the addition of examples, cases and negotiator profiles. So when the Copenhagen Business School Press kindly offered me the opportunity of a new edition, it became possible to tighten the writing, update the existing Negotiator Profiles and the Resource List, and add new cases as well as new Profiles for Myanmar, Slovakia, Ireland, and Sweden. A light-hearted comparison of the Swedish and Danish cultures rounds out the added material.

Whenever I am working on European projects these days, important insights gained from my talented colleagues in the Sears Florence Office keep coming back to me. Thank you Anna, Anita, Renzo, Adriana, Franco and all the rest of that marvelous group who contributed so much to this book.

When Southeast Asia is on the front burner, it's those hard-working colleagues of the Sears Singapore Office I'm indebted to.

And when I'm dealing with South Asian issues, it's K.B. Agrawal, a stalwart of the Sears New Delhi Office for many years, who since then has become a successful entrepreneur in a very difficult business environment. Thank you, K.B.!

Dear reader, the new millennium brings new challenges for both practitioners and students of international business. I sincerely hope this third edition of Cross-Cultural Business Behavior will help you meet those challenges.

RRG
Oregon, Wisconsin
July 2002

8

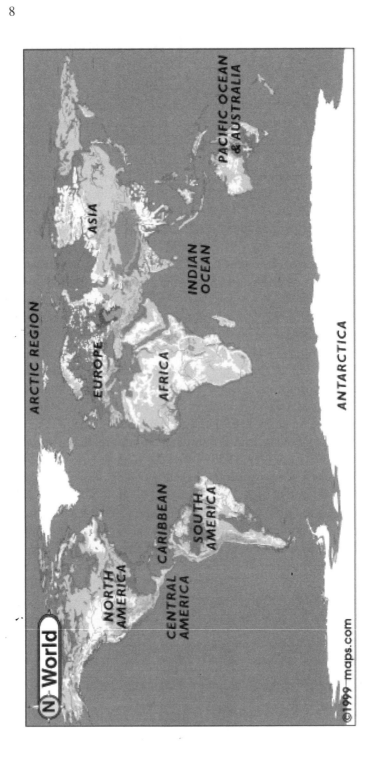

Introduction

This is intended as a practical guide for the men and women in the front lines of world trade, those who face every day the frustrating differences in global business customs and practices.

Cultural differences frustrate us because they are confusing and unpredictable. This book aims to reduce that confusion and introduce some predictabilty by classifying international business customs and pratices into logical patterns.

Scientists today believe the human brain is programmed to think in terms of patterns. Certainly I for one seem to learn and remember complex information more readily when it is organized according to some logical system.

With this in mind, over the last decade ot so I have worked out a simple way to catagorize those cultural variables which cause international deal makers the most problems. Thousands of managers and business school students who have attended our Global Management seminars tell me our "Patterns" approach makes sense. Time after time seminar participants come up after a presentation to say, "Now I understand what went wrong at that negotiating session last year!"

The Sources

The material for this book comes from three decades of observing myself and others spoiling promising deals because we were ignorant of how business is done. The cases are based on incidents drawn from the author's 35 years in marketing, sourcing, managing and leading seminars around the world. Chapter 10 is a partial exception in that a number of examples were drawn from conversations with business travelers in international airport lounges and hotel bars.

My 26 years as an expatriate manager in Germany, Austria, Italy, Brazil, India and Singapore was an especially rich source of material. I owe an enduring debt to colleagues in the Florence, Frankfurt, Vienna, Sao Paulo, New Delhi and Singapore offices I managed for their personal support over many years as well as for invaluable insights too numerous to mention.

For one to whom learning languages has never come easily, seeing coworkers in Florence and Frankfurt switch instantly and fluently from Italian, German or French into Spanish, English or whatever was a truly humbling experience. It was the same story in Singapore where some colleagues spoke English, Mandarin and Malay along with Cantonese, Hokkien and Teochew.

This linguistic virtuosity was inspiring because I believe bilingual or multilingual ability is an essential springboard to intercultural competence. And intercultural competence is or should be the goal of every effective expatriate manager and international negotiator.

The sources for the Negotiator Profiles which make up Part Two were the more than one thousand business negotiations I have conducted in some 55 different countries. Organized loosely according to the *Patterns* expounded in Part One, the Profiles are intended as thumbnail sketches of the negotiating behavior a visitor can expect to encounter in the markets covered.

The writings of anthropologist, scholars of intercultural communication and researchers provided insights over the years which helped me formulate the Patterns. Among the works I have found especially useful are those by Edward T. and Mildred Reed Hall, Geert Hofstede, Robert Moran and William Gudykunst. Obviously none of these experts is responsible for the shortcomings which will inevitably show up in this book.

Three academic institutions have been instrumental in sharpening the focus of this book:

– *The Export Institute of Singapore*: Site of the 'Going Global!' seminars and other programs we have conducted since 1994. The participants in these programs – both Singaporean and expatriate managers – have constantly stimulated my thinking with their questions, comments, and criticisms. My special thanks to Executive Director Ng Wei Min and his outstanding staff.

– The *Niels Brock Copenhagen Business College:* Where I had the privilege of lecturing several times a year to a wide range of bright young Danish students preparing for careers in international business. Mogens Gruelund, Elsebeth Riis-Petersen, Hanne Baumann, Flemming Steen, Jens Graff, John Knudsen, Ulla Regli and so many other Danish colleagues have provided ongoing support and creative ideas.

– The *Management Institute of the University of Wisconsin*: Organizer of the popular three day "Negotiating in the Pacific Rim" workshops attended by both novices and veterans of international marketing and sourcing from all over the United States. It has been a pleasure working with Professor Linda Gorchels and my genial colleague George Seyk in Madison since 1994.

Two truly great Danes played key roles in getting this book out of my head and onto paper. Jens Graff – friend, colleague, marketing professor and author – has had the patience to listen to my theories of international business behavior for years.

In 1995 Jens introduced me to Lauge Stetting, the thoughtful savant in charge of the Copenhagen Business School Press. For me Lauge´s most outstanding virtue is his patience: an important attribute when working with dilatory writers such as myself.

Still and all, the primary impetus for writing the book came from just one person: My wife Hopi, who has shared the joys and frustrations of international living with me for 36 very eventful years.

One major source remains to be acknowledged. Namely, the multiple culture shocks and cultural adjustments which Hopi and our six children – Richard, Lester, Reed, Thor, Kamala and Clio – helped me weather.

Moving from one country to another almost inevitably causes culture shock, and the severity of the shock is directly proportional to the cultural distance between the two counties concerned. In our case for example, moving from Europe to India was an especially severe culture shock.

Repeated shocks and adjustments tend to make us sensitive to the cultural differences which divide cultures. But we have found that those repeated adjustments also made us aware of the myriad similarities that bind us all together.

入鄉隨俗

Ru xiang sui su

Part One

1. Patterns of Cross-Cultural Business Behavior

Here are a few of the questions you will find answered in the pages that follow:

- Have email, video-conferencing and Web-conferencing reduced the need for international business travel and face-to-face meetings?
- What cultural gaffe caused top executives of a major Saudi Arabian company to break off promising negotiations with a California firm?
- Where did a Danish export manager go wrong when he lost a lucrative contract by inadvertently insulting a Mexican customer?
- Why did a North American importer end up with 96,000 cotton shirts he couldn't sell because they were improperly labeled?
- What did a world-famous European brewery do to cause their Vietnamese partners to abruptly halt negotiations on a joint venture project?
- Which all-important rules of protocol did a Canadian executive violate when he deeply offended a potential Egyptian customer?
- How do successful global marketing companies such as McDonald's overcome troublesome cross-cultural variations in taste preferences?
- Do business cultures change?

Two Iron Rules of International Business

Why is a thorough knowledge of international business customs and practices especially important for people involved in international sales and marketing? It's because of Iron Rule # 1:

- In International Business, the Seller Adapts to the Buyer.

What if you are the buyer in an international transaction? Well, then cultural differences are important only if you want to negotiate the best deal!

But suppose it is not a buy-sell transaction. Suppose you are traveling abroad to negotiate a joint-venture agreement, a merger or acquisition, or a strategic alliance? Now who is expected to do the adapting? That's where Iron Rule # 2 comes into play:

– In International Business, the Visitor Is Expected to Observe Local Customs.

The Chinese proverb *Ru xiang, sui su* says the same thing with fewer words: "Enter village, follow customs." Is this just another way of saying, When in Rome, do as the Romans do?" No. I disagree with that old saw. My advice is not to mimic or copy local behavior. Instead, just be yourself. But of course, 'being yourself' includes being aware of local sensitivities and honoring local customs, habits and traditions. This book will have served its purpose if it helps readers follow the two Iron Rules.

Let's now preview the Patterns of Cross-Cultural Business Behavior.

– Deal-Focus vs. Relationship-Focus

This is the 'Great Divide' between business cultures all over the world. Deal-focused (DF) people are fundamentally task-oriented, while relationship-focused folks are more people-oriented. Of course, relationships are important in business everywhere. It's a question of degree. But deal-focused people need to know for example that in RF cultures you need to develop rapport *before* talking business.

Conflicts often arise when deal-focused marketers who are unaware of this fundamental difference try to do business with prospects in relationship-focused markets. Many RF people find DF types pushy, aggressive and offensively blunt. In return, DF types sometimes consider their RF counterparts dilatory, vague and inscrutable.

– Informal vs. Formal Cultures

Problems also occur when informal business travelers from relatively egalitarian cultures cross paths with more formal counterparts from hierarchical societies. Breezy informality offends high-status people from hierarchical cultures, just as the status-consciousness of formal people may offend the egalitarian sensibilities of informal folks.

– Rigid-Time vs. Fluid-Time Cultures

One group of the world's societies worships the clock. The other group is more relaxed about time and scheduling, focusing instead on the people around them. Conflicts arise because some rigid-time visitors regard their fluid-time brothers and sisters as lazy, undisciplined and rude, while the latter often regard the former as arrogant martinets enslaved by clocks and arbitrary deadlines.

– Emotionally Expressive vs. Emotionally Reserved Cultures

Emotionally expressive people communicate differently from their more reserved counterparts. This is true whether they are communicating verbally, paraverbally or nonverbally. The resulting confusion can spoil our best efforts to market, sell, source, negotiate or manage people across cultures. The expressive/reserved divide creates a major communication gap, one largely unexplored in most books on international business.

Let us now move to Chapter Two, where we take a look at the "Great Divide."

2. The "Great Divide" Between Business Cultures:

Relationship-Focus vs. Deal-Focus

Whether marketing, sourcing, or negotiating an international alliance, the differences between relationship-focused (RF) and deal-focused (DF) business behavior impact our success throughout the global marketplace.

The vast majority of the world's markets are relationship-oriented: the Arab world and most of Africa, Latin America, and the Asia/Pacific region. These are markets where people avoid doing business with strangers. They get things done through intricate networks of personal contacts.

RF people prefer to deal with family, friends and persons or groups well known to them – people who can be trusted. They are uncomfortable doing business with strangers, especially foreigners. Because of this key cultural value, relationship-oriented firms typically want to know their prospective business partners well before talking business with them.

In contrast, the deal-focused approach is common in only a small part of the world. Strongly DF cultures are found primarily in northern Europe, North America, Australia and New Zealand, where people are relatively open to doing business with strangers

This Great Divide between the world's cultures affects the way we conduct business from the beginning to the end of any commercial relationship. For starters, the way we make the first approach to potential buyers or partners depends upon whether they are in DF or RF cultures.

Making Initial Contact

Because DF people are relatively open to dealing with strangers, export marketers can normally make direct contact with potential distributors and customers in these markets. Let's take the United

States as an example. Perhaps because they are raised in a highly mobile immigrant society, most Americans are open to discussing business possibilities with people they don't know.

Fig. 2.1

DEAL-FOCUSED CULTURES:
Nordic and Germanic Europe
Great Britain
North America
Australia and New Zealand

MODERATELY DEAL-FOCUSED:
South Africa
Latin Europe
Central and Eastern Europe
Chile, southern Brazil, northern Mexico
Hong Kong, Singapore

RELATIONSHIP-FOCUSED:
The Arab World
Most of Africa, Latin America and Asia

The success of business-to-business telemarketing illustrates this openness. Each year American companies buy billions of dollars worth of goods and services from total strangers. No wonder the USA is called the home of the cold call!

In contrast, telemarketing doesn't work so well in RF markets. For example, "telemarketing" in Japan refers to phoning *existing* customers or clients, something DF companies would call customer relations. Ringing up a stranger in Japan would be considered a strange act indeed.

Of course even in America, the larger and more complex the transaction, the more the buyer wants to know about the seller. But my point is, in DF cultures the marketer is often able to make initial contact with a prospective buyer without any previous relationship or connection. An introduction or referral is helpful but not essential.

This is the first of the several important differences between DF and RF business behavior.

Fig. 2.2 Making Initial Contact: DF vs RF Cultures

Direct contact	DF		RF	*Indirect contact*
	USA		Japan	

In sum, making business appointments in the U.S. is relatively quick and easy if you have the right product or service to offer, and if your market research is accurate, because America is the quintessential DF market. But cold calls rarely work in strongly RF business cultures such as Japan.

Often the best way to contact RF business partners is at an international trade show. That is where buyers look for suppliers, exporters seek importers, and investors search for joint-venture partners. Business behavior at such exhibitions tends to be deal-focused because most of the attendees are there for the express purpose of making business contacts.

Another good way to meet potential partners in RF markets is to join an official trade mission. All over the world today governments and trade associations are promoting their country's exports by organizing guided visits to new markets. The organizer of the trade mission sets up appointments with interested parties and provides formal introductions to them. These official introductions help break the ice, smoothing the way to a business relationship.

But suppose no relevant trade show is scheduled for the next few months, nor is an official trade mission planned in the near future. There is another proven way for us to make initial contact with distributor candidates in RF markets: we can arrange to be introduced by a trusted intermediary.

The Indirect Approach

Remember, RF firms do not do business with strangers. A good way to approach someone who doesn't yet know you is to arrange for the right person or organization to introduce you. A third-party introduction bridges the relationship gap between you and the person or company you want to talk to.

The ideal introducer is a high-status person or organization known to both parties. So if you happen to be good friends with a respected retired statesman who just happens to be well acquainted with one of your importer candidates, that's wonderful. Alas, such cases of serendipity are rare in the real world of international trade.

A good second best might be the commercial section of your country's embassy in the target market. Embassy officials are accorded high status in relationship-oriented cultures, and of course it is part of their job to promote exports.

Chambers of commerce and trade associations are other potential introducers. And what about your bank? If you want to do business in Korea and your bank lacks strong representation there, you'd better look for an international bank which does.

Or perhaps one of your golf buddies works for a company that has an active office in Shanghai, Seoul, Tokyo, or Riyadh. Maybe they can put in a good word for you. Freight forwarders, ocean and airfreight carriers and international law and accounting firms are other good sources of effective introductions.

Recognizing the importance of third-party introductions in their RF culture, the Japanese External Trade Organization (JETRO) is also willing to provide that service to reputable foreign companies.

In fact, having a proper introduction in Japan is so critical that specialized consulting firms have come into existence there whose main function is to introduce *gaijin* to Japanese companies. Of course, using a consultant is likely to cost you more than other ways of obtaining an introduction.

Pulling Guanxi

In the RF world, people get things done through relatives, friends, contacts and connections – in other words, though relationships. It's who you know that counts. The Chinese call these networks of relationships *guanxi,* a word well-known throughout East and Southeast Asia.

Of course, knowing the right people, having the right contacts, helps get things done in deal-focused cultures as well. Again, it's a matter of degree. Even in an extremely DF market such as the U.S., people use 'pull' or 'clout' to get things done. Knowing the right person can be very helpful.

But although it is a difference of degree, it's still a key difference. In strongly RF markets, initiating a business relationship can *only* be done if you know the right people, or if you can arrange to be introduced to them. Just try setting up a joint venture in China for example without having *guanxi* or "pulling guanxi" – using someone else's personal connections.

The bottom line is this. In relationship-oriented markets, plan to approach your potential customer or partner indirectly, whether via a trade show, a trade mission or a third-party introduction. The indirect approach is critical throughout the RF part of the world.

A case that took place in Singapore during the 1990s illustrates how essential contacts and introductions are to success in relationship-oriented markets, where people do not do business with strangers.

Case 2.1: "Exporting to Taiwan: *Guanxi* in Action"

You are the new marketing manager of Glorious Paints, a Singapore manufacturer of marine paints. It is a fast-growing company headed by three young, Western-educated directors.

Last year the marketing director led Glorious Paints to its first overseas sale, selling a large quantity of paint to Australia and New Zealand. Director Tan achieved this success by first sending information to potential distributors along with cover letters requesting appointments, then meeting with each interested candidate firm at their offices. After that Mr. Tan negotiated a distribution agreement with the company he decided was best qualified to handle that market area. This entire process took about four months and sales volume is already exceeding expectations.

Following that success you were hired to expand exports to other Pacific Rim markets. The director called you into his office to discuss market research showing that Taiwan is a very promising market with high demand and little local competition. So you were instructed to set up distribution there using the approach that had worked in Australia/New Zealand.

By searching a number of data bases you came up with the names and contact information for a number of Taiwanese importers, agents, representatives and wholesalers involved in the paint business. Next you sent off brochures and product information to these prospects, enclosing a cover letter requesting an appointment to discuss possible representation. You expected perhaps five or six of the companies to reply, as happened in Australia and New Zealand.

To everyone's surprise, six weeks went by without a single response. At a strategy session Mr. Tan pointed out that many Taiwanese are not comfortable corresponding in English, so you fired off a second mailing, this time in Chinese. But after another two months not a single prospective distributor has answered your letters.

Mr. Tan is upset with your lack of progress in this attractive market. He has called an urgent meeting for this afternoon and expects you to come up with a solution. As you sit stirring your tea the questions revolve in your head like the spoon in the teacup. "What have I done wrong? This strategy worked fine with the Aussies. Why not with the Taiwanese? What do we do now?"

But what if You're the Buyer?

Because exporters are responsible for actively seeking overseas customers, we might assume that contacts and connections are less important for international buyers. But buyers engaged in global sourcing quickly learn the limits to this assumption.

First of all, many international buyers proactively seek suppliers. Secondly, exporters need to have a certain level of trust in their prospective buyers. Even letters of credit are not absolute guarantees of payment, and insisting on cash in advance severely restricts one's market potential. For those reasons, in RF resource markets contacts and introductions can be as much a necessity for overseas purchasers as for sellers.

In fact, it was as an international buyer that the Great Divide between deal-focused and relationship-focused business cultures first became apparent to me. After a stint with a Chicago export management company I was recruited by Sears Roebuck and spent more than a quarter-century managing international buying offices around the world and coordinating the company's global sourcing activities. A large part of my buying career involved developing competitive sources of supply in Latin America, central and eastern Europe, the Asia/ Pacific region, the Middle East and Africa.

Early on I found out that in the countries I later came to call relationship-focused it was smart to get introduced to potential suppliers before visiting them. And it was also smart to spend time building a relationship with management before touring the factory and asking all the questions a buyer needs to ask a prospective vendor.

That procedure was quite different from the procedure we followed in the countries I later referred to as deal-focused. In those resource markets we could usually evaluate several factories a day. We would dash in, skip the coffee to save time, check out the equipment, get a feeling for how production was flowing, ask a series of rapid-fire questions, and then rush out to the next factory.

But I soon found that this "wham-bam, thank you ma'am" approach did not work in relationship-oriented markets. There our hurry-up, task-oriented approach failed to elicit the information we needed. Instead we evaluated only one or two manufacturers a day. We sipped a leisurely tea, coffee, or a cold drink with management. In the Balkans that often meant tipping back a slivovitz or two at 6:30 in the morning. We took our time, showed our interest, demonstrated our commitment to learning as much as we could about their company. That extra time always paid off in terms of better and more reliable information.

Later, when I again became involved in overseas sales and marketing, the significance of the Great Divide became even more obvious to me. But before we go any further, here's a good example of how contacts, or connections, or guanxi, can be as important for international buyers as for international marketers.

Dealing in Dhaka

Around 1989 we decided it was time to open a sourcing and quality control office in Bangladesh, a rapidly growing exporter of garments. As regional director for South and Southeast Asia based in Singapore, this task fell to me.

The first step was to arrange for legal registration. This is complicated because setting up an office in Bangladesh requires the approval of several different ministries and government agencies.

To handle the registration we talked to several local law, accounting and consulting firms. They all said the approval process would take up to a year and quoted varying fees of up $10,000, hinting at "special expenses", meaning bribes for the responsible officials. Unwilling to engage in bribery, we shelved the idea of a Dhaka office.

Then a few weeks later one of my Hong Kong contacts happened to phone me to ask a favor. "An old friend of mine from Bangladesh is checking into the Mount Elizabeth Hospital near your office tomorrow for a major operation. The poor guy will be all alone in Singapore. Would you please stop by and give him my best wishes for a swift recovery?"

The old friend turned out to be a charming, well-read gentleman who had headed two different ministries in a previous Bangladesh government and was now a consultant in Dhaka. Chatting with him about many things that day, I also mentioned our wish to develop long-term suppliers in his country. After the operation I dropped by again with a couple of novels to wish him well.

Two days later the ex-minister phoned to thank me and offer his help. "Your company's plans will obviously help promote Bangladesh exports. If you wish, I will arrange to get your office registered within a month. Can you pay me $900, the cost of my airfare?" I quickly agreed, and three weeks later our Dhaka office was a legal entity – the fastest liaison-office registration ever recorded in Bangladesh.

How did he do it? Since he was personally acquainted with all the officials involved, the ex-minister was able to hand-carry our registration documents from one agency to another, have a chat and a cup of tea, and get those papers signed without delay. And also without any 'special expense'.

This incident shows that in relationship-oriented markets having the right contact can be just as important for buyers as it is for sellers. In the next chapter we will look at how to build those all-important relationships in RF cultures.

3. Deal First or Relationship First?

In deal-focused markets you can usually get down to business after just a few minutes of small talk. And you can learn most of what you need to know about your potential DF counterpart in a matter of days, rather than the weeks or months it may take in strongly RF cultures such as China and Saudi Arabia.

Deal-focused buyers and sellers socialize over drinks, meals and on the golf course. But they also build rapport right at the bargaining table in the course of hammering out an agreement.

Of course, DF exporters and importers will want to learn a lot more about each other before they are ready to sign a distribution agreement. But that can come later. Meanwhile the two sides are sizing each other up while they discuss price, payment terms, specifications, quality, quantity, delivery dates, and all the other issues involved in an international distribution agreement. They talk business right from the start and get to know each other as discussions proceed.

Getting to Know Each Other

It takes time, patience, and sometimes a cast-iron liver to develop a strong relationship in some RF markets such as Japan, South Korea and Taiwan. Getting inebriated together seems to speed up the rapport-building process in East Asia, but normally only for men. While there are increasing exceptions these days, women usually don't fit in at these quasi-adolescent male bonding rituals.

The best way to get to know your local counterpart varies from one RF culture to another. In much of the Arab world, steaming platters of rice and lamb take the place of booze. Brazilian and Mexican executives love to talk about their art, music, literature and films. And then there is golf. In many parts of the world today a five iron closes the culture gap faster than a fifth of Scotch.

Yes, building trust and rapport with your customer is important everywhere in the world, not only in relationship-oriented markets.

The big difference is that with Arabs, Africans, Latin Americans and most Asians, you have to develop that climate of trust before you start talking business. In RF markets, first you make a friend, then you make a deal.

You Need to Develop a Personal Relationship

In RF markets the relationship you build with your counterpart will have a strong personal component in addition to the company-to-company aspect. Your customer or partner will want to know that you personally, as well as your company, are committed to the success of the venture.

Because of this personal element it is important that continuity is maintained as far as possible throughout the relationship. So if you are promoted or transferred to another assignment, take care to personally introduce your replacement.

Bureaucracy in RF Markets

Business negotiations usually take longer in RF than in DF cultures, for two reasons. First, it often takes more time to arrange an indirect approach. And then comes the lengthy process of building trust and developing a personal relationship.

When negotiating with government officials and public sector companies in relationship-focused markets, a third factor – bureaucratic inertia – often comes into play. Of course, officials everywhere tend to be cautious. They seem to find it safer to postpone a decision or to deny your request rather than to give their approval. Moreover, red tape often slows the process of getting things done. But in RF cultures suspicion of strangers, especially foreign strangers, often make officials even more hesitant to move things along.

That's why it took Volkswagen over nine years to negotiate the opening of an automobile factory in Shanghai with the government of China. And why McDonald's required more than 12 years to work out an agreement with the then-Soviet government for raising the first Golden Arches in Russia.

Visitors should load their briefcases with an extra-large supply of patience when preparing to do business with bureaucrats in many RF markets.

The Continuing Importance
of Face-to-Face Contact

The telecommunications revolution permits rapid correspondence with business partners around the world today. Telex, fax, email, telephone and video-conferencing enable us to stay in constant touch with our international counterparts.

But these technological marvels have not eliminated the need for face-to-face contact with our relationship-focused customers and partners. RF business people are less comfortable discussing important issues in writing or over the telephone. They expect to see their suppliers and partners in person more often than is necessary in deal-focused markets.

This cultural difference has assumed increased importance in the aftermath of 11 September 2001 in the United States. A number of our corporate clients and participants at Global Management workshops have expressed concern about the risks of international air travel. They want to know if they can substitute phone conferences and video conferencing for personal meetings with customers and business partners.

My response is to remind them that while modern technology can largely replace face-to-face-meetings with deal-focused counterparts, our RF customers will still expect to see us in person when major problems need to be discussed. A recent case involving U.S. exporters and a Malaysian distributor is relevant here.

Case 3.1: "Getting Paid in Malaysia"

During the period from autumn 1997 to autumn 1998 the value of the Malaysian ringgit in U.S. dollars declined by about 70%. For Malaysian importers, this sharp devaluation meant the cost of goods and services invoiced in U.S. dollars had more than tripled within the space of a year.

The ringgit devaluation caused serious problems for Rah-Tel, a large Kuala Lumpur-based importer and distributor of telecommunications equipment. Back in 1996 the owner and managing director, Mr. Abdul Rahim bin Mohsin, had succeeded in negotiating open-account payment terms with two American telecommunications equipment exporters.

By November 1997 Rah-Tel owed about US$130,000 to Grober Exports, an export management company, and about double that amount to King Tools, a marketer of equipment and services.

Mr. Rahim explained his difficult financial situation to both creditors in a series of faxes, emails and phone calls. He pointed out that while the US dollar value of his purchases had increased by three times, his local Malaysian customers were not prepared to pay him more than the ringgit amount they had previously negotiated. So Rahim requested a delay in payments, hoping the ringgit would recover its former value soon.

King Tools replied by email in December 1997, granting a 90-day extension but requiring Rah-Tel pay in full after that.

Grober Exports responded at first with several phone calls and e-mails. Then Grober executives made personal visits to Kuala Lumpur, one in November 1997 and another in May 1998. Within days of each of these visits Rah-Tel wired Grober's U.S. bank about 35% of the amount due them, thus accounting for 70% of the debt. Rahim then paid the remaining balance in September 1998, so Grober's debt recovery, albeit with a long delay, was 100%.

As of December 1998 King Tools had received none of the money owed them by Rah-Tel. At that point they decided to write off the entire amount as an uncollectable debt.

We ask our seminar participants why the Malaysian distributor paid Grober and not King Tools. Participants with negotiating experience in RF markets are usually quick to point out the importance of the two visits Grober Exports made to Kuala Lumpur. "When you've got something important or complex to discuss in relationship-oriented markets, you'd better do it in person," explained one veteran global marketer.

The Role of the Contract

Deal-oriented business people rely primarily on written agreements to prevent misunderstandings and solve problems. U.S. business people in particular tend to take a rather impersonal, legalistic, contract-based approach when disagreements and disputes arise. I have an American friend who says, "If you took all 862,496 lawyers in our country and laid them end to end ... Hey, come to think of it, would-n't that be a *super* idea!"

Many U.S. companies bring a lengthy draft contract and a lawyer to the negotiating table with them. They then proceed to discuss the proposed agreement clause by clause, consulting the legal adviser every time a question arises. This approach makes sense in America, the world's most litigious society. But it can be counter-productive in RF cultures where business people rely more on personal relationships rather than on lawyers and detailed contracts. In strongly RF markets a better approach is to keep the lawyers in the background until the later stages of the discussions, conferring with them during breaks.

Contrasting perceptions of the contract also cause misunderstand-ings between RF and DF cultures. For example, a Korean partner might expect to renegotiate the terms of a contract as conditions change, even if the agreement had just been signed in New York a month ago. The Koreans would expect their close relationship with their U.S. counterpart to facilitate such a renegotiation.

The New Yorkers on the other hand are likely to misinterpret an early request for changing the contract terms as a sign that their new Korean partners are tricky, fickle and unreliable. RF cultures depend primarily on relationships to prevent difficulties and solve problems, while deal- focused cultures depend on the written agreement to fulfill the same functions.

As more companies from opposite sides of the Great Divide gain experience from doing business globally, we can expect these misun-derstandings to slowly diminish. In the meantime however, business people need to be alert to cross-cultural differences that can wreck even the most promising international business deal.

4. Communicating Across The Great Divide:

Direct vs Indirect Language

RF and DF business cultures also differ in the way they communicate. Deal-oriented negotiators tend to value direct, frank, straightforward language, while their relationship-focus counterparts often favor a more indirect, subtle, roundabout style. In my experience this communication gap is the greatest single cause of misunderstandings between RF and DF business people. Confusion arises because the two cultures expect quite different things from the communication process.

Harmony vs Clarity

It is all a question of priorities. When communicating with others, the priority for DF business people is to be clearly understood. They usually say what they mean and mean what they say. German and Dutch negotiators for example are known for their frank, even blunt language.

RF negotiators in contrast give top priority to maintaining harmony and promoting smooth interpersonal relations. Because preserving harmony within the group is so important, RF people carefully watch what they say and do to avoid embarrassing or offending other people.

Fig.4.1 The Cross-Cultural Communication Gap

Direct language DF_____RF *Indirect language*

Over the last 35 years I have noticed that the nearer the RF-end of the continuum a culture is located, the more vague and indirect people are with their language. On the other hand, the nearer they are to the

DF end, the more frank and direct people tend to be. (However it's useful to note that while Germans and German-Swiss are in many respects slightly less deal-focused than Americans, they are definitely more direct in their verbal communication behavior.)

Things get interesting when the two parties in a negotiation come from opposite poles, as is the case for instance when most North Americans and Japanese interact. For example, I've had the pleasure of negotiating with Japanese companies ever since 1971 and cannot recall hearing the word 'no' even one time.

Most Japanese, Chinese and Southeast Asian negotiators I have encountered seem to treat 'no' as a four-letter word. To avoid insulting you they may instead murmur "That will be difficult" or "We will have to give that further study." Popular variations are "Maybe" and "That will be inconvenient." Educated and well-traveled Japanese are aware of their preference for avoiding that naughty word. Which is why Japanese politician Shintaro Ishihara titled his famous 1989 book, *The Japan That Can Say No.*

Mind you, one of our four sons speaks the language fluently and worked for a large Japanese company in Tokyo. While there he dated a number of Japanese young ladies and although he won't admit it, I think he may have heard 'no' once or twice!

Case 4.1 illustrates the contrasting approaches to business communication in RF and DF cultures.

Case 4.1: "Bilingual Labels"

As one of North America's largest importers of cotton garments, Great Northern Apparel of Toronto decided it was high time to start sourcing men's dress shirts in China. From an industry contact in the United States vice president Pete Martin heard about Evergreen Garments, a large manufacturer in Guangzhou specialized in supplying the U.S. market.

After considerable correspondence Pete Martin flew to Guangzhou to finalize the purchase agreement for 8000 dozen shirts. Discussions with the Evergreen Garment people proceeded amiably. Pete and the Evergreen team needed a full week of meetings to agree on fabric construction, size and color breakdown, packing, delivery, price, payment terms and the other details of a large transaction.

Exhausted from these lengthy negotiations, Pete was really looking forward to the signing ceremony. At this point however Pete remembered that Evergreen had not yet exported garments to Europe or Canada and thus might not be familiar with Canadian labeling requirements. So he explained that all apparel sold in Canada must have labels with the fiber content and laundering instructions in both French and English.

This news caused the Chinese side some concern because they lacked French-language expertise and strongly preferred to deal only with Chinese and English. Managing director Wang replied with a smile, "Mr. Martin, I am afraid that supplying labels in French and English will be difficult. This question will require further study."

Pete Martin repeated that bilingual French/English labels were required by Canadian law. "Please understand that we really have no choice on this – it's the law."

After a short discussion with his team, Mr. Wang again spoke up with a smile: "Mr. Martin, we will give your request serious consideration. I'm afraid it will be very difficult, but of course we at Evergreen Garments will do our best to solve the problem."

Relieved to have settled this final detail, Pete signed the contract of purchase and said his formal goodbyes to Mr. Wang and his Evergreen team.

Seven months later Pete got a call from the quality control chief at the Great Northern warehouse. "Mr. Martin, we have a problem. You know those 96,000 shirts that just came in from China? Well, they've got bilingual labels on them all right, but they're in English and Chinese!"

Pete Martin was stunned. He thought Evergreen had agreed to supply French/English labels. How would you explain to him why the shirts were delivered with the wrong labels?

Nonverbal Negatives

Many RF people also have subtle ways of saying no with body language. Some Arabs lift their eyebrows to politely refuse a request – the nonverbal equivalent of the American slang expression, "No way, José!"

In many cultures clicking the tongue with a 'tsk-tsk' sound indicates a negative response.

Japanese and Thais often smile and change the subject or simply say nothing at all. I have found that extended silence during a meeting with East Asian negotiators often means, "Forget it, Charley!"

The Myth of the 'Inscrutable Oriental'

Some suspicious deal-driven negotiators think this indirectness is designed to confuse or mislead them. It is in fact the RF-DF communication gap which gave rise to the myth of the 'inscrutable Oriental.'

But verbal subtlety and indirectness is only part of the story. To DF types, East and Southeast Asians seem inscrutable also because they hide their emotions, especially negative emotions. In these cultures showing impatience, irritation, frustration or anger disrupts harmony. It is considered rude and offensive. So people there mask negative emotion by remaining expressionless or by putting a smile on their face.

Thais for example seem to smile all the time. They smile when they are happy, they smile when they are amused, they smile when they are nervous, they smile even when they are absolutely furious. Thai people smile because to openly display anger would cause everyone concerned to lose face.

Communication and 'Face'

In the highly relationship-focused cultures of East and Southeast Asia, both sides lose face when a negotiator on one side of the bargaining table loses his temper. The person who displays anger loses face because he has acted childishly. And by openly showing anger he or she has also caused the other party to lose face. It doesn't take much of that to bring a promising negotiation to a lose-lose impasse.

As an unfortunate example, let's look at what happened recently during a long drawn-out negotiation in Vietnam. Executives from one of northern Europe's largest breweries had been haggling for months with a local public sector company over the details of an agreement to build a joint-venture brewery in central Vietnam.

Towards the end of a particularly frustrating day the leader of the European team could simply no longer mask his irritation. First his face got bright red. Shaking with anger, he clenched his fist so hard the wooden pencil he was holding suddenly snapped in half.

At that sound the room instantly become silent. A moment later the entire Vietnamese team rose as one man and stalked out of the conference room. The next day a three-line fax arrived at the headquarters of the European brewery informing them that the Vietnamese would never again sit down at the same table with "such a rude, arrogant person" as the head of the European team.

What to do now? Months of painstaking discussions had already been invested in this complex project. To save the deal the Europeans decided to repatriate the offending manager and replace him with a stoic type famous for his poker face. Some months later the agreement was duly signed, and visitors to central Vietnam can now imbibe lager and pilsner to their heart's content.

What could the deal-focused head of the northern European team have done to prevent that fiasco? When I asked participants in one of our recent Global Management seminars that question, the best answer was "Take a walk!" Exactly. Call for a recess. Have a cold drink. Go for a brisk walk. Do whatever it takes to relax and cool down.

For a Caucasian, your face turning red is an involuntary response one can't control. But you can take a break before something snaps.

While Westerners associate the concept of 'face' primarily with East Asian and Southeast Asian societies, it is in fact a cultural universal. Italians call it *honore*, Anglo-Saxons refer to it as self-respect. Nowhere in the world do human beings enjoy rude and offensive behavior. We tend to feel uncomfortable when others are angry with us or when we are embarrassed, mocked or singled out for criticism.

People in relationship-focused culture are often especially sensitive to face, perhaps because RF cultures are group-oriented. One's self-image and self-respect depend very much on how one is viewed by others. That is why business visitors need to be especially conscious of how their verbal and nonverbal messages may be interpreted in RF cultures.

Miscommunication Across Cultures

The strong East Asian concern for covering negative emotion can be confusing to outsiders from deal-focused cultures. When we moved from Germany to Singapore in 1988, my wife and I decided to try learning Mandarin on weekends. We hired Stefanie, a pleasant young woman who had recently immigrated from Taiwan to tutor us.

My lessons were interrupted late that year when my mother passed away and I had to fly back to Wisconsin to attend the funeral. Unfortunately, I had barely returned to Singapore when my brother phoned again to break the sad news that our father had passed away. As you might imagine, this was a very difficult time for me.

It happened to be a Saturday when I got back from this second funeral, and Stefanie dropped by to enquire why I had missed over a month's worth of lessons. Suffering from grief compounded by jet lag and exhaustion, I blurted out that both of my parents had just died.

A stricken look flashed across the young woman's face for just a fraction of a second, and she gasped. Then Stefanie suddenly laughed out loud, right in my face. And proceeded to giggle for several seconds thereafter.

Now, intellectually I was quite aware that people from certain Asian cultures hide their nervousness, embarrassment or severe stress with a laugh. I also knew I should have broken my sad news much more gently. After all, Stefanie was a Chinese person raised in the Confucian way. She revered her parents. For her the sudden realization that she could perhaps lose both of them almost at the same time must have come as a terrible shock.

Nevertheless my immediate reaction to her laugh was visceral. I felt as though I had just been hit very hard in the stomach. Even though I understood rationally what had happened, I had difficulty relating to Stefanie after that incident. A few weeks later she stopped coming and we had to find a new Mandarin tutor.

'Low-Context' and 'High-Context' Communication

We have seen that RF negotiators tend to use indirect language in order to avoid conflict and confrontation. The polite communication of Asians, Arabs, Africans and Latins helps maintain harmony. The meaning of what they are saying at the bargaining table is often found more in the context surrounding the words rather than in the words themselves. U.S. anthropologist Edward T. Hall, guru of cross-cultural communication, coined the useful term 'high-context' for these cultures because you need to know the context surrounding the words in order to understand what is meant.

In contrast, when northern Europeans, North Americans, Australians and New Zealanders speak, more of the meaning is explicit. That is, the meaning is contained in the words themselves. A listener is able to understand what they are saying at a business meeting without referring much to the context. Hall called these 'low-context' cultures.

For a Chinese executive trying to do business in Amsterdam this difference in communication styles quickly becomes obvious, as it does for a Swede or German trying to close a deal in Beijing. That's because China lies at the high-context/RF end of the culture continuum, while Sweden and Germany are perched at the low-context/DF end.

Less obvious are the differences between cultures that are located fairly close together on the continuum. For example, let's look at Greater China: the constellation of the PRC, Hong Kong (culturally distinct from the rest of China) and Taiwan. We will add Singapore as well because although the population of the Lion City is only about 77 percent Chinese, the business culture is strongly Chinese-oriented.

Fig. 4.2 Greater China

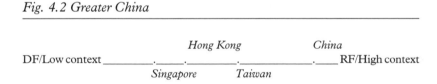

Figure 4.2 shows that while China – the mother culture – is located at the RF and high-context end of the continuum, Taiwan, Hong Kong and Singapore are spotted at varying distances away. Business people doing business in these three outposts of Chinese culture notice that while they are definitely more RF and indirect than say Australia, they are also more deal-focused and direct than most of their counterparts in the PRC.

Old Pacific Rim hands know that Hong Kongers and Singaporeans are somewhat more open to direct contact than PRC Chinese, require a shorter time for building rapport, and tend to use more direct language.

Equally interesting, research by a Danish scholar reveals similar fine gradations of cross-cultural business behavior among markets at the deal-focused and low-context end of the spectrum. Professor Malene Djursaa of the Copenhagen School of Business studied the interaction of over 50 Danish, German and British businessmen, and published her findings in the June 1994 issue of the *European Management Journal*.

Although all three of these European cultures are unmistakably low-context, they also display significant differences – differences that can cause problems for people doing business in the three markets. While the British are clearly more low-context and deal-focused than Arabs, Mexicans or Koreans, at the same time they are also more high-context and RF than their Danish and (especially) German counterparts.

Fig. 4.3

DF/Low context _____._____*Denmark*._____ RF/High context
                  Germany   *UK*

In lengthy interviews with business people of these three related cultures, Professor Djursaa learned for example that Germans find personal relationships to be more important in the UK than back home. The interviews also reveal that the British employ more roundabout, indirect language than the Danes. Further, the Danes reported that they get down to business more quickly than the British, but less quickly than the Germans.

The research of Hall, Djursaa and other scholars confirms what many business people have learned from experience: differences in cross-cultural communication create invisible barriers to international trade.

Variations in verbal and nonverbal behavior can cause culture clashes. But a skilled interpreter can often smooth over verbal problems. That's what is going on when an interpreter takes several minutes to render in Japanese or Chinese what a DF speaker just said in a couple of short sentences. Part of the translator's task is to cloak overly blunt statements with the proper amount of polite circumlocution.

Another feature of indirect, high-context communication in some traditional Asian cultures is extreme reluctance to report bad news. A case from Indonesia is pertinent here.

Case 4.2: "The Reluctant Messenger"

Anita is the sourcing manager of Blue Genes, a major Dutch importer/wholesaler of denim garments. She is worried about late delivery of 6000 fancy denim jackets ordered from Bali Jeans, her supplier in Indonesia. The contract shipping date from the Jakarta airport was last week, and she still has no word from them.

Last year Bali shipped two small orders, both of them within two weeks or so of the contract delivery date and without major garment defects. Based on that positive experience, Anita ordered 500 dozen jackets this season at a pretty good price.

On-time delivery is critical this time because her company's major retail customers will cancel if she ships late, leaving Blue Genes to eat the goods. Since these are big-ticket fashion jackets, the firm would take a heavy financial loss in addition to alienating regular customers

Bali Jeans answered Anita's last two fax inquiries promptly, reporting both times that production was "on schedule." But now, the fact is they are late.

As Anita sits steaming, her assistant pops in with a short fax from Mr. Suboto, marketing manager of Bali Jeans: "We regret to inform you that due to late delivery of piece goods we are running slightly behind on production. Expect to deliver within two weeks. Please immediately extend L/C validity by 45 days. Signed, Suboto."

Groaning out loud, Anita asks herself "How could this happen? Why didn't Suboto inform us right away when he found out that the fabric was late?" Obviously, if they are asking for an L/C extension of 45 days they will not deliver "within two weeks" as Suboto now claims.

Had she known about this delay two weeks ago Anita could have at least partially satisfied Blue Genes' most important retail customers by shipping them some quantities of a similar style from China. But being unaware of the problem in Jakarta, her company sold all those Chinese jackets yesterday to a German retail group. Now Blue Genes is completely out of stock and out of luck.

What cultural factor(s) may explain failure Mr. Suboto's failure to inform Anita earlier about this delay?

It is not that Bali Jeans management doesn't care about your business. Like some other Southeast Asians, Mr. Suboto tends to postpone reporting bad news. And perhaps he was also hoping that at the last moment a miracle would happen to solve the problem ...

"Saying It Like It Is" vs. "Saving Face"

Even when indirect RF and direct DF people are both speaking the same language, English for example, they are really speaking different languages. A Dutch or German negotiator will choose his words carefully so that his counterparts will understand exactly what he is saying. He wants no ambiguity, no beating around the bush.

Meanwhile his Arab, Japanese or Indonesian counterparts are choosing their words even more carefully, but for a different reason. RF negotiators want to make sure that no one at the meeting will be offended. They want no rude directness, no crude bluntness, no loss of face.

I personally come from a deal-oriented background. When an Australian, a German or a Dane describes me as a direct, straightforward person, I take it as a compliment. That's because in DF cultures directness and frankness are equated with honesty and sincerity.

But those same adjectives coming from a Japanese or Chinese person would more likely be meant as criticism. Why? Because in RF/high-context cultures, directness and frankness are equated with immaturity and naiveté – even arrogance. In strongly RF cultures only children and childish adults make a practice of saying exactly what they mean. They just don't know any better!

Two Different Meanings of 'Sincerity'

As a final illustration of the differences in DF and RF communication styles, let's look at the contrasting meanings of the word 'sincerity.' To English speakers from the deal-centered part of the world, sincerity connotes honesty and frankness. A sincere friend for instance is one who tells you the truth even when that truth happens to be unpleasant.

In contrast, for RF people a sincere friend is one who always shows his willingness to be helpful. For example, suppose an Arab businessman asks a deal-focused person for a favor which the latter knows he will not be able to do. The DF friend would probably show his sincerity by responding, "Very sorry, I won't be able to do that because ..."

The Arab however would regard such a person as a very fickle friend indeed. A sincere friend would instead reply, "Of course! I will do my best and let you know ..." In relationship-oriented cultures you show sincerity by declaring your willingness to help out, even when you cannot or will not do the favor.

In the next chapter we move on to the division between formal and informal business cultures.

5. Formal vs. Informal Business Cultures:

Status, Hierarchies, Power and Respect

Many promising international deals fall through when negotiators from informal cultures confront counterparts from more formal cultures. In this chapter we will look at several examples.

Formal cultures tend to be organized in steep hierarchies that reflect major differences in status and power. In contrast, informal cultures value more egalitarian organizations with smaller differences in status and power.

Why does this matter when we are doing business? Because contrasting values can cause conflict at the conference table. Business people from formal, hierarchical cultures may be offended by the easy familiarity of counterparts from informal, relatively egalitarian societies. On the other hand, those from informal cultures may see their formal counterparts as stuffy, distant, pompous, or arrogant.

Such misunderstandings can be avoided if both sides are aware that differing business behaviors are the result of differing cultural values rather than individual idiosyncracies.

Culture Clash in Germany

I learned about the informality/formality divide the hard way in the early 1960s when my employer, a Chicago export management company, transferred us to Germany to expand sales in Europe.

My first appointment was with our largest account, an importer/distributor of hand-tools located in Stuttgart. I spent that day in meetings with the boss of the company, Doctor Wilhelm Müller, and found myself saying "Herr Dr. Müller" and "Dr. Müller" the whole day. This formality was a bit oppressive for a young man from the United States, one of the world's more informal cultures. So returning to Frankfurt that evening I phoned my German friend. "Hans baby,

I'm really tired of all this medieval formality. How many times do I have to meet with this guy before I can start calling him 'Willi'?"

Laughing heartily, Hans straightened me out on the formality issue right then. "You're asking when you can start calling Dr. Müller by his first name? Well, the answer is *niemals, Dummkopf!* Never, you dummy!"

Of course Hans was right. I spent the next two years addressing this distinguished gentleman in the proper German way. And when his wife joined us once for lunch I called her "Frau Doktor." Why? Because those are the proper forms of address in Germany, a relatively formal society. This anecdote actually illustrates both Iron Laws of International Business. The seller adapts to the customer, and the visitor respects local customs.

Later I learned that most of Europe follows the same rules of formal address. Your French contact is likely to remain Monsieur Dupont, not René. And for years in Italy we addressed the head of our largest supplier with the honorific 'Commendatore' until we got to know him well enough to call him Gustavo.

By way of contrast, my most recent meeting in Sydney, Australia started with a hearty "G'day mate! Let's 'ave a beer!" Now that, dear reader, is an example of an informal culture!

Formality is all about status, hierarchies, power and respect. Whereas informal cultures are supposed to value status equality, formal cultures value hierarchies and status differences. Ignorance of this distinction can cause serious problems across the international bargaining table. A participant in one of our export marketing seminars in Europe related an incident that illustrates this point.

Case 5.1: "How to Insult a Mexican Customer"

José Garcia Lopez, a Mexican importer, had been negotiating with a Danish manufacturing company for several months when he decided to visit Copenhagen to finalize a purchase contract. The business meetings went smoothly, so on the last day of his visit Sr. Garcia confided that he looked forward to signing the contract after his return to Mexico.

That evening the Danes invited Sr. Garcia out for an evening on the town. Flemming, the 40 year-old export manager and his 21 year-old assistant Margrethe hosted an excellent dinner and then took their

Mexican prospect on a tour of Copenhagen nightspots. Around midnight Flemming glanced at his watch.

"Sr. Garcia, as I mentioned to you when we discussed your visit, I have a very early flight tomorrow to Tokyo. So you'll forgive me if I leave you now. Margrethe will make sure you get back to your hotel all right and then drive you to the airport tomorrow morning. I wish you a good flight!"

Next morning in the car on the way to the airport José Garcia was uncharacteristically silent. Then he turned to the young assistant: "Margrethe, would you please tell your boss I have decided not to sign that contract after all. It is not your fault of course. If you think about what happened last evening I believe you will understand why I no longer wish to do business with your company."

To repeat, formality has to do with relative status, organizational hierarchies, and how to show respect to persons of high status. That is why international marketers always should know whether they are dealing with formal or informal cultures. Figure 5.1 shows 'Who's Who' in this world of egalitarian and hierarchical cultures.

Fig. 5.1

VERY INFORMAL CULTURES
Australia
Denmark
USA, Canada
Norway, Sweden
New Zealand

FORMAL CULTURES
Most of Europe and Asia
Mediterranean Region and the Arab World
Latin America

In formal, hierarchical cultures, which account for most of the world, status differences are larger and more important than in egalitarian, informal cultures. Formality in addressing people is one important way of showing respect to persons of high status.

Showing Respect in Europe

Let's take Dr. Wilhelm Müller as an example. I addressed this German gentleman formally because that is the German custom. But the cultural value behind that venerable custom really has to do with showing appropriate respect. First of all, Wilhelm Müller was considerably older than I was. And in formal cultures age confers status.

Secondly, Herr Müller had earned a doctorate, an academic distinction of great importance in Germany. One acknowledges that distinction by including the title when addressing such a person. This bit of protocol is important because today over 40 percent of top managers in German manufacturing concerns hold a doctorate, usually in engineering.

Showing Respect to the Customer

The third and supremely important reason for according respect to Dr. Wilhelm Müller is valid far beyond Germany and Europe. Namely, this guy was my customer. International marketers must remember that all over the world these days the customer is king. (Except in Japan, that is. Because for Japanese businesses the customer is GOD! We can all learn something from the way our Japanese colleagues and competitors treat their customers.)

Hierarchies and Status in Asia

People from egalitarian societies are often unaware of the importance of status distinctions in hierarchical cultures. During the five years we lived in Singapore we were friends with an American couple who invited us to dinner several times. At the first party there were a number of Singaporean couples present, but none of the locals accepted subsequent invitations.

The American couple had no idea why their Singaporean friends no longer came to dinner, but my wife and I knew. You see, these particular Yanks happened to be strongly egalitarian. They liked to have their maid sit at the dinner table with them. Now, like most Asians, Singaporeans respect authority, honor social hierarchies, and value clear status differences. Feeling uncomfortable sitting at the same table with a Filipina maid, they said nothing but simply stayed away.

As the world's most egalitarian people, Scandinavians sometimes have a special problem doing business in strongly hierarchical cultures. Recently an associate of mine from a Nordic country visited good friends of ours in Bangkok. Svend politely shook hands with the host and hostess, and then with their Thai maid as well. Much to Svend's surprise the maid immediately burst into tears, ran out and spent the whole evening sobbing in her room.

Our Bangkok friends are a Thai-American couple. They gently explained to Svend that as a *farang* – a Caucasian foreigner – he automatically enjoys high status, whereas a domestic worker is of lower status. In Thailand people that far apart in social status do not shake hands. So when Svend grabbed her hand she thought he was making fun of her, and was absolutely mortified.

The sharp divide between egalitarian and hierarchical societies can act as an invisible barrier to exports. Marketers from informal cultures often do not know how to show respect to high-ranking persons from formal cultures, who may be easily offended by perceived slights.

The bottom line for export marketers and deal-makers in today's global marketplace is that ignorance of cultural differences is not an acceptable excuse for failure. Case 4.2 shows how you can lose business due to ignorance of cultural differences.

Case 5.2: "How to Insult an Egyptian Customer"

A major Canadian high-tech manufacturing firm was deep in negotiations with an Egyptian public sector company. Vice President Paul White was pleased to learn that the head of the Cairo-based company was leading a delegation to Toronto with a view to concluding negotiations.

White was even more pleased when upon his arrival Dr. Mahmud Ahmed hinted strongly that discussions were moving along nicely and that a favorable outcome was likely. After all, this contract represented the largest and most profitable deal White's company had worked on to date.

Quite aware of the importance of relationship-building, Paul invited the Egyptian delegation to an elegant reception and buffet dinner at the prestigious Grand Hotel, with Dr. Ahmed as the guest of honor.

Dr. Ahmed was his usual charming, affable self when he arrived at the party and warmly shook hands with Paul. After a few minutes of chit-chit the Canadian led his chief guest to the drinks table stocked with wine, liquor, fruit juices and soft drinks. "Well now, what can I offer you to drink, Dr. Ahmed?"

"Oh, nothing for me right now," replied the Egyptian with a smile. The two men conversed pleasantly about sports, music and other mutual interests for a while and then White guided his guest to the buffet table loaded with delicacies Dr. Ahmed was known to especially like. Paul was surprised when Dr. Ahmed once again declined politely, saying that he wasn't hungry.

Puzzled by his guest's lack of interest in food and drink, Paul wondered what the problem might be. Then the Canadian host was drawn into conversation with some of the other guests and did not notice when Dr. Ahmed left the party early.

At the negotiating session next day Dr. Ahmed was cool and distant. No progress at all was made towards an agreement. That afternoon Paul learned that the head of the Egyptian company was complaining vociferously to his colleagues about the "rude and offensive treatment" he had undergone at the dinner party. "I certainly do not intend to do business with such discourteous people," he was heard to say.

With the delegation due to leave Canada in three days, Paul White was desperate to know what was happening. Was this a negotiating ploy -- a pressure tactic? Or had his team really offended Dr. Ahmed somehow? If so, what could he do now?

The two preceeding disaster cases were real-world examples of how *not* to do business in formal cultures. Now let's look at an example of how to do it right.

Showing Respect in Asia

An American consultant with a decade of business experience in South Asia arranged for his Chicago client to meet with the Minister of Textiles in Bangladesh. The Chicago company had asked for a favorable decision on a complex issue involving garment quota allocations, but was not optimistic about the outcome. A U.S. competitor who had made a similar request the previous month had seen their application summarily rejected by mid-level bureaucrats in the ministry.

It was a sweltering day in Dhaka and the minister's shiny new window air conditioner was not in operation. This caused the visitors considerable discomfort, because at the consultant's insistence they were dressed in dark wool suits with starched shirts and ties. The two Westerners sat steaming and dripping sweat while the minister chatted away amiably, cool and comfortable in airy white muslin.

After about an hour and a quarter of what seemed to be aimless conversation, the minister stood up and with a broad smile informed the petitioners that he had decided to grant their request.

The consultant learned the next day from a government contact that the minister had deliberately not turned on his room air conditioner for the meeting. The contact hinted that His Excellency may have been 'testing' the Western visitors.

Nonverbal Ways of Showing Respect

The general lesson here is that when dealing with government officials in hierarchical countries it is important to show proper respect and deference. This advice is particularly important for Europeans, Americans and Australians negotiating with senior officials in countries with a history of Western colonial domination. Bureaucrats throughout South and Southeast Asia can be easily offended by overly casual behavior on the part of Westerners. Innocent informality may be misinterpreted as disrespect. Wearing a suit and tie to meetings during the hot season sends a positive signal of respect, and keeping one's jacket on in a non-air conditioned office signals even greater respect.

Australian, Scandinavian and American managers attending our seminars sometimes complain that they are at a competitive disadvantage globally because businessmen from hierarchical cultures already know all about formality, status differences and how to show respect, while those from egalitarian societies may not.

These managers have a valid point. A key rule of international business protocol is that when in an unfamiliar situation, always err on the side of formality at first. That may mean for instance addressing people by their surname and title rather than first name, dressing more formally, and following local etiquette when shaking hands and exchanging business cards.

So when calling on prospects in a hierarchical culture, the Japanese or Germans in their dark suit, white shirt, polished shoes and polished manners may indeed have an initial advantage over some of their more informal Aussie, Yankee or Nordic competitors.

Status Barriers

However, there are four classes of international business people who have to operate at an even greater disadvantage when trying to sell goods to strongly hierarchical buyers. These are:
- People on the lower rungs of the corporate ladder in their own company,
- Young people of either sex,
- Women,
- Men and women of any age involved in international sales and marketing.

The reason is that formal cultures tend to ascribe status according to one's age, gender, organizational rank, and (especially in most parts of Asia) whether one is the buyer or the seller. Therefore a woman who is a young export sales specialist potentially suffers under a quadruple handicap when operating in formal, hierarchical cultures such as Japan, South Korea and the Arab world.

Which makes our next case quite interesting. Case 5.3 is about a woman who succeeded as a very young export marketer in all three of these tough markets in spite of her four-fold handicap. (As with all the other cases in this book, this incident actually took place.)

Case 5.3: "Women in International Business"

In certain hierarchically organized cultures women rarely gain senior positions in commercial organizations. Especially in South Korea, Japan and Saudi Arabia, men are traditionally accorded higher status in the business world than females. The top positions in most companies are held by men who are not used to dealing with women in business on the basis of equality.

In direct contrast, many women in more egalitarian cultures around the world are successful entrepreneurs as well as executives in major corporations. The two opposing views of the role of women in business can lead to a culture clash when females try to do business in traditional, hierarchical societies. Despite the potential problems however, some enterprising women refuse to be shut out of promising markets by what they regard as male chauvinist attitudes.

A bright young Danish woman we'll call Tonia is a case in point. Tonia was a tall, striking blonde of about 20 employed by a Singaporean jewelry manufacturer. She was also studying international marketing part-time at the Export Insitute of Singapore. Having heard about the gender barrier, Tonia asked one of her EIS lecturers: "Which major markets in the world would you say are the most difficult for a woman to do business in?"

"Saudi Arabia, Japan and South Korea," replied the lecturer without hesitation.

The next day Tonia asked for a meeting with her boss, the marketing manager of the jewelry company. She volunteered to undertake a sales mission during the semester break to those very markets, and after some careful preparation left on a two-week trip to Tokyo, Seoul and Riyadh. The next semester Tonia proudly reported to the class that she had been able to sell her company's fine jewelry successfully in not just one, but all three of those particularly tough markets. Not only that, she had even been offered a job as marketing manager by one of her new customers!

The Gender Barrier

Although the gender barrier unquestionably exists in hierarchical cultures, being an obvious foreigner may lower that barrier significantly. For example, while there are millions of Japanese women working for companies in Japan, they are almost all 'office ladies' performing clerical duties. Japanese women in a business setting are automatically assumed to be secretaries and treated accordingly by the overwhelmingly male management. So Japanese women generally lack the status necessary to interact effectively with corporate decision-makers.

But those same male executives often see a foreign female as a 'gaijin' first, and only second as a woman. Knowing that foreign women sometimes hold managerial positions, many Japanese executives are willing to give them a chance.

The Youth Barrier

The age barrier is a different matter. The most common question from young international marketers and managers of either sex attending our training seminars is, "Since being young is such a handicap to doing business abroad, what are we supposed to do?"

I usually start by reminding the questioner that youth is actually an advantage in some markets, the USA in particular. But without a doubt, a person of tender years will find it difficult to be taken seriously by older business people in hierarchical cultures.

The ultimate solution of course is to grow older. But that's going to happen soon enough anyway. What to do in the meantime? I recommend this three-step procedure for young export marketers. (Because "the customer is king," youth is not such a major handicap for a buyer.)

How to Overcome the Youth Barrier with Hierarchical Buyers

– Get introduced by an older man. Preferably by the oldest male you can find who is still able to walk. This ploy works because enough of his maleness (if you are a woman) and his seniority will rub off on you to get you started. But be nice: after the introduction let that old guy go back to sleep while you run the meeting!
– Be an expert in your field. This works because just about everywhere in the world today expertise confers status. Once they get over the shock of your youthfulness, customers in hierarchical markets have the same concerns as their egalitarian counterparts, and your quiet competence gives them confidence that you will provide them with good service. A note of caution here. Remember to show them your expertise rather than tell them about it. The only thing worse than a show-off is a young show-off.
– Learn the local business protocol. Since you will probably be making your sales presentation to an older male who is a buyer, you are of course heavily outranked. It's something like a private soldier trying to sell to a general. So you must know how to show proper deference without actually groveling. (Although here I am reminded of a certain Sears Roebuck buyer who used to post a sign for the benefit of his suppliers, "GROVELING IS GOOD!")

Other Status Factors

While age, gender, organizational rank and whether one is buying or selling are the key determinants of status and power in most hierarchical societies, other factors such as family background, level of education and knowledge of 'high culture' also confer status in certain markets.

For example, in Latin America and much of Europe a deal-focused business person whose interests are limited to making money tends to be looked down upon. Higher status goes to the individual able to converse intelligently about art, music, literature, history, philosophy and the cinema. Business visitors who would like to be well regarded in those markets should consider brushing up on such subjects.

How to conduct business in other cultures without offending customers and business partners is such an important issue we are devoting a separate chapter to International Business Protocol. But first let's take a careful look at another Cultural Divide, the one between rigid-time and fluid-time cultures.

6. Time and Scheduling:
Rigid-Time vs Fluid-Time Cultures

Globetrotting business travelers quickly learn that people look at time and scheduling differently in different parts of the world. In rigid-time societies punctuality is critical, schedules are set in concrete, agendas are fixed, and business meetings are rarely interrupted. Edward T. Hall invented the term 'monochronic' for these clock-obsessed, schedule-worshiping cultures.

In direct contrast are 'polychronic' cultures, where people place less emphasis on strict punctuality and are not obsessed with deadlines. Polychronic cultures value loose scheduling as well as business meetings where many several meetings-within-meetings may be taking place simultaneously.

Fig. 6.1

VERY MONOCHRONIC BUSINESS CULTURES
Nordic and Germanic Europe
North America
Japan

MONOCHRONIC
Australia/New Zealand
Russia and most of East-Central Europe
Southern Europe
Singapore, Hong Kong, Taiwan, China
South Korea

POLYCHRONIC BUSINESS CULTURES
The Arab World
Africa
Latin America
South and Southeast Asia

Alert readers will note a couple of particularly interesting entries in this chart. One is Japan, which was classified as polychronic by Edward T. Hall back in the 1960s. But today the Japanese are as schedule-obsessed and clock-conscious as the Swiss.

The other is Singapore, a polychronic Southeast Asian entrepot just 30 years ago and today a moderately monochronic business culture. Both countries are proof that culture does change, albeit slowly.

Of course, orientation to time varies not only among different countries but often within a given country as well. As we will see below with Italy, there can be regional variations. Another example is Brazil, where temperate Sao Paulo is relatively monochronic whereas Rio is strongly polychronic. Similarly people in the more industrialized southern coastal provinces of China are more clock-conscious than those in the less-developed interior. And your South Korean meeting is more likely to start on time if it takes place in Seoul than in a small town in the countryside.

Europe: The North/South Divide

For international business people the problem is that contrasting conceptions of time and scheduling cause conflicts. Let's look first at Europe, where the meaning of punctuality for instance varies according to whether you are in the northern or southern part of the Continent.

Suppose you are an export marketer scheduled to meet your Hamburg customer at 9:00 am tomorrow. Knowing how important *Pünktlichkeit* is to Germans, what time should you arrive at his office in order to be considered punctual? Veterans of the German market agree that 8:55 am would be just about right. Getting there at nine on the dot would of course be technically acceptable, but arriving five minutes ahead of time shows that you share your customer's obsession with being on time.

The worst thing would be to show up late. Tardiness signals lack of discipline. Some Germans feel if you are ten minutes late for a meeting you may well be ten weeks late with your delivery. *Pünktlichkeit* and *Zuverläßigkeit* (reliability) are closely related concepts in this most monochronic of cultures.

Let's say your next sales meeting is in Munich. The laid-back Bavarians are more relaxed about time, so you could arrive right on time – possibly even two minutes late – without destroying your chances for a sale. And you can still be confident that your local counterpart will be punctual.

Where the Clock Slows Down

But when you hop across the Alps for your meeting in Milan, the rules change. There your customer or contact may well show up ten minutes or so late without feeling obliged to apologize. And as you travel south through Italy you find that schedules become even more fluid. In sunny Rome your local counterpart is likely to waltz in half an hour after the agreed time and greet you as though nothing at all is wrong.

At this point some of our seminar participants usually ask, "But what about that famous saying, "When in Rome, do as the Romans do." Doesn't that mean that in Italy for example we can be relaxed about punctuality as well?"

That's not the way things work in global business. If you are an international marketer, the "When in Rome ..." rule of thumb is trumped by a higher rule we have already invoked: "The seller has to show respect to the buyer." Being on time is a key way of showing respect – even in a polychronic culture.

The polychronic approach to time becomes more obvious as you move further south. By the time you reach Naples, 45 minutes' tardiness is considered no big deal. And then of course comes Sicily. According to my Florentine friends, if your Sicilian counterparts show up at all on the day of the meeting, they are considered punctual!

This European example with its soupçon of exaggeration is meant to contrast the rigid-time business cultures found mostly in temperate latitudes with the more relaxed, fluid-time cultures located primarily in hotter climes. For whatever reason, the closer you get to the equator the slower the clock seems to run.

But now dear reader, here's a little quiz: just one question. In the example of the north/south divide in Europe, did you perhaps feel I was putting down the Italians, criticizing their lack of punctuality? If that was your impression it shows you were probably raised in a monochronic culture where punctuality, tight scheduling, firm agendas, rigid deadlines and uninterrupted meetings are important virtues.

On the other hand, if you did not think I was criticizing southerners, you more likely grew up in a polychronic culture. That is, in a society where people spend less time worshiping the clock and more time attending to strong interpersonal relationships.

The following case points up ways of responding to tardiness in differing situations.

Case 6.1: "Waiting in Rome I"

Your new responsibility is to expand your company's sales in southern Europe. You decide to begin your market tour in Rome, where you are to meet your largest Italian customer.

Dottore Renzo Bianchi's email said he would meet you in the hotel lobby at 19:30 for a drink before going out to dinner at his favorite trattoria. But it's 19:50 before Dottore Bianchi finally appears. He approaches with a wide smile, shakes your hand and begins to chat animatedly without any kind of explanation or apology for being so late.

1. What are you going to say to Dottore Bianchi about his tardiness?
2. Explain your reasoning.

"Waiting in Rome II"

Your responsibility in your company is to look after the company's purchases in southern Europe. You decide to begin your tour of vendor facilities in Rome, where you are to meet your largest Italian supplier.

Dottore Paolo Verdi's email said he would meet you in the hotel lobby at 19:30 for a drink before going out to dinner at his favorite trattoria. But it's 19:50 before he appears. Smiling broadly, Dottore Verdi offers you a brief apology for being late as he joins you at the hotel bar, then begins to chat about dinner plans.

What is different about this situation, and why?

It's about Time ...

In fluid-time cultures business people may be tardy for your meeting because they had to help a friend or family member solve a problem. Or perhaps an earlier meeting ended later than expected. In polychronic cultures it is inexcusably rude to end an ongoing meeting just because you happen to have another one scheduled.

The Indonesians have a delightful expression for polychronic time. They call it *jam karet* or 'rubber time' – flexible, s t r e t c h a b l e meeting times, schedules and agendas. Indonesians tend to place a higher value on human relationships than on arbitrary schedules and deadlines.

The contrast between polychronic and monochronic cultures is magnified these days by the monumental traffic problems found in many developing countries. On a recent visit to Bangkok I spent three and a half hours getting from one side of the city to the other for a meeting. Traffic can be even worse in Cairo. Unless you anticipate that degree of traffic gridlock in certain cities and plan accordingly, even Germans and Swiss visitors might occasionally find themselves a minute or two late for a meeting.

Centuries ago when all societies on Earth were polychronic, a sundial was accurate enough to keep track of time. Then some sadistic inventor had to go and ruin a good thing, developing that cruel torture instrument we know as the clock. Now when the bloody alarm goes off at 6:00 am, monochronic people wonder whether worshiping the clock is such a great idea after all.

Polychronic Culture Shock

Consider the case of a fluid-time person undergoing her first collision with a monochronic culture. Not long ago a Malaysian business-woman flew to the USA for an important conference scheduled for 10:00 am on a Monday. She arrived in Boston late that Sunday evening, had trouble falling asleep because of jet lag, and overslept a little the next morning.

That Monday the Malay lady had difficulty finding the meeting location in her rental car, got lost and finally arrived well after lunch – four hours late for her meeting. The Americans she was supposed to meet came out of the conference room to tell her, "Oh sorry, right now we're in the middle of our afternoon meeting. And our calendar seems to be kind of full this week ... Well let's see, can you make it for Wednesday of next week?" But since she had to be back in Kuala Lumpur by that date our Malay lady never was able to reschedule that important meeting.

Not long after her return to Malaysia this charming polychronic woman attended one of our Global Negotiator seminars in Southeast Asia. During the lunch break she related that sad story as an example of how rude and schedule-obsessed Americans can be. "So there I was in Boston, having flown halfway around the world just for that meeting. And those people did not even have the common decency to rearrange their schedule for a foreign visitor who was a little late. Can you believe it?"

As we have learned, the meaning of "a little late" differs according to whether you are in a monochronic or polychronic culture.

Monochronic Culture Shock

Monochronic people are equally prone to culture shock when doing business in polychronic markets. I often hear northern Europeans and North Americans complain about the 'rude behavior' of business contacts in the Middle East, Latin America as well as South and Southeast Asia. "They always keep me waiting and then continually interrupt the meeting to take phone calls and receive unscheduled visitors."

Many rigid-time visitors are convinced that their counterparts in Rio de Janeiro, Bangkok or Casablanca deliberately keep them waiting as a negotiating power play. Why do you suppose monochronic travelers think that way? Because in London, Stockholm or Amsterdam, if the person you are to meet keeps you cooling your heels without a damn good reason, it probably *is* a power play. All of us tend to interpret the behavior of foreigners in terms of our home culture.

The next case concerns a young U.S. expatriate manager who has just taken up his first assignment outside North America and Europe. This incident illustrates what can happen when a monochronic businessperson encounters polychronic business behavior for the first time.

Case 6.2: "Waiting in New Delhi"

Richard was a 30 year-old American sent by his Chicago-based company to set up a buying office in India. The new office's main mission was to source large quantities of consumer goods in India: cotton piece goods, garments, accessories and shoes as well as industrial products such as tent fabrics and cast iron components.

India's Ministry of Foreign Trade had invited Richard's company to open this buying office because they knew it would promote exports, bring in badly-needed foreign exchange and provide manufacturing know-how to Indian factories.

Richard's was in fact the first international sourcing office to be located anywhere in South Asia. The MFT wanted it to succeed so that other Western and Japanese companies could be persuaded to establish similar procurement offices.

The expatriate manager decided to set up the office in the capital, New Delhi, because he knew he would have to meet frequently with senior government officials. Since the Indian government closely regulated all trade and industry, Richard often found it necessary to help his suppliers obtain import licenses for the semi-manufactures and components they required to produce the finished goods his company had ordered.

Richard found these government meetings frustrating. Even though he always phoned to make firm appointments, the bureaucrats usually kept him waiting for half an hour or more. Not only that, his meetings would be continuously interrupted by phone calls and unannounced visitors, as well as by clerks bringing in stacks of letters and documents to be signed. Because of all the waiting and the constant interruptions it regularly took him half a day or more to accomplish something that could have been done back home in 20 minutes.

Three months into this assignment Richard began to think about requesting a transfer to a more congenial part of the world – "somewhere where things work." He just could not understand why the Indian officials were being so rude. Why did they keep him waiting? Why didn't the bureaucrats hold their incoming calls and sign those papers after the meeting so as to avoid the constant interruptions?

After all, the government of India had actually invited his company to open this buying office. So didn't he have the right to expect reasonably courteous treatment from the officials in the various ministries and agencies he had to deal with?

Three decades as a monochronic person doing business in polychronic markets has taught me how to avoid some of the frustration. Here are three practical tips for rigid-time business travelers:

– Find out in advance which of the markets you are going to visit are in fluid-time cultures. Forewarned is forearmed.
– Bring a well-filled briefcase. Instead of wasting time in the reception area twiddling your thumbs, compulsively looking at your watch, and muttering curses, catch up on all that paperwork you never seem to have time for or read a good book. It makes the time go faster.
– Above all, BE PATIENT!

Punctuality

Punctuality may also vary according to the occasion. Take Singapore, where business meetings usually start within five or ten minutes of the scheduled time. In contrast, wedding dinners are guaranteed to begin at least two hours after the time given on the invitation – by which time some of the weaker guests have fainted from hunger. Many of my Lion City friends fortify themselves with an early dinner at home as a precautionary measure.

Or take Sao Paulo. I got used to business conferences starting 20 or 30 minutes late there, so when I received a dinner invitation for eight I decided to arrive about 8:30. But that proved to be quite a shock for the hostess: She was just getting out of the shower when I rang the doorbell. That's how I learned that an 8:00 pm dinner invitation in Brazil means you are supposed to arrive no earlier than nine and preferably closer to ten.

Not so with the Norwegians. My wife and I were invited along with several other expat couples to the home of Norwegian friends in Singapore. We all arrived at the house a few minutes before seven and stood around outside chatting with each other until exactly 7:00 pm, when one of the Scandinavian guests rang the doorbell. The monochronic Norwegians expect you to appear on time for any engagement, whether social or business.

Some rigid-time business people refer to Latin cultures as *mañana* societies. This kind of put-down doesn't seem to bother my Brazilian friends who tell me, "Brazil is the Land of Tomorrow. The only problem is, tomorrow never comes!" But for polychronic folks in general the issue is really one of priorities. What's more important, they ask, people or an abstract concept like time?

Agendas: Fixed vs Flexible

Monochronic meetings tend to follow an agreed outline or agenda. At a typical negotiation in Germany, Switzerland or Sweden you can expect to start off with a few minutes of small talk and then proceed in linear fashion from Item 1 to the last item on the agenda with no major digressions.

In France or Italy however the 'warm up' chat is likely to last several times as long. And if there is any agenda at all you may start with Item 5, proceed to Item 2 and then wander off in several different directions at once. Polychronic meetings tend to follow their own inner logic rather than a fixed outline. The important thing is that everyone has his or her say.

What's more, in a decade of working with Italians, French, Spanish, and Portuguese, I found that in the end we usually accomplished what we came to do. The longer warm up time served to get us all on the same wave length. And some of those 'senseless digressions' led us to creative solutions which helped us reach agreement.

As a monochronic person living for more than a decade in Latin Europe, Latin America and South Asia, I now find the polychronic way equally congenial. In international business one soon learns that there is usually more than one way to achieve your goal. So choose the approach that best fits the local circumstances.

Schedules and Deadlines

Some strongly polychronic cultures have an aversion to rigid deadlines. Many traditional Arab businessmen for example believe it is impious and irreligious to try to see into the future. God, not man is in charge of what will happen. The Arabic term *Insh'allah* – 'God willing' – expresses that belief.

With counterparts from polychronic cultures it can be a mistake to set rigid deadlines and try to enforce them. Instead I recommend the following approach:

- If you need something delivered or some action taken by say March 1, get your polychronic counterpart to agree on February 1 or even January 15.
- During the whole time leading up to the deadline, stay in frequent touch with your counterpart. Face-to-face contact is the best way to expedite matters.

In other words, put a comfortable margin in your scheduling and then maintain a close relationship with your counterparts. Let's remember that while it is rude to be tardy in a monochronic culture, it is equally rude to patronize people from polychronic cultures who refuse to bow down in worship of Chronus, the old god of time.

Let's now consider another important division between business cultures.

7. Nonverbal Business Behavior:

Expressive vs. Reserved Cultures

In Chapter 3 we looked at the verbal communication problems faced by people doing business across cultures. In this chapter we consider the difficulties caused by differences in nonverbal communication.

People of other cultures misunderstand our body language just as they may misinterpret the words we speak or write. Fortunately however, we can learn the highlights of another culture's nonverbal language much quicker than we can its verbal language. There are three types of interpersonal communication:

- Verbal communication has to do with words and the meaning of words.
- Paraverbal language refers to how loudly we speak those words, the meaning of silence, and the significance of conversational overlap.
- With Nonverbal communication (also called body language) we communicate without using any words at all.

Expressive vs. Reserved Cultures

Varying degrees of expressiveness in paraverbal and nonverbal behavior cause unexpected problems for international managers and negotiators. Let's look at a relevant incident.

In 1989 and 1990 I made numerous trips from Singapore to Thailand in connection with setting up a Bangkok office for the U.S. company I was working for. As regional director for South and Southeast Asia, one of my responsibilities was to help our local manager recruit Thai staff.

With the help of a Thai human resource consultant we placed recruitment ads in Bangkok newspapers, screened the applicants and selected about 10 young Thais for employment interviews. While the interviews with the men went smoothly enough, the female candidates were not responding well at all. That was a serious problem because qualified English-speaking office workers and management trainees are not easy to find in Bangkok. And now for some reason my interviewing approach seemed to be turning off a number of promising candidates.

I asked our consultant what the problem was. She thought for a moment and then began talking around the issue politely, obviously trying hard to spare my feelings. (Remember, Thais tend to be relationship-focused, high-context, hierarchical people. She did not want to offend a *farang* client – especially not a white-haired one.)

Finally our advisor managed to gently convey the message that I was talking too loud, as well as using too much facial expression and too many hand gestures. She explained that many soft-spoken Thai women tend to interpret a loud voice as a sign of anger, and that my animated facial expressions and gestures warned the women that I might not be quite right in the head.

So here was an angry, insane 'farang' trying to interview potential employees. Small wonder those Thai women were not particularly interested!

This was a problem of undue expressiveness. During my eight years in Italy as a manager responsible for southern Europe and the Mediterranean region, I had gradually become more expressive in order to be understood there. But now in Thailand, a very restrained culture, the exuberant Latin communication style was causing a problem.

Fig. 7.1

VERY EXPRESSIVE CULTURES
The Mediterranean Region
Latin Europe
Latin America

VARIABLY EXPRESSIVE
USA and Canada
Australia and New Zealand
Eastern Europe
South Asia, Africa

RESERVED CULTURES
East and Southeast Asia
Nordic and Germanic Europe

So for the rest of the interviews that week I tried hard to modulate my voice, maintain an expressionless face (except for a smile of course) and keep both hands folded in front of me. It worked, and we were able to hire several bright young Thai men and women who were a credit to the company.

Figure 7.1 reveals which markets are emotionally expressive and which are more reserved.

Note that Latin Europe and the Mediterranean area are among the world's most expressive cultures while Thailand is the opposite – one of the most reserved. So the culture clash related above is understandable. But as we will see in the next case, problems can arise even when cultures involved are somewhat closer together.

Case 7.1: "Baffled in Bangkok"

Jane Reynolds was the executive director of an important trade association in Singapore. An outgoing, enthusiastic American who was successful in gaining the cooperation of the association's members, she had lived in Singapore for ten years and got along with people there very well.

Jane was pleased when she was asked to chair the annual meeting of a Thai women's organization in Bangkok. Although Mrs. Reynolds was an experienced speaker and discussion leader, this was the first time for her to chair a conference in Thailand. When Jane asked friends and colleagues for advice, they warned her that Thai women tended to be somewhat shy in public. They would probably be hesitant to offer their views and opinions in front of a large group.

So Jane was delighted when during the morning session first one and then two other Thai participants quietly offered useful comments and suggestions. She showed her delight in characteristic fashion. Getting up from the table with eyebrows raised and arms waving, Mrs. Reynolds exuberantly thanked the three women and praised them for their contributions, making sure to speak loudly enough that all the attendees would be able to hear.

The meeting then continued, but for some reason there was no more input from the floor. In fact the Thai women stopped responding to the chairperson's questions as well, remaining silent for the remainder of the conference.

After the meeting two of the Thai members who had spoken up approached Jane and tearfully asked, "Why were you so angry with us this morning? We don't know what we did to upset you so." Jane hastily replied that she wasn't angry or upset at all, but the two women just mumbled their goodbyes and walked sadly away.

Jane Reynolds returned to her hotel that afternoon completely baffled by the reaction of the Thai participants. She wondered why things had suddenly gone wrong at the conference after such a promising beginning ...

Paraverbal Negotiating Behavior: Vocal Volume and Inflection

Reserved, soft-spoken business people also run into problems when negotiating with more expressive counterparts. A few years ago in Egypt two American buyers were negotiating a contract with a large public sector manufacturing company located in Alexandria.

Raymond was an expressive, somewhat loud-mouthed Yank, while Clem was unusually restrained and soft-spoken for an American. Clem led off the discussion of contract terms in a low monotone. After about 15 minutes first one, then another, and finally all three Egyptian negotiators fell sound asleep at the conference table, despite having swallowed toxic-level doses of high-octane Turkish coffee.

Raymond had spent enough time in that area to know that Egyptians tend to be rather expressive communicators. They like to speak loudly enough to be heard clearly, often raise their voices to emphasize important points, and are known to literally pound the table when further emphasis is called for. So after a few minutes of Clem's low monotone the three Egyptians apparently concluded that this guy had nothing really important to say, and proceeded to drift off.

The two American visitors of course saw this as a problem. A negotiation with one side fast asleep is unlikely to be extremely fruitful. So the buyers called for a short break during which the officials gulped down more coffee and Clem decided to leave the meeting for a tour of the city.

When the four men reconvened Raymond continued the discussion in a voice that was loud, clear and spiced with vocal inflection. By the time Clem rejoined the meeting that afternoon the two sides had reached agreement on the major points. It's amazing what negotiators can achieve when they are wide awake and paying attention!

"But wait a minute! Aren't the sellers supposed to adapt to the buyers?" Yes – unless of course that buyer really wants the deal. And happens to know how to close the communication gap.

Paraverbal Negotiating Behavior:
The Meaning of Silence

Expressive people tend to be uncomfortable with more than a second or two of silence during a conversation, while people from reserved cultures feel at ease with much longer silences. Japanese negotiators for example often sit without speaking for what seems like an eternity to voluble Mexicans, Greeks or Americans. After three or four seconds the latter feel compelled to say something – anything – to fill that awful silence. If nature abhors a vacuum, people from emotionally expressive cultures abhor any lull in the conversation.

Unfortunately the loquacity of expressive people tends to irritate the reticent Japanese, who seem to value the space between the spoken words just as much as the words themselves. Negotiators from reserved cultures do not feel the need to engage in constant, stream-of-consciousness blabbing the way many of their expressive counterparts do.

Paraverbal Behavior: Conversational
Turn-taking vs Conversational Overlap

'Conversational overlap' is a twenty-dollar term for interrupting another speaker. While expressive people regard interruptions as a normal part of conversation, overlap is considered rude by people from reserved societies. For instance, northern European and North American negotiators are often frustrated by the constant interruptions they experience while conducting meetings in Italy, Spain or the former Yugoslavia.

Scandinavian researchers have studied conversational patterns during business negotiations between restrained Swedes and their more expressive Spanish counterparts. They found that Spanish negotiators interrupt Swedes about five times as often as Swedes interrupt Spaniards. Since Scandinavians find interruptions disruptive and rude, it is easy to see how irritation and conflict can arise during meetings with expressive southerners.

Then there's Asia. The super-polite Japanese not only take turns to carefully avoid overlap. They go a step further, often pausing five or ten seconds before taking their conversational turn.

My experience is that problems occur with overlap unless both sides know about this cultural difference. Latins and Arabs tend to think the Japanese are at loss for words or indecisive, while the Japanese may find their voluble counterparts rude and insulting.

We know by now that at a sales meeting it is primarily the seller's responsibility to adapt his or her conversational behavior to that of the customer. During joint venture or strategic alliance talks, however, each side should strive to meet the other half way. But remember, people negotiating across cultures can make those adjustments only if they are aware that the potential for a communication conflict does exist.

Having considered differences in paraverbal language, now let's look at body language, also called nonverbal communication.

The Four Key Elements of Nonverbal Negotiating Behavior

Veterans of cross-cultural business meetings find that differences in these four facets of body language are potentially the most disruptive in international negotiating sessions:

PROXEMICS: Spatial Behavior, Interpersonal Distance.
HAPTICS: Touch Behavior.
OCULESICS: Gaze Behavior, Eye Contact.
KINESICS: Body Movement, Gestures.

Distance Behavior: The 'Space Bubble'

Every human being is surrounded by an invisible envelope of air called a 'space bubble' which varies in size according to (a) where in the world we grew up, and (b) the particular situation.

For example, two Anglophone Canadians who have just met at a social event are likely to stand about an arm's length away from each other. But the space bubbles of the same two Canadians making love shrink to zero: they are (hopefully!) meeting skin to skin.

No spatial confusion exists as long as the people involved share similar-sized comfort zones. The difficulties begin in cross-cultural situations when different-sized space bubbles collide.

Figure 7.2 shows the approximate range of same-sex space-bubble sizes across cultures in a business situation.

Fig. 7.2 Distance Behavior: The Use of Space.

CLOSE: 20 to 35 cms. (8 to 14 inches)
The Arab World
The Mediterranean Region
Latin Europe
Latin America

DISTANT: 40 to 60 cms. (16 to 24 inches)
Most Asians
Northern, Central and Eastern Europeans
North Americans

Space: When Worlds Collide

Some Arab men show their friendliness to other males by moving in so close you soon know what they had for lunch. If you are a large-bubble person you will probably instinctively step back, which signals the Arab you don't like him. Not at all a good way to start a productive business relationship! On the other hand, a small-bubble business visitor meeting his East Asian or northern European counterpart risks being taken for an aggressive person, perhaps even one intent on intimidation.

Our first few weeks in Italy I unconsciously tried to avoid those friendly Latin space invaders by keeping a conference table or desk between us. But gregarious visitors from various parts of Italy and the Mediterranean basin would either walk right around to my side of the desk or lean towards me way across the table. Which made me feel they were constantly "getting in my face" – a revealing American phrase which connotes aggressive, threatening behavior. However, once I understood why Latins and other Mediterranean peoples like to get so close I felt more comfortable during business meetings there.

Expressive people also engage in more physical contact in public than men and women from more emotionally reserved cultures. Figure 7.3 classifies cultures by the degree to which touch behavior is accepted.

Fig. 7.3

> *HIGH CONTACT CULTURES*
> Arab World and Mediterranean Region
> Latin Europe and Latin America
>
> *VARIABLE CONTACT*
> Central and Eastern Europe
> North America, Australia/New Zealand
>
> *LOW CONTACT CULTURES*
> Most of Asia
> UK and Northern Europe

How Touching!

Differences in touch behavior are serious enough for problems to arise even between cultures located fairly close together on the chart. For example, Americans do too much shoulder patting, elbow grabbing and back slapping to please most British people. But on the other hand, Latin Americans often accuse Yanks of being snobbish and standoffish because they do not engage in enough physical touching.

Similarly, the variation between the British and the French is surprisingly large considering that these two European countries are separated only by a narrow channel of water. Some years ago researchers studied comparative touch behavior in Paris and London cafés by counting the number of times couples touched each other on the hand, arm, shoulder etc. They counted about 100 touches in Paris and ... you've probably guessed it ... exactly zero times in London. Even though the French are known to be a tactile people compared to the Brits, so large a variation between people of neighboring cultures warns us of what to expect when we venture abroad.

Touching: How?

Touch behavior regarded as proper in one culture may be less appropriate in another. Shortly after we relocated to New Delhi I was surprised by an incident that occurred during a trip to Bombay.

After a pleasant morning business meeting my Indian counterpart casually took my hand while we were walking to a restaurant for lunch. Now, at that point I had to make a quick decision. If a man wants to hold hands with me in Chicago, London or Frankfurt, I know exactly what is going on. In those cultures men who hold hands with other men are sending a clear nonverbal message of sexual interest. But here I was in India. Does same-gender handholding mean the same thing in South Asia?

There in the monsoon heat of Bombay, where holding hands is a sticky affair, I was literally in a bit of a sweat. Then I remembered having seen a couple of our male friends in New Delhi holding hands with other men from time to time. I was glad to recall that it was just a gesture of friendship. And even gladder that I had not hastily pulled my hand away – that would have been a rude move indeed in India.

Touch Behavior: Shaking Hands Across Cultures

Among business people the world over the handshake is the most common form of physical contact. Figure 7.4 lists a few of the variations.

Fig. 7.4 THE HANDSHAKE

Germans	Firm, brisk and frequent
French	Light, quick and frequent
British	Moderate
Latin Americans	Firm and frequent
North Americans	Firm and infrequent
Arabs	Gentle, repeated and lingering
South Asians	Gentle, often lingering
Koreans	Moderately firm
Most Asians	Very gentle and infrequent

Most Europeans shake hands each time they meet and again when they take leave. North Americans shake hands less often than Europeans, but more firmly than most Asians.

The Eyes Have It

Perhaps the subtlest form of body language is gaze behavior. We are easily confused when people use either stronger or weaker eye contact than we do. Figure 7.5 displays the variations.

Figure 7.5

INTENSE EYE CONTACT
The Arab World and the Mediterranean Region
Latin Europeans and Latin Americans

FIRM
Northern Europe and North America

MODERATE
Korea and Thailand
Sub-Saharan Africans

INDIRECT EYE CONTACT
Most of Asia

I conduct business with negotiators at both ends of the gaze-behavior spectrum. When meeting with Arabs, Turks and Latin Europeans I try to look them firmly in the eye whenever we are conversing. People from very expressive cultures value strong, direct eye contact.

Eye Contact in Expressive Cultures

Living in Florence taught me the importance of appropriate gaze behavior. One day I was walking to the train station accompanied by my friend Paolo. It was only a ten-minute stroll and I thought we had plenty of time. However, every time Paolo had something to say he would grab me by the shoulders and turn me towards him so that we could look directly into each other's eyes. Since Paolo spoke every few steps, I ended up missing my train. From that day on I mentally doubled my estimated walking time when in the company of a Latin European.

Where I grew up you chat with your companions as you walk side by side, automatically scanning the surface in front of you so as to sidestep the dog droppings. But in the truly expressive societies of this world, that kind of walking and talking is considered cold and impersonal. Emotionally expressive people like to read your eyes and your face as they talk to you. Direct eye contact is a critical element of correct body language.

Italian gaze protocol in an automobile is especially interesting. Our first month in Florence found me on the *autostrada* headed for Milan at 140 kilometers an hour (over 85 mph) with my colleague Giorgio driving. Giorgio was briefing me on the complex negotiation scheduled for that afternoon, and wanted to be sure I understood every single detail. So he kept studying my face intently to see if I was getting it while waving his free arm to emphasize the importance of what he was telling me.

I couldn't believe it. Here we were, hurtling around curves and roaring through dimly-lit tunnels at high speed in a car driven one-handed by a guy whose eyes were focused more on the passenger next to him than on the road ahead.

Half way to Milan I broke my long silence to croak, "Okay, Giorgio, it's my turn to drive now!" And for the next eight years I did most of the driving. For some reason I was never able to get used to that particular facet of Italian gaze behavior.

Eye Contact in the Pacific Rim

Business visitors to East and Southeast Asia should prepare themselves to encounter the opposite style of gaze behavior. There, a direct gaze may be interpreted as a hostile act. Many Japanese and other Asians feel uncomfortable with strong eye contact. So I try not to stare the Japanese in the eye across the conference table, for example. Singaporean Chinese have asked me, "Why are you looking at us so fiercely?"

Intense eye contact makes many Asians think you are trying to intimidate them, to 'stare them down.' In Malaysia and Singapore, both countries with very little violent crime, a man staring at another male is assumed to be provoking a fight. And a woman who makes more than fleeting eye contact with a man is assumed to want sex with him right then and there.

Some visitors think to avoid such problems by donning sunglasses. Unfortunately that solution creates another problem. In Southeast Asia it is rude to have dark glasses on when conversing with someone unless that person is also wearing sunglasses.

Body Stance and Eye Contact

One more aspect of gaze behavior is of interest to globetrotting negotiators. In the expressive, intense-gaze cultures of the Mediterranean region, two men talking to each other will stand practically nose to nose, directly facing each other. This stance allows plenty of opportunity for eye-reading and face-reading.

By way of contrast, in the more moderate-gaze cultures of the UK and North America, two business people usually converse at right angles to each other. Anglo-Saxons feel less need for reading each other's expressions and some feel uncomfortable with too much face-to-face contact.

Nonverbal Communication: Kinesics

Two aspects of kinesics are of special importance for international negotiators: facial expressions and hand and arm gestures. Emotionally expressive people employ plenty of both, while their brothers and sisters from the more reserved cultures are famous for 'poker faces' and little bodily movement.

Expressive negotiators gesticulate to add emphasis to what they are saying as well as to send nonverbal messages. Those from reserved cultures value restrained nonverbal behavior and discourage open display of emotion. Latins seem to wear their hearts on their sleeves. They trust people who show their feelings openly and distrust those who mask their emotions. In contrast, the taciturn Japanese and Germans may regard such displays as childish and immature.

Facial Expression: Raised Eyebrows

Negotiators are likely to encounter raised eyebrows in many parts of the world. But flashing one's eyebrows sends different signals in different cultures.

Fig. 7.6

North Americans	Interest, surprise
British	Skepticism
Germans	"You are clever!"
Filipinos	"Hello!"
Arabs	"No!"
Chinese	Disagreement

What this list shows is that the same expression can have a different meaning, sometimes even the opposite meaning, in another culture. The same applies to hand and arm gestures.

Ambiguous Gestures

Use of Left Hand. The left hand is considered unclean in Muslim, Hindu and Buddhist cultures. Avoid touching people or handing them objects such as your business card with the left hand. An American expatriate manager in Indonesia, the most populous Muslim country, learned that it was all right to sign documents with his left hand but he had to hand them to people with his right.

A participant in one of our "Negotiating in the Pacific Rim" seminars at the University of Wisconsin's Management Institute asked what to do in Thailand. He had traveled to Bangkok enough to know that the left hand is considered unclean there. But he also knew that to show respect to high-status persons you have to hand them a gift or a business card with both hands.

We explained that Thais and some other Asians have found a neat way to dodge the horns of the two-hand dilemma. The approved procedure is to offer the object in your right hand cupping your right elbow with the left hand. Thus both arms are involved, showing respect, while only the (clean) right hand actually touches the object being passed.

Showing the Sole of Your Shoe. The bottom of your shoe or your foot are also regarded as unclean in the same cultures. Foreign visitors should avoid crossing their legs in such a way that the sole of their shoe is visible to anyone.

Fist in Palm. Giving my first presentation in Southeast Asia, I emphasized the key point by pounding the palm of my left hand with my right fist. When several people in the audience gasped or tittered

I knew I had committed a faux pas. After the talk two local people kindly told me that bit of body language is similar to an obscene sexual gesture.

Index Finger: Pointing. Throughout East and Southeast Asia it is rude to point at anyone with your forefinger. Instead, use your whole hand, flat with the palm down in Japan, fist clenched with the thumb on top in most of the ASEAN countries. You may also jerk your chin in the direction you wish to indicate. The subtlest way is to simply glance in the direction you wish to indicate.

Index Finger: Beckoning. During one of my seminars at a business college in Copenhagen, a professor opened the lecture room door and signaled to a colleague by crooking her index finger in the familiar Euro-American beckoning motion. Her gesture provided me with a perfect opportunity to explain that all over Asia, that particular sign is reserved for calling dogs and prostitutes. A repeated scooping motion of the right hand is the polite way to beckon those who happen to be neither pets nor ladies of the night.

Tapping Your Head. Non-Europeans are constantly amazed that body language can vary so widely within this tiny appendage of the Eurasian land mass. A good example is the head tap.
- In France, Italy and Germany, if you tap your forehead or temple with your finger while looking at someone you are saying nonverbally, "Hey, you are stupid!" Be especially careful using that sign in Germany, where it is called *Vogelzeigen* and will cost you a hefty fine if the *Polizei* catch you doing it
- In Spain or Great Britain that same gesture is self-referential and means, "I am so clever!"
- In the Netherlands, watch carefully. If a Dutchman taps the right side of his head with the index finger vertical it translates, "You are a very smart person." But if he taps his forehead with the finger horizontal he is saying, "You are an idiot!"

The 'Thumbs Up' Sign. Be careful with this one too. While the raised thumb is slowly becoming a universal sign for "Great!" it isn't quite there yet. In Germany and other parts of Europe for example it signifies the numeral one. But in the Eastern Mediterranean and parts of Europe it is a rude sexual sign.

The Peace Sign. The forefinger and second finger extended with palm facing outwards meant "V for Victory" during World War II. Today it means "Peace." But if you accidentally reverse your hand and flash the sign with your palm facing inwards, you've really done it. Should that happen you had better be bigger than the person you just insulted, because the peace sign reversed means roughly the same thing as "flipping the bird" – raising your middle finger with the palm in.

The A-OK Sign. The thumb-and-forefinger circle is easily the most dangerous and ambiguous of gestures. Of course most of its multiple meanings are harmless enough:

- American astronauts: "Everything OK. All systems go!"
- For the Japanese the circular shape looks like a coin, so it means "Now we are talking about money."
- In the south of France it symbolizes the zero, so it indicates quite the opposite: "nothing" or "worthless."
- But in the Iberian peninsula, Brazil and some other parts of Latin America, parts of Europe and Russia, LOOK OUT! In those cultures it is used as a vulgar sexual suggestion. The risk of giving offense is so great I've stopped using the A-OK sign entirely for fear of using it in the wrong place.

The Cultural Relativity of Business Behavior

The susceptibility of gestures to misinterpretation reminds us of a universal truth: behavior which is polite and proper in our culture may be rude and offensive in another. To help international business travelers avoid damaging blunders, our next chapter focuses on global business protocol.

8. Global Business Protocol and Etiquette

This is a good place to review Iron Law # 1 of international business, which states that it is the visitor's responsibility to understand local business customs and practices. That responsibility is twice as great if the visitor is on the sales and marketing side, because Iron Law # 2 dictates that the Seller is expected to adapt to the Buyer's customs and practices.

Which brings us to the issue of business protocol, that is, the rules and norms of proper business behavior in a particular culture. International marketers and negotiators who flagrantly violate these rules risk alienating their local counterparts.

It's true that to err is human, but aren't we supposed to aim for Zero Defects these days? Maybe a reasonable goal would be to commit fewer blunders than any of our competitors. To achieve that goal we have to know a good deal about international business protocol. A good starting point is to learn as much as possible about local sensitivities before visiting a particular market. The following case shows what can happen when we do not.

Case 8.1 : "A Slip of the Tongue"

TransOceanic is a worldwide logistics services company involved in freight forwarding and container consolidation, based in the United States. For almost six months they had been working hard to expand their network of local representatives throughout the Middle East. TO's number one regional priority was to conclude a representation agreement with Arabco, one of Saudi Arabia's largest and most established logistics companies.

To achieve this goal, Regional Manager Ted Goodfellow of TransOceanic had been meeting once or twice a month with Arabco. By now the two companies had agreed on all the financial, legal and technical issues. Ted was now back in Riyadh to wrap up the final details and sign the contract. This visit was largely a formality – both sides clearly wanted this agreement.

During the pleasant meeting with the top Arabco executives Goodfellow casually mentioned, "We at TransOceanic are really looking forward to working with you here in the Persian Gulf!" At that there was a moment of shocked silence on the Arabco side of the conference table. Then the three senior executives arose and strode angrily out of the room, breaking off negotiations.

Bewildered, Ted looked at the two junior Saudis who had remained behind. He hated to see six months of hard work going up in smoke. "What happened here?" he asked the young Arabs across the table. "Did I say something wrong?"

After some hesitation one of the Arabco employees explained that in Saudi Arabia, the body of water in question is called the *Arabian Gulf*. By misnaming it Ted had unintentionally implied that the Gulf belonged to Iran, a country which Saudi Arabia at that time considered hostile and threatening.

The bosses of Arabco were now too upset with Ted to listen to an apology from him. "Well, what should we do then to get these talks back on track?" asked Ted. At this the young Arabs shrugged, smiled faintly and ushered the American to the door. On the way back to his hotel Ted Goodfellow focused his mind on finding a way to repair the damaged relationship.

This regrettable incident happened in the early 1990's to a friend of mine. We use this and similar cases in our negotiation seminars to demonstrate the importance of understanding local sensitivities.

Fortunately, these days books, newsletters, magazine articles, workshops, audio cassettes, video tapes and CDs are available to help the globe-trotting negotiator. For example, I like to read Roger Axtell's *Do's and Taboos* books, published by John Wiley & Sons in the USA. They are always fun to read and help you prepare for visits to new markets or refresh your memory on markets you haven't been to for a while.

Patterns of International Business Protocol

Another way to learn the business protocol and etiquette of unfamiliar cultures is to apply the concept of cultural patterns outlined in the preceding chapters. Because our brains are programmed to think in patterns, this approach works for the busy people who attend our Global Management seminars.

As an example, let's recall the rules for making initial contact with a potential customer or partner abroad. When working with relation-ship-focused markets such as Japan, South Korea, China, Saudi Arabia and Brazil, you will recall that protocol demands an indirect approach. We need to be introduced by a credible third party. On the other hand, with deal-focused cultures such as the U.S., Canada and Australia a direct approach may work just as well. International business protocol can be that simple.

Things get more complex however when we start planning for the first meeting with our new contact. We'll see that our "patterns of culture " approach explains some, but not all protocol behavior.

Meeting Protocol: Dress Code

Climate and culture both play a role in sartorial behavior. In the tropics and hot desert climes businessmen often wear an open-necked shirt and cotton trousers. But even in those markets it may be safer to wear a suit coat or blazer to the first meeting just in case. For meetings with government officials in RF, hierarchical cultures this formality takes on greater importance.

In most parts of the world business women can choose between a good dress, suit or blazer and skirt. For men a dark suit, conservative tie and dark socks will cover most meetings with high-status individuals. Here are a few culture-specific hints:

– Visits to Latin Europe and Latin America require special attention to the style and quality of both men's and women's apparel and accessories. *La bella figura* is a key Italian value, for instance.
– In the Middle East some of your business contacts will judge you partly by the quality and price of your briefcase, watch, pen and jewelry. Wear and carry the best you have.
– Older Germans often feel more comfortable doing business with men whose shoes are well polished.

- Throughout Asia it is a good idea to wear slip-on shoes such as high quality loafers, because custom requires you to remove your footwear when entering temples, homes and some offices as well.
- Americans pay special attention to the condition of your teeth, so some visitors include a stop at their dentist's office for a cleaning as part of their preparation.
- In Muslim and Hindu cultures female visitors should dress modestly, showing as little bare skin as possible. In India for instance my wife Hopi and I have both had the experience of traveling with women who against our advice started out wearing sleeveless blouses or tank tops, pleading the extreme heat. These visitors inevitably received so much unwelcome attention that by the second day they donned more seemly attire. Hopi's advice is to observe how Indian women dress to beat the heat. That is, while you needn't necessarily don a sari, do wear only 100 percent cotton during the hot seasons, silks in the cooler seasons.

Meeting Protocol: Punctuality

In rigid-time cultures it is imperative to be on time for scheduled meetings. But even in polychronic cultures the visitor is expected to be punctual, in order to show respect. And remember, if our counterparts keep us waiting in a fluid-time culture, they are not being rude. They are being themselves – polychronic!

Nonverbal Greetings: Handshake, Bow, Salaam, Namaste or Wai?

For men being introduced to female counterparts, one of the few rules of etiquette that is almost universally valid is to wait for the woman to offer her hand. In most deal-focused cultures today businesswomen expect to shake hands with men.

In some RF cultures however women may not want to shake a man's hand. For example, in India male travelers should be prepared to exchange the elegant *namaste* gesture (called *namaskar* in the south), pressing the palms of both hands together at about chin level with perhaps a slight dip of the head. With Thai women the similar *wai* gesture is usually appropriate, although a few Bangkok women I do business with feel comfortable shaking hands.

Regarding Japan, we are frequently asked by Europeans, Americans and Singaporeans about bowing. In my experience non-Japanese often look awkward when attempting to bow. So my Japanese friends recommend nodding your head respectfully while shaking hands, maintaining gentle eye contact while doing so.

Nonverbal Greetings. Kissing: Hand, Cheek, Lips ... Or None of the Above?

Non-European visitors tend to be perplexed by the variety of kissing rituals in the multicultural mosaic that is Europe. Here are some guidelines:

- Don't worry about kissing or being kissed the first time you meet.
- At subsequent meetings foreigners are excused from the kissing if they do not wish to participate. This will be a relief to many Asians who feel ill at ease with the strange and embarrassing custom of kissing people in public.
- This is for men who do decide to join in: When kissing a woman's hand or cheek, you don't actually touch the skin. Just kiss the air a few millimeters (a small fraction of an inch) from her hand or cheek.
- Cheek-kissing: The proper Brits usually kiss just once (on the right cheek), the French twice (left, right) and the passionate Belgians three times: left, right, left.
- The reticent Germans seem to do very little cheek kissing. Like the Italians and Spanish, a German is more likely to kiss her hand.
- In Vienna, though you may still occasionally hear an Austrian gentleman murmur, *Küss die Hand, gnädige Frau!"* a foreigner need not feel obligated to actually kiss the lady's hand.
- For non-European women: When a man raises your hand to his lips, the appropriate response is to react as though this is about the fifth time it has happened to you today. Just acknowledge the gallant gesture with a slight smile.
- Some male visitors to Russia may not be quite comfortable with being kissed on the lips by Russian men while enfolded in a great bear hug. My advice: Have another vodka and enjoy.

Meeting Protocol: Forms of Address

The more formal the culture, the more likely you will confine yourself to using the person's family name plus any applicable title or honorific. This is sometimes a problem for Yanks and Aussies doing business in East Asia.

For example, you really do not need to know the full name of a senior Korean, especially if he is your customer or potential customer. "Manager Kim" or "Chairman Park" show the appropriate degree of respect in this hierarchical society. Visitors to Japan who interact with women should remember that the polite prefix *san* can mean 'Miss', 'Ms' or 'Mrs' as well as 'Mister.'

The Chinese normally have three names of one syllable each, of which the first is the family name. So your counterpart Yi Er Man should be addressed as "Mr. Yi" rather than "Mr. Man." But be careful. To accommodate foreigners Chinese often reverse the names when they have their business cards printed. Those ever-polite Japanese sometimes do this too. When in doubt, just ask.

Indonesia's largest ethnic group, the Javanese, commonly have only one name. But middle class Javanese may have two, those of the upper class three names. In neighboring Malaysia be conscious of the fact that there is a complex hierarchy of nobility reminiscent of medieval Europe. If your counterpart qualifies as a 'Tan Sri' for instance, be sure to use that title both in correspondence and in person.

In Spain and the Hispanic countries of Latin America, look for two family names. The Mexican Pablo Garcia-Mendoza for example would be 'Señor Garcia' to you. Unless of course he is a university graduate, in which case he becomes *Licenciado* ('Licenciada' for a woman) Garcia.

What about the more informal cultures? In the USA the saying goes, "I don't care what you call me just as long as you call me for dinner." Nevertheless, physicians and surgeons are normally addressed as "Doctor" on all occasions. PhD's on the other hand are usually called "Dr." only when he or she is 'on duty.' (In the UK a male surgeon named Smith is properly addressed as Mr. rather than Dr. Smith.)

Even in the informal USA there are hierarchies. Whereas at a Silicon Valley startup company everyone may be on a first-name basis, in larger, more traditional corporations top executives are often addressed as Mr., Miss, Ms. or Mrs. – at least in the office. Back in the 1980s at

Sears Roebuck and Co. we commonly addressed only the CEO and vice presidents with "Mr." – about a dozen executives in all.

Verbal Greetings

Many cultures employ standard expressions as verbal greetings. For instance Americans often say, "Hi, how are you?" Some Asians and Europeans seem to be confused by this rhetorical question, thinking the Yank is actually asking after their health. In fact it's a meaningless expression calling for the automatic response, "Fine! How are you?" whereupon everyone gets right down to business.

I remember a meeting in Amsterdam at which two friendly, low-context Dutchmen complained that Americans are superficial people because, "When you ask how we are, you really don't give a damn, do you?" Some Germans agree with that statement. Unlike Americans, a German is likely to ask "*Wie geht es Ihnen?*" only if you have been ill and she wants to know if you have recovered.

But Europeans also employ various meaningless mantras when being introduced to someone for the first time. Germans for example may say "*Sehr angenehm,*" meaning it is a great pleasure to meet you. Now, excuse me. How do they know whether it's going to be such a great pleasure when they don't even know me yet? My German friends blame it on a borrowing from the English "Pleasure to meet you" or from the French "*Enchanté!*" (literally "I'm enchanted to meet you!").

My favorite greetings are the ones I heard almost every day for several years in Singapore. The lift operator in our office building on Orchard Road used to ask me either, "Have you had your lunch?" or "Have you had your rice?" whenever I entered the elevator. Passengers in the lift who were new to Southeast Asia must have wondered why the old gentleman would ask me that at 7:30 in the morning. (The polite answer is of course, "Yes, thank you. Have you had yours?" regardless of the time of day.)

Meeting Protocol: Exchanging Business Cards

Many Asian visitors to the United States are struck by how casually Americans treat that little bit of cardboard. An American is likely to stuff the card in his back pocket, toss it onto the desk, scribble on it, or perhaps pick his teeth with it at the lunch table.

More formal cultures tend to treat the name card with more respect. I always enjoy observing the ritual of the *meishi* in Japan, for instance. There the 'meishi' or business card is exchanged with great ceremony. It is presented and received with both hands, scanned carefully for four or five seconds, placed respectfully on the conference table and then later put reverently into a leather (not plastic) card wallet.

Business visitors to the Pacific Rim will note that the ceremony of the meishi has spread to most parts of East and Southeast Asia, a hierarchical part of the global marketplace. There we are expected to treat the name card with the same respect we show the person who gave us the card.

Giving and Receiving Gifts

In contrast to most DF cultures, RF people value exchanging gifts because it is an accepted way to build and cement strong personal relationships. On these questions the wise business traveler relies on local contacts or consults some of the guides mentioned in the Resource List of this book. The following tips are intended to give the reader an idea as to the complexity of exchanging gifts across cultures.

Business Gifts

- WHAT to give: Be aware of culture-specific taboos. Avoid sharp objects such as knives: in some cultures they symbolize the ending of a relationship. In China avoid clocks and watches, which bring bad luck because the word for clock sounds like another Chinese word that refers to death.
- Good choices are quality writing instruments, branded whisky or cognac (in non-Muslim cultures), picture books about your city, region or country, and products your home country is famous for.
- WHEN to give: In Europe, after the agreement is signed. In Japan and most other Asian countries, at the end of the meeting. Note that North America is not a gift-giving culture. Many companies have strict policies concerning gifts, especially for people with purchasing responsibilities.
- HOW to give: In Japan the wrapping of the gift is at least as important as the gift itself. In Japan and the rest of Asia, present and receive any gift with both hands – except in Thailand, where you

hand over the present with your right hand supported by your left. In Asia your gift will probably be unwrapped after you leave. In Europe and North and South America it will more likely be opened in front of you.

While the nuances of gift giving are important, not every blunder is fatal. For example, a few years ago a Chinese delegation came to Copenhagen to sign a contract for a large purchase of railway equipment. On the last evening the Danes presented each of the senior Chinese with an expensive and tasteful gold desk clock.

The next morning on the way to the airport the junior member of the visiting delegation whispered to his young Danish counterpart, "You know, one really should not give clocks to Chinese people. Clocks remind us of death, bring bad luck." Then as the Dane was groaning inwardly with dismay the Chinese smiled and added, "But that's all right. No one in this group is superstitious."

Hostess Gifts: Europe

Let's say you are invited to dinner at the home of your potential joint venture partner. You should bring flowers for the hostess, right? Well, let's consider a few taboos:

– Red roses are out unless you are romancing the hostess.
– Yellow roses brought by a male guest in France signifies he is romancing the host.
– Red carnations are bad unless you know your hosts are good Socialists.
– Mums, calla lilies, white asters and dahlias are no good because they are for funerals.
– Remember to bring an uneven number, except that bouquets of six and 12 are OK.
– In Germany and some other countries don't forget to unwrap the bouquet before presenting it to the hostess.
– If it is to be fairly large dinner party, remind yourself to have the flowers delivered earlier in the day: your hostess will be too busy attending to guests to find a vase and water for your silly blooms.

So how about a bottle of wine instead? That's also a bit tricky in Europe because your host might get the impression you think his wine cellar is inadequate. If you absolutely must bring wine, select a very fine bottle from a renowned winemaker, preferably one from your home region if you come from a wine country.

"Well then, what IS the best choice for a hostess gift?" Candy or cakes. A box of fine chocolates, for example. Or a tin of the very best biscuits (cookies). And something for the children would be a very good idea.

Meeting Protocol: Refreshments

In Asia and the Middle East, business visitors will be offered hot tea or coffee. Savvy travelers wait for their host to take a sip before putting cup to lip. They also always accept the offered beverage, a symbol of hospitality, and avoid asking for anything that has not been explicitly offered. To request a Coca-Cola for example could cause your hosts loss of face if it does not happen to be available.

Wining and Dining

Here again the no no's are many and varied, so the smart visitor relies on local advisers or culture-specific guides. Just think about food and drink taboos:

– Observant Muslims do not drink alcohol or eat any pork product. Many avoid shellfish as well. Jews share some of these food taboos.
– Hindus avoid both beef and pork; most are in fact strict vegetarians.
– Buddhists are often also strict vegetarians, but many Thai Buddhists enjoy beef so long as someone else has done the slaughtering for them.
– Timid travelers may have trouble with spicy, strong-smelling or unfamiliar foods. Some of our friends in Singapore, Malaysia and Thailand love to torment first-time visitors by ordering durian – the 'King of Fruits' – for dessert. This Southeast Asian fruit has a mild, somewhat custardy flavor but exudes a most unusual fragrance. To put it delicately, it stinks like a stopped-up sink – or worse. I did learn to savor durian in cooked form as a pudding, but can't eat it raw without holding my nose.

Some food and drink faux pas are serious, such as offering your Muslim guest a pork chop or your Hindu friend a T-bone steak. Other mistakes are simply amusing. Most Italians for example drink cappuccino only in the morning, before about 10:00 am. So when we lived in Italy I loved to go into a coffee bar around 3:00 pm and order, *"Un cappuccio, per favore!"* just to enjoy the startled expression on the *barista's* face. Unless he caught on quickly to my foreign accent, that barista would think he had just met one very weird Italian indeed!

Amusement aside, knowing the rudiments of local business protocol shows your counterpart that you are a serious and committed potential supplier or partner. And making fewer blunders gives you an edge over your less conscientious competitor.

In the next chapter we examine an especially touchy issue: corruption and bribery.

9. Culture, Corruption and Bribery

This guide to negotiating across cultures would be incomplete without a look at how to do business successfully in some difficult markets where corruption is rife and bribing government officials is accepted practice.

The international bribery issue is repeatedly mentioned by Global Management clients and seminar participants around the world as an issue of concern. Most of them ask, "How can I do business around the world without having to pay bribes?" This chapter is an attempt to answer that question.

Official corruption in certain major markets prompts business people to make under-the-table payments in order to get things done. In some countries these payments are sanctioned by custom even though they are illegal under local law. Regardless of how bribes are regarded locally, however, most of the business executives who attend our Global Management seminars want to know how to avoid them.

The Downside of Bribing Officials

Today the U.S. government is the only one in the world which legislates heavy penalties – fines and prison sentences – for any of its citizens caught bribing overseas officials. In contrast, many European countries not only condone such payments, they permit their companies to claim foreign bribes as a tax deduction.

Nevertheless, business people of any nationality have good reasons for avoiding the bribery trap:

– Ethics. This is a cultural variable. Many societies regard bribery as an unethical practice, which corrupts both the giver and the recipient of the bribe.
– Corporate Ethics. The regulations of many companies prohibit bribery.

- Expense. Illegal payments can become a major business expense. Hong Kong companies report that bribes account for about five percent of the cost of doing business in China. In Russia the cost is said to range higher, in Indonesia perhaps still higher.
- Local Law. Even countries where official corruption is widespread have laws on the books prohibiting the bribing of their government employees. While such laws may be only sporadically enforced, the foreigner unlucky enough to get caught is likely to face a capricious legal system as well as unpleasant prison conditions.

Now let's look at why official corruption and bribery are greater problems in some countries than in others.

Reputable organizations study the bribery issue. One of them is Transparency International, a Berlin-based group. TI publishes an annual Corruption Index of over 50 countries based on surveys of international business travelers. Similarly, Hong Kong-based Political and Economic Consultancy (PERC) has surveyed expatriate managers to come up with a corruption rating for many Asian countries.

Poverty and Corruption

The lists compiled by TI, PERC and other organizations reveal that poverty is a common trait of so-called 'corrupt' countries. For example, TI often lists Nigeria, Pakistan, Kenya, Bangladesh and China as among the most corrupt countries. All of these are low-income developing economies. India and Indonesia also regularly belong to the 'Top Ten.'

By way of contrast, New Zealand, Denmark, Sweden, Finland and Canada, consistently listed by TI as among the least corrupt countries, are among the world's richest. PERC's Asian surveys point to the same conclusion: the poorer countries such as India, China and Indonesia rank highest in official corruption, while the richer economies – Japan, Hong Kong and Singapore – are the least corrupt.

The poverty-corruption link probably stems from the fact that in low-income countries government officials are poorly paid. Low salaries tempt some (not all) government employees to supplement their income with 'dash' or *la mordida*. Apparently, need tends to breed greed.

Bureaucratic Red Tape Breeds Corruption

Besides being poor, economies perceived as relatively corrupt also tend to be over-regulated – tangled in red tape. Commercial regulations are typically written in such a way as to give bureaucrats discretionary authority to arbitrarily decide an issue for or against a company. This authority provides venal officials with powerful leverage for extracting bribes.

Low government salaries combined with bureaucratic red tape probably account for most illegal payments demanded by officials in so-called corrupt economies.

Unfortunately however, this analysis means little to executives trying to conduct honest business in poor, over-regulated economies. While international trade plus deregulation will eventually bring wealth to developing countries, negotiators want to know what to do NOW – before 'corrupt' countries manage to move up the income ladder. Experience reveals five rules for avoiding bribes even in markets where illegal payments are commonplace.

Rule #1 is the simplest: Never assume you have to give a bribe, even in supposedly highly corrupt societies. Look for another way. He who expects to pay a bribe will end up doing exactly that.

Rule #2 is also simple: "Just say no." Tell the bribee your corporate policy forbids such payments. Of course, this ploy seems to work best for companies with sought-after products or a very big pencil. In other words, those with clout. For example, during the 1960s and 1970s IBM had little trouble introducing its products anywhere. Foreign markets were anxious to have state-of-the-art IBM equipment and knowhow. Case 9.1 provides another example.

Case 9.1: "Using Your Clout"

Giant U.S. discount retailer Wal-Mart is also in a position to say no. According to apparel industry sources in Jakarta, when company founder Sam Walton visited Jakarta in the mid-1980s top Indonesian officials asked him why Wal-Mart was not sourcing any garments or other products in his country. The legendary "Mr. Sam" replied that he refused to buy goods in any market where it was necessary to bribe officials for the privilege of doing business.

Sam Walton was referring to the fact that Indonesian customs officials routinely demanded large bribes for clearing imports of materials and components which local manufacturers needed in order to produce finished goods for export. The government reacted swiftly. Within weeks the responsibility for determining the value of imports was removed from Customs and given to SGS, a private Swiss firm renowned for its probity.

The reorganization worked. By 1986 Sears Roebuck and other big retailers were able to source shoes, apparel and other consumer goods without the added cost and delays of official corruption.

Offer Legal Travel Perks and Favors

Rule #3: When a government employee asks for or hints about a bribe, look hard for legal and ethical ways to meet his or her needs instead. Here are three proven ways:

– Offer an expense-paid visit to your plant or your home office, to a training course in your home country or to attend a business-related meeting, to a course or conference in a third country. All travel expenses are paid, and often a daily cash allowance is added to the package. Such perks are well received in countries where shortage of foreign exchange makes overseas travel a rare privilege. At the same time, a legitimate business purpose is served.
– Make an appropriate donation. According to the business press, an American multinational found that a high official was blocking a proposed telecommunications deal in Southeast Asia. After the U.S. firm donated funds to build an ultra-modern hospital in the official's home district, that deal was immediately approved.
– Do a personal favor, something you would do for a friend or relative. For instance, help the official get his son, daughter, nephew or niece into a university in your homeland or in a third country.

Be Creative

Rule #4: Look for creative ways to accomplish your goals without giving in to graft. The next case illustrates this point.

Case 9.2: "Using Your Head"

A foreign company headquartered in Singapore had to send technicians to Indonesian factories on a regular basis. About half of the company's techs had to slip a fifty dollar bill to the Jakarta airport immigration official on duty in order to get an entry visa stamped in their passports. It was always the same techs who were asked for the bribe.

Trying to figure out why only some of his travelers had to pay, the managing director one day examined his employees' travel documents. In the passports of the techs who were paying the bribes he soon noticed tiny pencil tick marks in the lower right-hand corner of their visa stamps. But the visa stamps of those who weren't paying showed no such marks.

Discussing the matter with his technicians the boss soon figured out that immigration officials were routinely demanding 50 dollars from travelers new to Indonesia. They then marked the visa stamps of those who complied to show fellow officials that "this guy pays." On the other hand, if you refused they just shrugged and stamped your passport anyway, because of course no such payment is required.

That day the director erased all the pencil marks from his techs' passports and briefed them on the scam. Since then his company's travelers have paid no more bribes to immigration officials.

Rule #5: Learn the culture of the country. Culture gives us invaluable clues to evading the bribery trap.

Culture and Corruption

Societies in which illegal payments are common happen to share a number of cultural values. Three of these values are of particular interest to us here:

- They are relationship-focused; personal connections are crucial.
- They are strongly hierarchical, valuing wide status differences.
- They are polychronic, with a relaxed attitude toward time and scheduling.

In the rest of this chapter we will discuss how these three characteristics can provide clues to help business visitors avoid the bribery trap.

But first a word of caution. Obviously, these three common cultural values *per se* have nothing to do with official corruption. Cultures which are relationship-focused, hierarchical and polychronic need not be corrupt. The point here is that the societies identified by international business people as the most corrupt happen to share these particular cultural traits. Anthropologists and sociologists may find such correlations interesting. But for business people what counts is that these shared values suggest effective ways to avoid making illegal payments.

Relationship-Focused Cultures: The Importance of Contacts

While contacts are useful to business people everywhere, in RF cultures personal connections are absolutely essential. You have to know the right people – it really is who you know that counts. *Guanxi*, meaning relationships or connections, is not the only word used to express this concept. The Egyptians have a similar expression, *wastah:* an intermediary or personal contact. The Russian word *blat* carries many of the same connotations.

While the term varies from country to country, the concept is the same: in RF cultures you need good contacts to do business. That's because RF-culture people tend to be uncomfortable dealing with strangers. Strangers are outsiders not to be trusted. So to do business or solve a problem in these countries a foreigner simply must have the right connections.

The RF value can lead unwary business visitors into the bribery trap. For example, on their first visit to a relationship-focused market foreigners often lack the right local contacts. Some think that spreading 'baksheesh' around is the best way to expedite the lengthy process of developing good relationships.

After all, they may say, the exchange of gifts and favors is part and parcel of building guanxi. And expensive gifts are a form of bribery. However, the good news is that even in so-called corrupt countries it is possible to develop effective relationships without bribing anyone. The next three cases provide examples.

Case 9.3: "Using Your Contacts"

An expatriate manager in New Delhi got a rude shock one morning when he opened a letter from the municipal authorities. The letter informed Richard that under new city zoning regulations he had exactly 30 days to vacate the building in which his office was located. If he did not move out on time he would be jailed.

Richard quickly phoned several Indian friends and business acquaintances who confirmed that the officials were serious. For example, the manager of the Central Bank of India branch nearby had just been arrested for not relocating the branch in time.

Since the zoning change affected a large number of businesses in New Delhi, hundreds of people were racing around desperately looking for new locations, which were in short supply. Richard knew he needed to obtain an extension giving him more time to find office space, and the only official authorized to grant extensions was the director of the Delhi Housing Authority.

Next morning the anxious expat arrived at the DHA building at 6 am. When he finally pushed his way into the director's inner sanctum Richard observed the harried bureaucrat brusquely rejecting one application for extension after another. But when the director saw Richard, his face lit up. "Ah, how nice to see you again! That dinner party last month was truly delightful. My regards to your wife. Now, what can I do for you?" Five minutes later a much relieved expat manager left the DHA with a 90-day extension.

Analysis: In a RF culture, when you have developed a pleasant social relationship with someone, that person will often try his or her best to help you in time of need. This relationship may enable you to get the job done without bribery.

Case 9.4: "Building Effective Relationships."

An international sourcing team working for a U.S. department store group was in Cairo trying to bring a local flannel shirt manufacturer up to speed. As they were leaving their hotel for the airport, a senior Egyptian government official they knew rushed up out of breath to ask a favor.

He explained that the wife of Egypt's president was the sponsor of a charitable enterprise, a garment factory set up to provide jobs for orphan girls. The first lady wanted to know what it would take to upgrade the factory to international quality standards.

The two apparel specialists, an American and an Italian, hesitated at first because they had an important meeting the next day in Florence. In the end however they agreed to undertake a thorough evaluation of the factory. They followed up with a report recommending ways to improve quality, and arranged for a production engineer from their company to make a more detailed analysis a month later.

While this special effort caused the team to miss their meeting in Italy, it paid off handsomely in terms of improved government relations. For the next few years the U.S. retailer enjoyed excellent government support for its business activities in Egypt.

Analysis: By doing a small and quite legal favor, the Italo-American team established relationships which smoothed the road for others from their company to do business successfully in Egypt.

Case 9.5: "Building Effective Relationships II."

When Richard's New Delhi office was upgraded to a regional office for South Asia, he had to begin making frequent trips abroad. This became a major hassle because as a foreign resident he was required to obtain two separate clearances each time he wanted to leave the country. Richard's lawyer was able to obtain the tax clearance but for the police clearance he had to apply at the Foreigners' Regional Registration Office in person. These visits normally took the better part of a day.

That all changed however when Richard was introduced to the chief of the FRRO at a New Delhi cocktail party. It turned out the two men shared an interest in Indian military history. After an hour or so of pleasant conversation Colonel Singh said goodbye, adding "Now don't forget. Any time you need a clearance just have the desk sergeant bring you straight to my office."

For the remainder of his stay in India Richard was able to have his paperwork taken care of in an hour or so while enjoying a fascinating conversation. In RF cultures it's who you know that counts. The right personal contacts can save you time, money and frustration.

Polychronic Cultures: The Meaning of Time

Another value which happens to be characteristic of 'corrupt' societies is a relaxed approach to punctuality, schedules and deadlines. Frustrated by seemingly inexplicable delays, executives from clock-worshiping monochronic cultures are often willing to make under-the-table payments in order to expedite a government decision. In this connection it's a good idea to remember that the English word 'tip' is probably derived from the phrase "To Insure Promptness."

Case 9.6: "Hands Up! Your Money or Your Time"

A multinational firm we'll call WMN, with a regional head office in Singapore, decided to open representative offices in Thailand, the Philippines and Indonesia. WMN's regional director in Singapore engaged a reputable international law firm in each country to handle the registration formalities.

While the rep offices in Bangkok and Manila were up and running within three months, it took two long years for the Jakarta operation to be approved and registered. In contrast XYZ, a major competitor of WMN, was able to set up its Jakarta office within just 90 days.

Analysis: WMN's post mortem revealed that the law firms they used both in Thailand and the Philippines enjoyed long-standing close relationships with the responsible government officials. In contrast, the law firm WMN retained in Indonesia turned out to lack these valuable connections.

Shortly after WMN's Jakarta office was finally registered, the Singapore regional director met an executive from XYZ company at a social function there. The latter readily admitted to having expedited the office registration process by handing out large 'facilitation payments.'

Lesson A: Except in Singapore, bureaucrats in Southeast Asia tend to move rather slowly. To speed things up you often have to either know the right people, or bribe the right people.

Afterword: XYZ company closed its Jakarta office less than three years after it opened because its 'operating expenses' had become too high.

Certain government officials kept coming back to the well for more. In contrast, WMN's Jakarta office is still there.

Lesson B: While an illegal payment may promise you a shortcut, it often leads to a dead-end. The bribe that buys you time today may cost you dearly tomorrow.

Case 9.6 mentions Singapore as a market where government works. The Lion City is a living example of the fact that effective government removes a major cause of bribery.

Hierarchical Cultures: Status, Power and Respect

The third relevant value of 'corrupt' countries is the existence of steep organizational hierarchies. In hierarchical societies, lower-ranking officials are often reluctant to make decisions, preferring to pass the buck to their superiors. Business visitors aware of this trait know the importance of negotiating with the highest-ranking official they can reach. Unfortunately, once they are in touch with the high-level official some foreigners assume they still have to pay a bribe in order to get a favorable decision.

Case 9.7: "To Solve Your Problem, Go to the Top of the Hierarchy"

A young Western manager responsible for the Middle East was guiding a delegation of three businessmen on their first visit to pre-revolutionary Iran. When he stepped up to the check-in counter at Isfahan Airport the clerk smiled and said cheerfully, "Sorry sir, the flight to Kerman is fully booked. No seats available today. Next flight in three days."

"But we booked this flight weeks ago! And our reservations were reconfirmed just last week. See, it's marked here on the tickets ..." The clerk shrugged and looked at the foreigner expectantly. Experience told the visitor that fifty dollars was the going rate to make the four seats suddenly available, but he had no intention of playing the game. "Well then, I guess I'll just have to talk to General Manager Zahid," he said, and turned away.

At this the clerk's smile suddenly vanished. "Oh, that will not be necessary. You're in luck: I have just found four seats for you!"

Analysis: A huge plaque in the departure hall advertised the name of the boss of the airport in letters so large a visitor could hardly avoid noting the man's name. However, the clerk became cooperative because he thought the traveler might know his boss personally. In Iran subordinates often live in fear of their superior's disapproval.

Afterword: As expected, the plane to Kerman was in fact empty except for the four foreigners.

Of course, getting to the top of the hierarchy is not always so easy. But remember Rule # 4? While using your brain is always a good idea, sometimes a bit of brawn comes in handy as well.

Case 9.8: "When It Is Not Easy to Get to the Boss"

The week Richard arrived in New Delhi to begin his expatriate assignment he found out that the waiting time for a telephone was a little over three years. Since it would be impossible to run his business without a phone, Richard made inquiries. Old Delhi Hands told him that $5000 under the table would get him a phone within a month. But Richard's employer had strict rules against bribery, so he wrote a letter to the director general of the local telephone company explaining in detail why he needed the phone. Then he made an appointment for a meeting.

Arriving at the telephone company for the meeting, Richard at first thought there was a riot in progress. He saw a mob of about 500 people screaming, waving pieces of paper and trying to push past uniformed guards to enter the building.

The expat's assistant enlightened him: "Oh, it's like this every day here. These people have been waiting years for a telephone and want to see the director general to plead their case. As I told you, you will have a very difficult time getting to see him."

Since he had a confirmed appointment, Richard decided to fight his way through the crowd. It took half an hour to bull his way into the director-general's office and stand in front of his desk. The big boss stood up wearily and shook Richard's hand. "Well, I can see you really want that telephone you wrote me about. Sorry about your torn shirt and your ear – my secretary will apply some iodine. You can be sure you will have a phone in your Jor Bagh office this week."

Analysis: Telephone instruments and connections are often in short supply in developing countries around the world. Business people who cannot or will not pay a bribe usually send a local employee to see a responsible official. Those local staffers accounted for most of the 500 people crowding around the telephone company's office. Why was Richard successful? Partly because his letter made a strong case for needing the phone.

But the main reason is that he stood out from the crowd of other deserving supplicants. He was the only foreigner in the mob. Equally important, Richard's shirt was in shreds and his left ear torn and bleeding. His willingness to endure abuse showed he really wanted that telephone. As promised, the phone was installed 48 hours later.

Afterword: However, the next week Richard found out he had another problem. It would take over 18 months to get a telex – also an absolute must for his office. When he phoned the director general about the telex, the latter listened for a moment and then interrupted Richard's plea with a chuckle: "Don't worry, you won't have to spoil another shirt coming to see me. I will see to it that you have your telex installed within three days."

In Case 9.8, getting to the boss obviously did pay off. However, there are times when even going to the boss is not enough to get the job done. Sometimes you may have to go to the boss's boss.

Case 9.9: "Going All the Way to the Top"

Though the Ministry of Foreign Trade had invited Richard's company to open a office in India, other government agencies such as the Ministry of Finance were obstructing his efforts. One day in September while the expat was trying to figure out how to gain the cooperation of these officials, a call came in from the office of Prime Minister Indira Gandhi.

The PM's social secretary phoned to say that Mrs. Gandhi wanted to buy Christmas presents for her grandkids, the children of her son

Rajiv and his Italian wife Sonia. "Since you represent Sears Roebuck in India, can you get us a Wish Book quickly?"

After thinking a moment Richard replied, "Yes of course. It will be our pleasure. But you will understand that we wish to present it to the Prime Minister in person." Later that day an official invitation to the PM's office was delivered by messenger.

Richard found Mrs. Gandhi in a conference with several of her key ministers. The PM glanced meaningfully at the officials gathered in the room, including the Minister of Finance, and asked the Sears manager: "I trust you are getting good cooperation from the various ministries?"

"Yes Prime Minister, your government's support is excellent" was Richard's reply. And as if by magic, from that day forward government officials in fact became very supportive indeed.

Analysis: The Ministry of Foreign Trade wanted Richard's company to succeed. The expat had notified MFT officials of his forthcoming meeting, and these people in turn had briefed the PM on the importance of Sears Roebuck's efforts in India. Mrs. Gandhi obviously scheduled the meeting so that her ministers would be on hand to get the message.

Richard's diplomatic reply allowed the obstructionists to save face. For the next few years Sears found it easier to do business in India, where government plays a very large role in the economy.

"But in a REAL Crisis You Would Still Make a Payoff, Right?"

We get that question from time to time at our seminars and on consulting assignments. While international executives tend to agree that bribes are avoidable in many situations, what happens when it really comes to the crunch? What about a life-threatening crisis, for example?

Case 9.10: "Life and Death in Delhi"

Like many other developing countries, India tries to conserve hard currency by promoting local production of expensive pharmaceuticals. New Delhi does this by licensing a domestic producer to develop a certain drug while banning all imports to guarantee the licensee a monopoly.

This import-substitution policy almost killed Richard's son years ago. When their four-year old son took a bad fall in Delhi, his parents took him to the local hospital with a fractured skull and massive brain concussion. Doctors told Richard and Hopi the little boy was dying of severe brain damage.

A few hours later the doctors reported there was still a faint hope, but the little guy would need several specific medications within the next 48 hours. The pharmacy however had bad news for the distraught parents. Three of the required drugs were unavailable because imports had been banned for the last two years, even though the domestic licensees were still not yet in production.

Since the boy had to be kept totally immobile he could not be evacuated. Hopi and Richard were stymied: They could neither get the life-saving drugs into the country nor get their dying son out of it.

Luckily however a desperate phone call and telex to friends in Europe put the three drugs on the next Lufthansa flight to Delhi. When the German captain landed at Palam Airport at 6 am he phoned Richard to report, "Yes, I do have the drugs with me. But Customs won't let me bring them in. Better bring a thick wallet – you know what I mean."

Hopi stood vigil at Lester's bedside while Richard left for the airport armed with two thick wallets, one stuffed with rupees and the other with dollars. But when the Chief of Airport Customs insisted it was impossible to bring banned medicines into the country, the expat didn't reach for either of those wallets. Instead Richard blurted out, "But Sir! While you and I are standing here arguing, my son is dying in the hospital."

At this news the Chief looked stricken. "What? Your SON? Why didn't you tell me it was your son? Well, never mind now, just follow me!"

With tears in his eyes the Chief personally stamped the sheaf of documents 'APPROVED' and showed Richard where to pay the 200 percent import duty. (That's where all those rupees came in handy: no checks or credit cards accepted.) He then personally escorted Richard all the way to the parking lot to make sure he got past airport security without delay.

Twenty minutes later Richard arrived at the hospital with the medications, just under the wire.

Analysis: Some strongly hierarchical cultures tend to value sons over daughters. This is the case for example in India, where poor families give up many daughters for adoption, but few sons.

Afterword: A hard-headed young man, the four-year-old defied the dismal prognosis by making a total recovery from the concussion. He went on to learn several languages including Chinese, earned his BA from the University of Wisconsin, his MA from the University of California, and has built a successful career in international communications.

Afterword II: When Richard and Hopi's daughter Clio heard this story a few years ago, she asked, "Dad, if it had been me, what would you have told that Customs officer?"

Richard didn't need to stop and think. He replied, "Clio, I would have told him exactly the same thing. I would have said, 'But Sir! My son is dying in the hospital!'"

In this chapter we cited cases from the real world of global business to illustrate the Five Rules for accomplishing your international business goals without paying bribes. We welcome input from readers who would like to share their own experiences with a view to helping others avoid the bribery trap.

10. Marketing Across Cultures:
Customer Focus in the Global Marketplace

So far we have dealt with the cross-cultural challenges faced by business people engaged in face-to-face selling, buying and negotiating in the global marketplace. In this concluding chapter of Part One we look at how cultural differences affect the people responsible for designing the products and planning the international marketing campaigns.

The marketing of industrial products is generally less impacted by culture than that of consumer goods. True, the people giving the sales presentations and negotiating the contract details have to be concerned with cultural variation regardless of product type. But whereas industrial goods normally require little or no product adaptation, that is not the case with consumer goods.

Consumer Goods: Food and Beverages

Let's start with food and drink. The management of Wal-Mart, world's largest retailer, has been learning a lot about adapting the company's offerings to local tastes and preferences outside the States. In the early 1990s, to crack the Japanese market the U.S. giant teamed up with that country's largest retailer. Wal-Mart soon found that Japanese consumers are more brand-conscious, more detail-oriented, and much more focused on packaging and presentation than Americans.

For example, small items such as oranges, apples and rice crackers have to be individually wrapped: an unaccustomed expense for the U.S. discounter. Local consumers also found Wal-Mart's store brand American cookies too sweet. So as Wal-Mart launches its own stores in Japan, it will face many new challenges of adaptation and localization. But such challenges are all too familiar to companies trying to market food and drinks across cultures.

What Americans call 'sweet corn' is a perfect example. Yanks have been chomping on this variety of maize since pioneer days, lightly boiled and brushed with butter and salt. But when U.S. producer Green Giant tried to market canned sweet corn in Europe during the 1960s they failed utterly, finally closing the canning factory they had built in Italy.

The problem was simple. When it comes to food and beverages, tradition and taste preferences are key elements in the purchasing decision. And except for northern Italians (who love *polenta*) Europeans regarded 'maize' or 'Indian corn' as animal fodder, not fit for human consumption. The market was not ready.

My family and I witnessed this cultural difference in the late 1960s when we lived outside of Vienna and raised sweet corn in our garden. It was a great hit with our American friends but we couldn't even give it away to our Austrian neighbors.

But living in Germany 20 years later we found that things had changed. Well-traveled Europeans had brought back tastes for exotic foods sampled on holidays around the world. So by the mid-1980s sweet corn could be found all over Europe. In Germany for example it was an essential part of the popular *amerikanischer Salat*. Food preferences change slowly, but they do change.

Disaster at Euro Disney

Differences between European and U.S. dining habits played a supporting role in bringing the Disney theme park near Paris to the verge of bankruptcy. Disney, one of the world's most successful global marketers, initially refused to adapt its food and beverage service formula to the European customer.

When it opened in 1993, Euro Disney's restaurants offered insufficient seating capacity. Whereas Americans visiting Disneyland and Disney World in the USA eat lunch anytime the spirit moves them, the French and other European visitors all wanted lunch at the same time, around 1 pm. Nor did European visitors accept standing in queue for an hour or so.

What made matters worse was that Euro Disney restaurants offered no wine or beer. That was because Disney's U.S. eateries are 'family restaurants' where alcoholic beverages are out of place. What did it matter that European traditions and expectations are totally different?

By 1993 Euro Disney had run up losses approaching one billion dollars, a huge sum even for such a large company. Disney management responded by putting a European in charge of the operation to make changes. Among the modifications made was an important addition to the menu: visitors can now quaff beer or sip wine at Disneyland Paris, which has moved into the black.

For the folks at Disney the European fiasco was a temporary blip in a brilliant record of success in marketing across cultures. But even this glitch could have been avoided had Disney execs studied the European history of McDonald's, another superstar of global marketing.

Marketing the Big Mac

The Golden Arches have successfully spanned cultural gaps for decades. McDonald's formula seems to work all over the world with only minor modifications. I happened to witness one such modification when the first Indonesian 'McD' opened in the early 1990s in Jakarta. Scanning the new restaurant's offerings, I was at first puzzled and then impressed when the word 'hamburger' appeared nowhere on the extensive. Big Mac, yes. Burgers, sure. But no hamburger.

Then it hit me. In the world's most populous Muslim country, any reference to 'ham' might well offend some customers. Few Jakartans would be likely to know that the word 'hamburger' is actually derived from the German city of Hamburg, and that burgers are made of beef, not pork.

Under the Golden Arches in India the word hamburger is also absent, but for a different reason: India's majority Hindus venerate the cow and would never tolerate beef on the menu. No pork sausages for breakfast either, since both Hindus and Muslims avoid pork products. So for a while the only meat offered was the Maharaja Mac, a mutton burger. And even that item has since been withdrawn from the menu.

Today the most popular items at McDonald's Indian restaurants are the McVeggie Burger and the McAloo, a spicy potato-based burger. These products are part of a distinct trend towards beefing up (sorry!) menu offerings for vegetarians, and McDonald's vegetarian items are now prepared in separate parts of the kitchen to avoid contamination with meat. Moreover, the mayonnaise used in India is made without eggs, and menu items have been spiced up to better match local tastes.

McDonald's is a highly successful global marketer because although they provide their customers with a basically identical eating experience wherever the Golden Arches appear, they also pay close attention to local tastes and expectations. Some more examples:

- In Singapore the Sausage McMuffin served at breakfast time is made from spicy ground chicken rather than pork. Some 15 percent of the Lion City's population is Muslim.
- In Japan the first Golden Arches arose not in suburban shopping malls as in the USA but in small satellite restaurants close to train and subway stations, serving mostly take-out customers.
- Responding to traditional Japanese tastes, teriyaki burgers often appear on the menu alongside the Big Mac. Mild curries, rice dishes and rice balls have been added from time to time in an attempt to beat tough local competitors.
- In Moscow, restaurant employees had to be specially trained to smile in the friendly McDonald's way, because Russians do not feel comfortable smiling at strangers.
- McDonald's first restaurant in Israel, near Tel Aviv, served kosher food. And its Mecca site in Saudi Arabia serves only halal beef, slaughtered according to Islamic law.
- Over the years European customers have been able to order black currant milk shakes in Poland, veggie burgers in the Netherlands, and salmon burgers in Norway.

These local variations on a global theme have helped McDonald's become the number one fast food provider just about everywhere. The Philippines is a rare exception. There the local Jollibee chain has relegated the Big Mac to second place. Jollibee caters to Filipino palates with sweet and juicy burgers, sugary spaghetti topped with hot dogs, beef with honey and rice, and mango-based desserts. The U.S. giant is fighting back with localized menu items such as spicier burgers, rice dishes and local *longganisa* sausage.

Euro Disney could have learned two things from McDonald's worldwide success. First, how to take a global strategy and localize it with appropriate tactical variations. Second and more specifically, how to handle an important cultural difference between European and U.S. dining habits. Americans tend to regard alcohol as a sinful indulgence to be kept out of 'family' restaurants.

When we lived in Europe during the 1970s and early 1980s, the Golden Arches were 100 percent alcohol-free, just like they were in the good old US of A. But during the latter half of the eighties European customers began to drift away to local restaurants where they could enjoy a mug of beer or a glass of wine with their meal.

After some internal debate McDonald's management decided to tweak their global strategy and allow their European franchisees to offer wine or beer according to their local customers' tastes and traditions. The lost customers soon returned.

While McDonald's reacted to local market requirements quickly in the 1980s, Euro Disney apparently needed the pressure of a near-billion dollar loss to make a similar menu adjustment in the 1990s. However, we should not forget that the Disney theme park in Japan has been a roaring success without any local modification at all. Perhaps the Asian success delayed Disney's response to the threat of a European failure.

Besides McDonald's, other U.S. global food marketers are also adapting their menus to cater to local tastes. Some examples:

– In India Dominos Pizza offers spicy vegetarian toppings such as "Peppy Paneer." Over 60 percent of their pizzas sold in India are now vegetarian, versus about 15 percent in the rest of the world.
– Burger King modified their Singapore menu by adding curried chicken and the Rendang Burger: slices of beef simmered in a hot and spicy sauce.
– Wendy's has offered their Japanese customers sandwiches filled with deep-fried pork cutlets served with a bowl of rice.
– In Japan Kentucky Fried Chicken (KFC) dropped mashed potatoes and gravy, adding french fries and chicken curry with rice while cutting the sugar content of its cole slaw in half.
– Dunkin Donuts sells some interesting local variations in Southeast Asia, including mango, durian and pandan flavors.
– In Singapore Pizza Hut offers several special toppings. The Singapura has beef with onion and chili flakes, the Kelong features sardines, onions and fresh chili while the Merlion is loaded with mutton and chilis. Meanwhile for Thai customers they add pineapple to the toppings and place little bowls of hot sauce on the tables.
– Shakey's offers the Temasek Special pizza in Singapore: marinated beef with cucumbers, satay sauce and chilis. Patrons can also create their own toppings with such ingredients as green peas and whole kernel corn.
– Campbell Soups has created a whole range of Asian offerings in its research and development laboratory in Hong Kong. Its first suc-

cess there was watercress and duck gizzard soup. Campbell actually learned about localization in its home market, making blander soups for the U.S. Midwest and spicier versions for the Southwest. This domestic experience helped them in the Mexican market, where they created a cream of chile poblano soup.
– Blue Diamond Growers, a world power in marketing almonds, flavors the nuts it sells in Mexico with chili peppers, cheese and lemon.

The Knorr Dry Soup Story

Fast-food companies are not the only ones with failures and successes in adapting products to local markets. Dehydrated soups were popular in Europe where we discovered them as American expatriates, but they were practically unknown on the other side of the Atlantic.

CPC International had the U.S. distribution rights for Knorr, a leading European brand of dry soups. Planning to introduce the Knorr line to the American market, CPC conducted some basic market research. When consumer test panels reacted favorably to the taste of the product, CPC proceeded to bring Knorr soups to market.

However, despite positive test results, sales turned out to be so disappointing that the company considered withdrawing the dry soups from the U.S. market. Such a move of course would have entailed writing off large market research and development expenses.

Subsequent analysis showed that although American consumers did like the taste of the dry soups, they were not willing to spend 15 to 20 minutes cooking and stirring the soup. U.S. consumers were used to "instant" canned soups which require only four or five minutes of heating before serving. Thus, while CPC marketers took U.S. taste preferences into account, they overlooked a countervailing cultural value: the American drive to save time in food preparation.

At this point the CPC people got creative. They decided to market the tasty dry soups as a base for sauces and chip dips. So they added to the Knorr packages directions for mixing the soup powder with sour cream and other liquids. This approach brought immediate success, and Knorr quickly gained a major share of the U.S. sauce and dip markets.

Chocolate

One would expect chocolate to be a major exception to the need for cultural adaptation. After all, chocolate surely is the universal flavor. It is popular all over the globe, right?

Ah yes, but not necessarily the *same* chocolate! Most Americans prefer bland milk chocolate, as do many Germans. The Dutch tend to like white chocolate and the French the dark, bitter variety. Russians didn't take to Mars "M & Ms" because they are not as filling as other chocolate confections. Asians seem to love the combination of chocolate with ginger.

Coffee

What about coffee, which seems to go so well with a bit of chocolate after dinner? People everywhere drink coffee. Well, it's the same story:

- Nescafe, the largest food company in the world, makes over 200 different varieties of coffee to suit local tastes.
- The Japanese love canned coffee, which is sold both hot and cold in vending machines all over the country.
- As you move from south to north in Europe, the preference moves from very dark to light.
- Greeks prefer it sweet and gritty, mixed with the grounds. Ditto the Egyptians.
- Italians prefer a caramelized roast yielding a darker color, strong taste and a distinctive aftertaste.
- The 'French roast' popular in France and other markets produces a medium to medium-dark color and flavor.
- Viennese love a full cup of medium-dark blended coffee topped off with sweetened whipped cream: the famous *Kaffee mit Schlagobers*.
- Most Germans and Scandinavians prefer lightly-roasted coffee with a slightly acidic taste.
- In the USA, be careful when you order "regular" coffee. According to the New York Times Magazine, regular means "black" in Chicago, "with milk" in Boston and "with milk and sugar" in Rhode Island. Regular can also mean non-decaffeinated coffee.

Milk

With coffee goes milk. An Italian company encountered strong consumer resistance in the U.S. to its brand of heat-treated milk. Despite the convenience – it does not require refrigeration – Americans prefer their milk fresh and cold. So whereas over 70 percent of the milk sold in Europe is heat-treated, in the U.S. the market share is under one percent.

This is no surprise to me. During our eight years in Italy none of our children was able to develop a taste for room-temperature milk.

Coca-Cola

After all those varieties of coffee it is refreshing to find one beverage that actually is standard: Coca-Cola, the best known of all global brands. Although some cola connoisseurs report variations in sweetness from country to country, the company insists the formula is the same everywhere in the world. And unlike many other mass-consumption items, the core product itself does not have to be modified to suit local tastes.

Nevertheless, other elements of the marketing mix do vary from market to market. At a party in Singapore, Coca-Cola's manager for Southeast Asia told me how he was able to overcome a distribution bottleneck in Bangkok. Instead of the big trucks Coke uses elsewhere to deliver to retailers, they employ dozens of little *tuk-tuks* which wriggle their way through tiny holes in the permanent gridlock that afflicts Thailand's capital. Creative adaptation again!

On the other hand, in China Coke has invested large sums in delivery trucks because of inadequate distribution. They also employ platoons of sales reps who travel around on motorcycles calling on retailors. Coca-Cola is also modifying the assortment offered in China. Under government pressure they have developed other soft drinks for the local market. They came up with Tian Yu Di, a soft drink in three flavors: lychee, mango and guava. In Hong Kong Coke's beverage assortment includes soy milk and flavored tea drinks.

To compete in the lucrative Japanese market – where the ad slogan once was "I feel Coke" – Coca-Cola had to bring out new sodas, fruit-based drinks and cold canned coffees every month. Oolong tea was one of the local favorites.

One more cultural difference: Coke finds that its sugar-free sodas sell much better in the diet-conscious U.S. than anywhere abroad.

Beer

Marketers of beer encounter a number of significant market variations. The Dutch brewer, Heineken, for example, tailors its advertising pitch to each market. In France and Italy, traditionally wine-drinking cultures, they market Heineken as a drink for all occasions. It seems to be working because beer consumption is rising rapidly in both markets.

Farther East the Dutch brewer targets young professionals, promoting Heineken as a taste of refined European culture. In the U.S. Heineken is also promoted as a status symbol, an upscale European import.

In perhaps the ultimate bow to cultural preferences, Heineken developed a special alcohol-free version of its low-alcohol Buckler brand for the Saudi Arabian market.

There's No Accounting for Taste

The significance of cultural preferences becomes clearer when we take a look at the wide range of foods regarded as delicacies in one country and disgusting in another. For instance, in the heart of Florence near the Straw Market you can get a steaming platter of boiled cow's stomach from a vendor's cart. And if you're lucky you can still find a Tuscan trattoria there serving cock's combs and thistle blossoms.

The French do not regard offal as awful. Cow's stomach is also served there, as are curried lamb's brains, pig's trotters and blanched pig's intestines. Another favorite is grilled sweetbreads (the thymus gland) skewered on licorice sticks.

People who find those menu selections a bit strange might prefer some of the goodies available in Thailand. These include crocodile filets fried with mustard sauce, and choice cuts of cobra and python served with steamed bamboo worms. Other taste treats are mountain frog, ground lizard and curried soft-shell turtle stewed in lemon-grass broth.

More familiar to some business travelers are such Chinese and Southeast Asian favorites as sea slugs, drunken prawns, soups made from bird's nests cemented together with bird saliva, crocodile steaks, and goat penis soup. The Vietnamese on the other hand seem to prefer armadillo meat washed down with coffee brewed from beans vomited by weasels.

And then we have the Japanese obsession with *fugu,* or blowfish. The blood, liver, gut and genitals of this delightful sea creature contain the lethal poison tetrodoxin. Chefs must pass a rigorous exam before being certified to serve fugu. Just as well, because when something goes wrong death is swift and very painful.

A Chacun Son Gout (To Each His Own)

All these widely-diverging taste preferences present opportunities for alert international marketers. Americans export the dark meat parts of chicken to Russia, Latin America and Asia because Yanks prize the bland white breast meat while other consumers prefer the juicy thighs and other cuts.

Australia's commercial fishermen used to discard the fins of the sharks they caught as inedible. Now they export the fins to China, Hong Kong and Taiwan where they are converted into the very expensive shark's fin soup.

American poultry processors have always thrown away certain parts such as chicken feet and turkey testicles as they prepare the meat for market. But in the late 1980s clever entrepreneurs realized that these 'inedible' poultry parts were regarded as expensive delicacies in Hong Kong and Taiwan. So they got rich by cleaning, packaging and exporting these treasures. In Greater China, boiled chicken feet are a popular snack food, and turkey testicles are regarded as potent aphrodisiacs – nature's own Viagra!

And finally, consider the lowly sea urchin. At least it used to be considered lowly along the coast of Maine in the U.S., where lobstermen used to throw them away. But in 1987 the Japanese learned of the availability of Maine urchins and began to import them. Japanese gourmets feast on the roe as well as on the undeveloped sex organs of immature sea urchins as an aid to sexual potency. As a result, Maine exports of these delicacies have jumped from zero in 1987 to over $75 million these days.

The Name Game

Focusing on the local customer also means being aware of how your brand name translates in different languages. A bartender in Frankfurt told me the after-dinner liqueur Irish Mist was a hard sell for quite a while because *Mist* in German means dung or manure.

The marketing people at an Italian toilet tissue manufacturer located near Florence once asked us whether their product would sell well in the UK. They couldn't understand why we recommended changing their brand name for English-speaking markets. After all, SOFFASS had always served them well in the home market ...

Globalize ... or Localize?

"Customer focus" was been a popular buzz phrase for years now. But we sometimes forget that customers' values, attitudes and beliefs differ around the world. The savvy international marketer knows how to focus on the local customer while still thinking globally.

We have seen that cultural differences create invisible barriers to trade. But at the same time – as we saw with chicken parts, shark fins, sea urchins, and turkey testicles – those very cultural differences also create new market opportunities.

Problems and opportunities: Two good reasons for learning what makes international customers tick.

Part Two

Forty Negotiator Profiles

Group A

Relationship-Focused – Formal – Polychronic – Reserved

The Indian Negotiator

In the Hindi language, *kal* means both 'yesterday' and 'tomorrow.' That makes *kal* (pronounced 'cull') an apt symbol for India: a land of the future hamstrung by the red tape of its bureaucratic past.

Bureaucratic Red Tape. Regulatory obstructionism provides one of the toughest obstacles for foreigners trying to do business in the world's second most populous country. With a population of over one billion, including some 150 million relatively prosperous middle class consumers, the Indian market is a powerful magnet for exporters and investors. Unfortunately, the unprepared business visitor is liable to get snarled up in the ubiquitous red tape.

Any Old India Hand will tell you that there are three keys to success in this enormous market. One is patience. Another is the right local partner. And the third is a basic grasp of the business customs and practices.

Patience will serve you especially well when dealing with officialdom. As we saw above, time has a different meaning in India. Taking the linguistic example a step further we note that *kal-kal* means "the day before yesterday" as well as "the day after tomorrow." Minutes don't count for much in this polychronic, fluid-time culture.

Meeting with a senior government official? Prepare to be kept waiting half an hour to an hour without the courtesy of an apology. Nor should you be surprised if your important meeting is interrupted every few minutes while the harried official across the desk takes phone calls, signs piles of documents and receives impromptu visitors.

It would be a mistake to interpret this behavior as rude or reflective of sloppy work habits. Clocks in South Asia tick to a slower beat – it's a question of culture and climate. My response is to carry a large briefcase stuffed with reading material and overdue expense reports. Over the years I slowly learned to regard that waiting time as an opportunity rather than a problem.

The right local partner will have the connections to reduce – but not eliminate – those frustrating delays. But avoid setting your hopes too high. While finding the right partner is an essential condition for success in India, it is hardly a sufficient condition.

Some knowledge of local business customs and practices will help you find the partner who is right for you. That same cross-cultural knowledge will also help you work effectively with your partner, client, customer or supplier. The following practical tips come from one who has lived in India twice and done business there off and on since 1969.

Communication. India is a linguistic mosaic with over 300 different languages – and that does not include dialects. While Hindi is the most widely spoken, 14 other major tongues are official languages. For instance, there are more speakers of Bengali in the world today than Russian speakers. Luckily English, usually spoken with a delightful lilt, is the language of international business. But do watch out. Indian English is sprinkled with local terms which sometimes confuse foreign visitors. If you hear your partner referring to "a lack of rupees" he may be talking about a *lakh* of rupees, meaning 100,000 of them. And if your customer shocks you by saying she has just 'fired' her assistant, that just means her employee got a reprimand.

The Family. Indian business culture of course reflects the basic values of the society. One such value is the importance of the family, which explains the structure of most small and medium businesses from Chandigar to Calcutta. Indians also value respect for age and authority. Young people are expected to defer to elders; white hair confers status.

Hierarchy, Status, Power and Caste. The concept of status leads logically to a discussion of caste. Hindus belong to whatever caste they are born into. They cannot move up the caste ladder by getting a PhD, by getting elected to high office, or by becoming a millionaire. Some 14 percent of Hindus fail to qualify for even the bottom rung of the caste ladder. These are the untouchables, formerly known as harijans, currently as dalits.

Some years ago a harijan named Jagjivan Ram was the Minister of Defense and the second most powerful political figure in the country. In New Delhi he was treated with all the outward signs of respect due his exalted status. But whenever he returned to his native village Jagjivan Ram was treated by his upper caste neighbors as just another untouchable, a social outcast. Culture changes at a glacial pace, even in a torrid climate like India's.

Relationship Focus. Europeans and North Americans also need to be aware that Indians are strongly relationship-focused. Budget plenty of time to get to know your counterpart before launching into your sales pitch. In India you need to make a friend before you make a deal.

But even though *who* you know is critical, you can't neglect the *what* either. You need to know the local do's and don'ts of relationship-building. When meeting and greeting people for example, many Indian women prefer to give the graceful *namaste* gesture (*namaskar* in the South) rather than shake hands. You return this greeting by placing both hands together just below the chin, finger tips up, while inclining your head in a slight nod.

Another charming South Asian custom is the garlanding of important visitors. Business visitors often wonder what to do with the garland after it has been draped around their neck. The appropriate response is to smile in thanks, remove it as soon as the flash bulbs stop popping, and carry it in your hand until your hosts relieve you of the fragrant burden.

Wining and Dining. When entertaining Indian guests, remember that most Hindus are serious vegetarians. And because of the importance of family you can expect some of your invitees to bring along a few friends or relatives to your dinner. For both of those reasons my wife always threw buffet dinners. The buffet format not only provides flexible seating for unexpected guests, it also allows the food to be displayed on two tables at opposite ends of the room: one for vegetarians, the other for the meat eaters.

Speaking of meat, don't forget that Hindus (80% of the population) do not eat beef and that neither Muslims (12%) nor Hindus eat pork. Hindus of course venerate the cow while both religious groups consider the pig unclean. That's why our four boys were raised on goat burgers rather than hamburgers during our years in India.

If you are a guest in a traditional Indian home, politely decline food or refreshments the first time they are offered. To accept immediately signifies greediness and poor breeding. By the same token, some of your Indian guests will similarly refuse. The gracious host or hostess responds by repeating the offer at least twice. It would be rude indeed to accept your guest's initial refusal at face value!

Negotiating Behavior. Once you have built a comfortable relationship with your local counterpart the negotiation process can begin. Be prepared for a tough, drawn-out bargaining session. Indian business people are often real experts at bazaar haggling, so remember to build some fat into your opening position.

At some point in the bargaining process you can expect your counterpart to play the poverty card. I first encountered this favorite Indian gambit years ago in Bombay while sourcing cotton apparel. Meeting with Naval Tata, then head of India's largest private industrial concern, I asked him why most Indian manufactured goods were priced well above world market levels. The distinguished head of the Tata Group thought for a moment and then answered: "You see, India is such a poor country. You should be willing to pay higher prices to our suppliers to help India develop."

Ever a patriot, Mr. Tata finessed the real answer to the question. The fact is, protectionism, over-regulation and poor infrastructure have made India a high-cost economy despite the low labor costs. To this day India remains a relatively high-cost producer of many goods, especially compared to China.

Recent progress with bureaucratic reform, privatization, and infrastructure improvement will gradually increase India's international competitiveness. The country's outstanding success with business process outsourcing shows what can be done. But don't come with unreasonable expectations. The red tape of yesterday will continue to burden India's economic future for years to come.

The Bangladeshi Negotiator

Western business people have tended to dismiss the market potential of this South Asian nation ever since Henry Kissinger called it an "economic basket case" in the 1970s. But despite its poverty, profitable opportunities still exist for foreign exporters, importers and investors.

Most market potential is concentrated in textiles, by far the country's most successful industry. Over one million people work in the 2000 or so garment factories which account for 60% of total Bangladeshi exports. U.S. apparel retailers and wholesalers buy half of those apparel exports, well over $1 billion worth. So manufacturers of textile machinery and supplies should be looking for export and joint-venture investment opportunities.

But poverty is not the only deterrent to commercial interest in Bangladesh. Bureaucratic red tape as well as major differences in business customs and practices are real barriers to trading with this developing country. Here are some key elements of Bangladeshi business culture.

The Right Local Contact. The right contact is one who knows how to cut through the jungles of red tape without having to pay *bakhsheesh*, the local term for a bribe.

Building Relationships. This includes relationships with government officials. The state controls most of the Bangladesh economy with a heavy hand, which causes frustration for business people. But the good news is that South Asian officials tend to be more open to dealing with foreign businessmen than is the case in East Asia.

Unfortunately, many foreigners bungle the chance to establish effective relationships with the public sector. They adopt a patronizing tone with Bangladeshi officials because of the country's poor economic condition. This is a major faux pas. It is important to show appropriate respect when meeting with government officials, who enjoy high status in the Bengali culture.

Orientation to Time. Pack an extra supply of patience when visiting Bangladesh. Poor infrastructure, frequent natural disasters and a relaxed attitude to scheduling combine to frustrate people accustomed to quick response and prompt deliveries. If you need goods shipped by March 15, consider stipulating January 15 in the purchase contract.

In most Bangladesh businesses all important decisions are made by the managing director, who typically is unwilling to delegate any of his authority. When this person is overburdened or "out of station," your urgent fax or email is likely to go unanswered.

The country's Islamic heritage is evident in attitudes towards time and scheduling. On one memorable flight from Chittagong to Dhaka in a rickety old Fokker, the Bangladeshi captain frightened some of the foreign passengers when he announced, "Despite this monsoon rainstorm we will land at Dhaka airport shortly, God willing."

Those of us familiar with the culture knew the pilot was simply translating the pious phrase *Insh'alla* into English. However, the elderly American woman sitting in front of me understood that our captain wasn't sure we would make it, and she promptly fainted.

Meeting Protocol. During meetings with senior government officials, be ready for anything.

Assistants and secretaries rush in with papers to be signed, incoming phone calls punctuate your carefully rehearsed presentation, friends and relatives drop in for a gabfest. The proper response is to stay calm, avoid showing impatience. While such behavior would be considered rude in monochronic cultures, it is normal meeting protocol in South Asia.

Meetings in the private sector are conducted closer to international norms.

Negotiations. The Bengalis are a friendly, hospitable people who enjoy the give and take of a lively bargaining session. Expect your negotiations to take more time than they would in deal-focused cultures. It is important to keep a smile on your face even if discussions become a bit heated.

Negotiating in Myanmar

Myanmar forms a cultural bridge between the ancient cultures of China and India. So business visitors with experience in those two markets will find familiar values, attitudes, beliefs and behaviors. However, Myanmar has been isolated for decades from the rest of Asia and the world, so negotiating business there presents special challenges.

About 70 percent of the 45 million people are Burmese. Among the numerous minority groups are the Shan, Karen and Arakanese, with ethnic Chinese and Indians accounting for about one percent each. Just as the Malays of Malaysia are defined as Muslims, most Burmese identify themselves strongly with Buddhism. Like Sri Lankans, Thais, Cambodians and Laotians, the Burmese follow the Theravada or Hinyana stream of Buddhism.

Key Values. Burmese are very proud of their ethnicity; many of them tend to look down on South Asians, Chinese, and other foreigners to the extent these outsiders behave in an "un-Burmese"way. The values, beliefs and behavior encompassed by 'Burmeseness' (*Bahmasan chinn*) include showing great respect for elders, being able to recite from memory important passages of Buddhist scriptures and to converse in idiomatic Burmese. The people of Myanmar also have a preference for reserved and indirect speech as well as modesty in dress and manners.

Another key value is *ko chinn sar-nar-hmu*: a strong feeling of empathy and deep consideration for the feelings of others. Friends (including "business friends") are expected to be sympathetic and empathetic in times of difficulty. Failure to show empathy is very likely to disrupt your business relationships.

Language of Business. Due to Burma's earlier history as a British colony, English used to be taught from kindergarten through university. In the 1960s however English instruction in the primary schools was swept away in a tidal wave of nationalism and xenophobia. Since the 1980s teaching English has made a comeback, so younger business people and most government officials speak it with some fluency.

Making Contact. As in most parts of Asia you are expected to approach potential business partners indirectly, via intermediaries such as your embassy, law firms or consultants. A direct approach would mark you as un-Burmese and perhaps undesirable as a partner. Since most of the economy is state-run, you will probably interact with government officials. Ministries are divided into corporations and directorates: the former deal in products, the latter in services. Corporations are headed by Managing Directors, directorates by Director Generals. The next highest rank is General Manager. Ministers sometimes attend meetings.

Relationships. Success in business depends on developing solid social relationships with your local partners. Plan to spend considerable time outside of office hours building rapport.

Verbal Communication. One reason Burmese value indirectness is to avoid imposing on others or causing loss of face. The important term *ah-har-hmu* refers among other things to the desire to avoid offending people or troubling them unduly. The result is that business visitors are likely to encounter indirect, evasive and roundabout language on a regular basis. People who are blunt are considered un-Burmese, crude and uneducated. "Yes" very often means, "I understand" rather than indicating agreement.

Few older Burmese say "thank you" for favors done or "sorry" when they make mistakes. To show that you are sorry, say "forgive me" or explain that your mistake was unintentional. To express an apology nonverbally, give a small gift or do the person a favor. Burmese who are proficient in English are more likely to use the polite words and phrases.

Hierarchies and Status. As is the case in most of Asia, age and seniority are much respected. Remember to pay most of your attention to the senior person present, as defined by age and rank within the company or organization.

Nonverbal Communication. Burmese smile often, sometimes to cover discomfort or embarrassment. Body language is very reserved; people tend to speak softly and use few gestures. The left hand is considered unclean; use only the right hand to pass objects to others.

Orientation to Time. Visitors are expected to be on time for meetings, but officials are likely to keep you waiting. Burmese tend to be relaxed about punctuality, schedules and deadlines.

Negotiating Style. Because foreigners are mistrusted you will probably need considerable time and repeat visits in order to reach agreement. In most cases decision-making is a slow process involving consensus-seeking; the final decision is made at the top. Business negotiations in Myanmar are conducted face-to-face.

Business Protocol and Etiquette

Dress Code. For men, a long-sleeved shirt and tie for private-sector meetings, lightweight suit when meeting senior officials. Women should dress modestly, usually in a suit, dress or skirt and blouse.

Names and Titles. Burmese names may cause problems for foreigners, especially since it is not uncommon for people to change their names. The traditional system is to name a child after the day of the week he or she is born on. It is very important to employ the correct honorific when addressing a Burmese. A working adult male named Myo Nu is addressed as U Myo Nu, an adult woman named Maung San would be Daw Maung San. The proper honorific for a male teacher or boss is Saya, for a woman Sayama.

Meeting and Greeting. People in Myanmar do not generally shake hands, but may do so with foreign visitors. It is a good idea to wait until a hand is offered. If not, a polite nod and smile is appropriate. Business cards are exchanged at the beginning of the meeting, using the right hand.

Meeting Behavior. Expect your first meeting to be primarily a 'get-to-know-you' session; serious business will be discussed at subsequent meetings.

Gift Giving. Good choices for business gifts include tasteful writing instruments, diaries and calendars. Once you know your counterparts, golf balls, cigarettes and good cognac or whisky are other possibilities. If the recipient politely refuses your gift, smile and insist until the gift is accepted. Gifts are not normally opened in front of the giver.

Appropriate hostess gifts include fancy fruit, chocolates and other sweets. Remember to remove your shoes before entering a home. Avoid giving knives, letter openers or scissors: in Myanmar cutting instruments symbolize the severing of a relationship.

Wining and Dining. Generally only Westernized Burmese drink alcohol. Most business entertainment is done over dinner (rarely at lunch or breakfast) in upscale hotels, and is relatively formal. A Chinese restaurant is often the best choice. Burmese usually expect to be coaxed repeatedly to take a second serving. Few people in Myanmar eat pork or beef.

The Vietnamese Negotiator

During the late 1990s Vietnam was expected to become the next Asian Tiger, but unfortunately it didn't happen. Fueled by the lifting of the U.S. trade embargo in 1994, Vietnam did experience a burst of international business interest at that time. Many foreign investment projects were initiated. But then frustration set in.

The much-hyped 'doi moi' reform movement brought few practical results, so today Vietnam remains saddled with a communist economy closer to Cuba than to China. Its per capita GDP is less than half of China's, even less than that of most African countries. The result is that Hanoi's nine new luxury hotels remain mostly empty these days.

Once the economy does finally open up however, international marketers and investors will certainly find opportunities in this large, potentially dynamic Southeast Asian country.

Language. A growing number of Vietnamese negotiators speak English, especially in the South. If you find it advisable to employ an interpreter, consider hiring your own linguist rather than relying on one supplied by your Vietnamese counterparts.

Get Introduced. Unless you represent a large, well-known company or have already met at a trade show or on a trade mission, the best way to make initial contact in Vietnam is to be introduced by a respected intermediary. Ask a bank, consultant, law firm, freight forwarder or your embassy to provide a formal introduction.

Build Relationships. As in the rest of Asia, developing rapport is a critical aspect of the overall negotiating process. Deal-making is easier once you have established a personal relationship with your counterpart. Socializing over drinks and dinner is a good way to build rapport.

Orientation to Time. While Vietnamese are often late for a meeting, they expect visitors to be on time. Showing up late indicates lack of respect for your local counterparts.

Hierarchies and Status. Younger, lower-ranking persons are expected to defer to older and higher-ranking individuals – and especially to senior government officials. Be prepared for a certain degree of formality in business meetings, although Vietnamese tend to relax as the relationship progresses.

Preserving Harmony. Vietnamese regard open displays of irritation, impatience or anger as rude behavior. They lose respect for people who cannot maintain a calm exterior under stress. Confrontation quickly disrupts harmony and leads to loss of face.

Face. You can cause your Vietnamese counterparts to lose face by losing your temper, embarrassing them, criticizing them in public or expressing sharp disagreement. Causing loss of face can completely disrupt a promising business negotiation. On the other hand, saving your counterpart's face can contribute to the success of your negotiation. For instance, if you need to correct a Vietnamese negotiator's mistake, call for a break and diplomatically point out the error over a cup of tea. Your sensitivity to face will go a long way towards building a strong relationship with the Vietnamese.

Verbal Communication. Vietnamese often employ indirect, vague, "polite" language. For most Vietnamese, avoiding conflict and maintaining a pleasant relationship are far more important than mere clarity of meaning.

You may find the Vietnamese somewhat reserved and formal until you have built rapport. Especially in the early stages of the relationship you will accomplish far more with face-to-face meetings than with letters, faxes and phone calls. Frequent travel to Vietnam is a definite prerequisite to success in business there.

Paraverbal Communication. Vietnamese tend to speak more softly than many Westerners. They also avoid interrupting other people since conversational overlap is regarded as extremely rude behavior. Wait until the Vietnamese negotiator has finished speaking before chiming in.

A laugh or a giggle frequently signals embarrassment or stress rather than amusement, so avoid joining in the general merriment at a meeting until you understand just what is going on. Avoid raising your voice at the bargaining table: A loud voice indicates anger or childishness in Southeast Asia.

Nonverbal Communication. Expect a gentle handshake and indirect eye contact. Strong, direct eye contact may be misinterpreted as an expression of hostility. A knuckle-crunching handshake is considered rude and offensive.

Body language is restrained: Vietnamese use few hand gestures. They may be startled or confused by wide, expansive gestures and arm-waving. Vietnam is a low-contact culture so expect little touching. Avoid arm-grabbing and back-slapping.

Vietnamese Negotiating Style

Sales Presentations. North Americans, Australians and some other Westerners often start presentations with a joke or humorous anecdote. In Vietnam this approach is inappropriate. Try not to over-praise your own product or company – let your brochures and testimonials speak for you. By the same token, avoid badmouthing your competitors. Instead, pass along to the Vietnamese clips of any critical articles that have been published about the competition.

Remember to hand out copies or outlines of your presentation in advance. Use visual aids wherever possible, especially where numbers are concerned. Check frequently to see whether your counterparts are following the presentation.

Bargaining Range. Vietnamese negotiators tend to bargain vigorously and very often expect their counterparts to grant major concessions on price and terms. It sometimes appears that they measure their success at the bargaining table by how far they are able to move you away from your opening offer. Counter this tactic by building sufficient margin into your initial bid. Always leave yourself room for maneuver, and squirrel away some bargaining chips for the end game.

Making Concessions. Be prepared for some spirited horse-trading and bazaar haggling. Take great care to make any concession conditional – always demand something of equal value in return. Give in to any demand with extreme reluctance and only after lengthy hesitation. This is the one and only occasion during the negotiation process in Vietnam when you should let your face show some negative emotion. It is okay to show how painful that last price concession was.

Expect the Vietnamese side to withhold any major concession until the end game while at the same time they continuously push you to concede point after point. Just keep smiling and ignore any outrageous demand. Alternatively, keep smiling while you make an equally outrageous demand of the other side. Be patient, stay cool ... and keep smiling.

Decision-Making Behavior. Decisions are made by top management. High officials and private-sector executives are very busy, so decisions almost always take time. Larger private-sector firms are often headed by 'retired' military officers; here again decision-making is slow. Some smaller entrepreneurial firms act more quickly.

Role of the Contract. Don't be surprised if your Vietnamese partner contacts you a few weeks after the signing ceremony with a request to renegotiate key parts of the agreement (such as price, for example). Vietnamese expect that because of their close relationship you will agree to discuss changes in the contract any time conditions change.

Business Protocol and Etiquette

- When meeting with senior government officials men should wear a dark suit and a conservative tie. For other business meetings a long-sleeved shirt and tie for men and a conservative dress or skirt and blouse for women are appropriate attire.
- Receive your counterpart's business card with both hands, scan it carefully and then put the card away in a leather card case or place it on the table in front of you. Present your own card with your right hand or with both hands.
- Vietnamese names follow the Chinese pattern. If you are introduced to Nguyen Van Tuan for example, Nguyen is the family name and the others are given names. Visitors should address Vietnamese by their family name – and title, if any.
- Vietnam is a gift-giving culture. A good choice would be an expensive branded cognac or whisky. Other ideas are items typical of your region or tasteful logo gifts. Present the neatly wrapped gift with

both hands. The recipient will probably put it aside and not open it until after you have left. When you are given a gift, accept it with both hands and a smile, but open it later.

- Entertaining and being entertained is an important part of building an effective relationship with your local counterpart. The major hotel restaurants in Saigon and Hanoi offer a selection of Chinese, French and local cuisines. Finding a good restaurant is more of a challenge outside the major cities – rely on local advice.

Maintaining the Relationship. Budget plenty of time, as well as travel and communication expense, in order to stay in close contact with your Vietnamese partners. Frequent visits to the market are essential.

The Thai Negotiator

The Thais form a bridge between the 'chopstick cultures' of Southeast Asia and the 'banana-leaf cultures' of South Asia. Thailand's customs, traditions and business behavior owe much to both China and India. Such diverse influences make this market a complex but delightful place to do business.

The Language of Business. Language is often the first problem business visitors encounter.

Thailand means "Land of the Free," reflecting the country's unique status as the only Southeast Asian country which was never colonized. One result is that relatively few Thais speak European languages. So while English-speaking negotiators rarely need an interpreter in former British colonies such as India, Sri Lanka, Singapore or Malaysia, it's a different story in Thailand.

That is why it's a good idea to ask whether you need to arrange an interpreter for the first meeting with your local counterpart. If you plan to set up an office or subsidiary, keep in mind that qualified English-speaking middle managers are hard to find in Bangkok.

Making Initial Contact. Most Thais are reluctant to talk business with people they do not know. That applies especially to any foreigner trying to sell them something. A good solution is to meet your prospects at a trade show or on a trade mission. Otherwise, arrange to be introduced by a person or organization of high status who knows both you and the Thai party.

Failing that, see if you have a friend with a non-competing company already represented in Bangkok. If so, ask him or her to introduce you.

Other sources of introductions are your embassy, the chamber of commerce or bank, plus trading companies, law firms or consulting firms. The key point here is that cold calls are unlikely to work in Thailand.

Maintaining Harmony. Once you have set up a meeting, the next cultural value likely to cause a problem is the importance of maintaining surface harmony during negotiations. Direct confrontation tends to disrupt the harmony of the meeting, so most Thais prefer indirect language.

A key Thai value is *kreng jai,* showing concern and consideration for the needs and feelings of others. Deal-focused Western visitors sometimes unintentionally offend by being too direct and by using pushy, hard-sell tactics.

A related value is *jai yen,* literally 'cool heart'. When the discussion gets lively, avoid raising your voice, displaying anger or openly criticizing your local partner. Maybe that's one reason Thais smile so much. They smile when they are happy, they smile when they are sad, they even smile when they are angry. Smiles and gentle words promote harmony; scowls and loud voices disrupt harmony.

'Face' Issues. Here are four proven tips for avoiding misunderstandings in this relationship-focused, face-conscious society:

– Avoid conflict and open confrontation at all costs.
– Avoid words or actions which might embarrass or shame someone, even unintentionally. For instance, never correct or criticize your Thai counterpart in front of other people. Remember that many Thais even feel uncomfortable if they are singled out for praise.
– Bear in mind that in this vertical culture, higher status people do not apologize directly to people of low status. Domestic servants or manual workers are likely to feel acutely embarrassed by a formal apology from a superior. A friendly smile and perhaps a small gift of sweets later accomplishes the same result without the embarrassment.
– If you have inadvertently offended someone of equal social status, such as a business partner, demonstrate humility. Smile and ask him or her to forgive your clumsiness. Thereafter smile a lot and spend as much time together as possible. Building a strong personal relationship is the best way to avoid giving offense and to recover from causing loss of face.
– Thais do not like to tell you bad news. If your local business partner delays telling you about a problem until it is too late, do not get upset. Thais seem to feel they are showing you respect by shielding

you from bad news. The way to bridge this communication gap is to develop a climate of trust with your local counterparts.

Hierarchies, Status and Respect. Thais accord high status to older people, especially older males. It is important to show appropriate respect to senior, high-ranking persons – particularly if they are customers or government officials.

Time. Visitors from clock-obsessed cultures encounter another challenge: A very relaxed attitude to time and scheduling. The tropical climate and relatively low level of industrialization plus (in Bangkok) the permanent traffic gridlock all conspire to frustrate business people from rigid-time cultures. Some visitors go so far as to change hotels in Bangkok each evening so as to be closer to the next day's meeting site.

Like most of their neighbors in South and Southeast Asia, Thais consider people more important than schedules and deadlines. Your Thai contact may keep you waiting because he was caught in a traffic jam, or perhaps because the meeting before yours took an hour longer than expected. In the Thai business culture it would be unthinkable to break off an ongoing meeting in order to be on time for the next one.

Business Negotiating Style

Your Sales Presentation. Take time to gauge the English-language capability of your audience before beginning your presentation. Use plenty of visuals and handouts, especially with materials having to do with numbers. Avoid the aggressive 'hard sell' approach.

Meeting Behavior. Avoid overly long meetings, break up lengthy discussions with some social activities. Thais tend to be put off by "all work and no play." *Sanuk* or 'fun' makes hard work easier to take.

Bargaining Behavior. Be prepared for a certain amount of bazaar haggling. It's a good idea to add a 'comfort factor' to your opening offer in order to make room for some tactical concessions later on price or terms. The decision-making process takes much longer than it does in more deal-focused cultures. Remember to bring a large supply of patience with you to the negotiating table.

Business Protocol and Etiquette

Dress Code. The way you dress can show either respect or disrespect. Men should wear a dark suit and tie when meeting a senior government official, while a long-sleeved white shirt and tie with neat trousers is appropriate in the private sector. Women may wear a modest dress, lightweight suit or skirt and blouse.

Meeting and Greeting. While a gentle handshake is appropriate when greeting Thai men, local women may employ the *wai* gesture: Both palms together at approximately chin level with the head slightly inclined. Raising the hands higher while bowing the head slightly more is appropriate when greeting a Buddhist monk. Thais avoid physical contact with people they do not know well.

Because the left hand is considered unclean, exchange business cards with your right hand only.

To show special respect you may also present your card with the right hand, cupping your right elbow with the left hand. It is polite to present gifts the same way, but be aware that Thais really do not expect business gifts.

The Name Game. Thai surnames tend to be long, multi-syllabic and difficult for foreign visitors to pronounce. Fortunately however, Thais are normally addressed by their first name preceded by *Khun,* as in "Khun Somchai." Similarly, visitors may be addressed as "Mr. Jim" or "Mrs. Linda."

Paraverbal and Nonverbal Communication. Thais tend to speak softly and use almost no gestures. This reserved communication style caused an expat manager a problem a few years ago while interviewing job applicants in Bangkok. When several of the female candidates seemed confused during the interviews, the manager's local HR consultant gently explained that he was talking too loudly and using too many hand and arm gestures.

The women interviewees interpreted the loud voice to mean the manager was angry with them, and the arm-waving to mean he was mentally deranged. Which of course explained why he had so little success during the first round of interviews. After all, who wants to work for an angry, insane employer?

While Thais employ more eye contact than most Japanese, for example, intense eye contact which would be appropriate in the Middle East or Latin America is considered 'staring' and makes many Thais uncomfortable.

The foot is even more unclean than the left hand. Visitors should never sit in such a way as to show the sole of their foot or shoe. Nor should we point to or touch an object with our foot or shoe. On a recent visit we observed the look of horror on a Thai hotel guest's face when a Western visitor shoved the Thai's suitcase aside with his foot to clear some space at the crowded registration desk.

Pointing at people with your index finger is extremely impolite. If you really need to point, aim your right fist thumb-first in the direction indicated. Or just jerk your chin in that direction.

Likewise, beckoning to someone by crooking one's forefinger is rude. So to call a waiter it is better to simply raise your hand the way you did in school and make eye contact. Or extend your right arm horizontally, palm down, and make a rapid scooping motion with your hand.

A tall *farang* (European-type foreigner) should try to avoid towering over his or her local counterparts. It is polite to bend over a little to reduce any natural difference in altitude.

Personal Relationships. In general, you will find that developing and maintaining solid personal relationships with your local counterparts is the key to business success in Thailand.

The Malaysian Negotiator

Malaysia is a diverse, multi-cultural, multi-ethnic society. Malays account for around 50 % of the population, ethnic Chinese about 30% and ethnic Indians (mostly of South Indian origin) 8 %. Non-Malay bumiputeras and a small Eurasian element round out the mix.

Business visitors interacting with the public sector will deal mostly with Malays, while in the private sector both Chinese and Malays are active. Ethnic Indians are more often found in the professions: law, medicine and education. It is important to remember that all Malays are Muslim, but not all Muslims are Malays.

Language of Business. The national language is Bahasa Melayu, but English is widely spoken, especially in the private sector. Visitors can usually conduct business without an interpreter.

Importance of Relationships. Getting to know your counterpart is an essential prelude to discussing a deal. Expect much of your first meeting to be taken up with general conversation. Sharing a meal helps you get to know your Malaysian contact, as do golf and sightseeing.

During the first meeting, stick to small talk and general topics until your counterparts signal they are ready to talk business. Good topics of conversation include travel, sightseeing, business conditions in your country and food. Avoid commenting on local customs, politics or religion.

Let your local counterparts decide when it's time to get down to business. Malaysians signal their readiness by asking specific questions about your project, your company or the purpose of your visit. Each time you re-visit the market, always take the time to update your counterparts on what's happened since your last meeting and socialize with them before getting down to business.

Orientation to Time. Business visitors are expected to be on time for meetings, while local counterparts are likely to be more relaxed.

Traffic jams make it increasingly difficult to be punctual for appointments in Kuala Lumpur. The wise visitor schedules no more than two meetings per day: good timings are 10 am and 2 pm.

Formality, Hierarchy, Status and Respect. This traditional culture accords high status to older people, people of high rank in organizations and to the Malay nobility. Younger business visitors should defer to senior Malaysians, particularly when the latter are buyers or potential customers. Politeness and formality in manners show respect to your counterpart.

'Face' Issues. Malaysians are sensitive to perceived slights. The easiest way to lose face and cause others loss of face is to display impatience, irritation or anger. Showing negative emotion disrupts the harmony of the meeting and may be interpreted as arrogance. Business visitors from more informal, direct cultures such as the U.S. sometimes unintentionally offend Malaysians.

Four tips regarding face:
- Avoid open conflict and confrontation during meetings; try to maintain surface harmony.
- Avoid words or actions which might embarrass or shame someone. For example, never correct or criticize your Malaysian counterpart in front of other people.
- Avoid overly-direct statements or remarks. Blunt speech may be interpreted as ill-mannered.
- 'Give face' to your counterparts by showing appropriate respect and observing local customs.

Indirect Verbal Communication. Malaysians maintain smooth interpersonal relations during vigorous negotiations by employing indirect, oblique language. Your local counterpart is likely to employ circumlocutions and evasive language to avoid insulting others. For instance, Malaysians often avoid saying the word 'no,' which is considered offensive. Hesitation, silence, changing the subject or giving a vague, roundabout response are all polite ways of saying 'no' without actually saying that rude word.

Paraverbal Communication. Most Malaysians are soft-spoken. Visitors should avoid raising their voice, engaging in loud, raucous behavior or interrupting people in mid-sentence. (While tolerated in some cultures, conversational overlap is considered offensive in Malaysia.)

Some Malaysians giggle or burst out laughing when they observe a mishap, for example when someone slips and falls down. While in some cultures laughter under such circumstances would be considered inappropriate, in Southeast Asian societies it is simply a spontaneous reaction to an awkward or embarrassing situation. No offense is intended.

Nonverbal Communication

Proximity: Like North Americans, northern Europeans and East Asians, Malaysians like to stand and sit at about an arm's length distance from other people.

Touch behavior: Malaysia is a low-contact society. In a business situation, avoid touching people except for a gentle handshake. Back-slapping and arm-grabbing are out of place.

Gaze behavior: Intense eye contact is considered 'staring' in Southeast Asia. It makes many Malaysians uncomfortable. And when we wear sunglasses in this tropical country, we should avoid conversing with someone from behind dark glasses. Indoors or out, this is considered rude.

Gestures: Malaysians use few gestures. They are likely to be startled or confused by our sudden hand and arm movements. Using your index finger to point or beckon is impolite. If you need to point, close your (right) fist and aim it thumb-first in the direction indicated. To beckon a waiter, raise your hand or extend your right arm and make a scooping motion with the fingers of the right hand. The left hand and the feet are regarded as unclean by both Muslims and Hindus. Avoid touching people or passing objects with your left hand. Likewise, avoid touching or moving any object with your foot and do not cross your legs in such a way that the sole of your shoe faces someone. In Malaysia, striking the open palm of one hand with the fist of the other is an obscene gesture. Standing with hands on hips signals anger or hostility to Malaysians.

Protocol and Etiquette

Dress Code. How we dress shows either respect or disrespect to our counterparts. Because of the tropical climate, men may find it uncomfortable to wear a suit. Nevertheless, males should don a dark suit, white shirt and tie when meeting a high level government official. For meetings in the private sector a long-sleeved white shirt and tie with neat trousers is appropriate. Women wear a modest dress, lightweight suit or skirt and blouse, being sure to cover the upper arms. Skirts should be at least of knee length.

Meeting and Greeting. Customs vary within this very diverse society. One common greeting is a gentle handshake accompanied by moderate eye contact. Here are some other practices:

Malays may offer a graceful *salaam*: with a slight bow, extending one or both hands to lightly touch the other person's hands, then bringing the hand(s) back to touch the greeter's heart.

Indians may use the equally graceful *namaste* or *namaskar* gesture, placing palms together with fingertips just below chin level, accompanied by a slight bow or nod of the head.

Male visitors should wait for women to offer their hand. If no hand is offered, the polite male just smiles and exchanges verbal greetings.

Exchanging Business Cards. With ethnic Chinese, exchange cards using both hands. With Malays and Indians, offer your card using your right hand with the arm supported at the wrist by the left. It is polite to study your counterpart's card before putting it away.

Refreshments. At business meetings you can expect to be served tea or a cold drink. If asked what you would like to drink, the polite response is, "Whatever you are having." Wait until your host has taken a sip before drinking.

Names. The name game is as complex as the culture. Customs vary among Malays, Chinese and Indians. In general, address each person you are introduced to with his or her title and name. If the person does not have a professional, academic or noble title, use Mr. or Miss/ Mrs./Madam.

Here are some culture-specific tips:

- With a Malay name such as Abdul Hisham Hajji Rahman, Rahman is his father's name and Hajji indicates the father visited Mecca. He is addressed formally as Encik ('Mr.') Hisham, less formally as Abdul Hisham. If Encik has made the pilgrimage he may be addressed as Hajji Hisham. A Malay woman is addressed with *Puan* plus her name. Remember that if her name is Noor binti Ahmad, she is addressed as Puan Noor -- Ahmad is her father's name.
- Chinese family names precede the two given names. For example, Li Er San is addressed as Mr. Li. If he gives his name as James Li, he may suggest you call him James, but wait for him to do so. Since most Chinese wives do not take their husband's name, they should be addressed with "Madam" plus their maiden name rather than "Mrs." plus the husband's name.
- Indian names vary by religion and also by region: that is, by the Indian region the person's ancestors came from. Indian Muslim names are similar to Malay names; a South Indian Hindu named S. Nagarajan is addressed as Mr. Nagarajan since "S" is the first initial of his father's name; an Indian Hindu from the north named Vijay Kumar would be Mr. Kumar, while his Sikh neighbor Suresh Singh is Mr. Suresh because the name "Singh" is common to all male Sikhs.
- Westerners are often addressed by their given name preceded by Mr., Miss or Mrs. So your Malaysian contacts may call you "Mr. William", "Mrs. Mary" or "Dr. Robert."

Titles. Titles are important in this rather formal, hierarchical society. Three common ones are Tun, Datuk (or Dato) and Tan Sri. Address Dato Abdul Hisham Rahman as "Dato." The king and the nobility are treated with great respect in Malaysia.

Gift Giving. Gifts are normally exchanged only between friends. If you or your company already has a relationship with your Malaysian counterparts, here are some do's and don'ts:

- A gift is normally not unwrapped in the presence of the giver.
- Gifts of food are good, but avoid alcohol for Muslims and pork products for both Muslims and Hindus. If invited to a dinner or party, fruit, candy and cakes are acceptable gifts.

– Avoid giving knives, letter openers or clocks to a Chinese: sharp objects suggest the cutting off of a relationship, while the Chinese word for timepiece sounds like the word for death.

Negotiating Behavior

Bargaining Range. Many Malaysians love to bargain. Since you may run into unanticipated cost factors, remember to build some margin into your opening bid or quotation. Smart negotiators keep a few bargaining chips in their back pocket for the all-important end game.

Lawyers, Contracts and Disputes. Malaysians prefer to resolve disputes in face-to-face meetings rather than via fax and email. They rely more on relationships than on contract clauses to resolve business disagreements. During the early stages of contract negotiations, it is wise to keep your lawyers somewhat in the background rather than at the bargaining table. To many Malaysians, the presence of lawyers may signal lack of trust.

The Indonesian Negotiator

Indonesia's business culture is complex due to the diversity of its demographic makeup. Its population of well over 200 million includes Javanese, Bataks, overseas Chinese, and 300 other ethnic groups. It is the world's fourth most populous country and by far the largest Muslim nation. Business visitors find the culture relationship-focused, hierarchical and relaxed about punctuality and deadlines. Indonesian negotiators tend to be soft spoken, friendly and polite.

The Language of Business. The national language is Bahasa Indonesia, similar to Malay. Perhaps because the country was colonized by the Dutch rather the British, English is not as widely spoken as it is in Singapore or Malaysia. So if you are meeting your local counterpart for the first time it would be wise to inquire whether an interpreter will be necessary.

If you plan to set up an office or subsidiary, keep in mind that English-speaking middle managers are often hard to find in Indonesia. To solve this problem many foreign companies recruit management in the Philippines where experienced managers fluent in English are easier to find.

Making Initial Contact. Most Indonesian executives are uncomfortable talking business with people they do not know -- especially foreigners who are trying to sell them something. Trade shows and official trade missions are good ways to meet prospective customers and partners. Another way is to have someone introduce you, preferably a person or organization who knows both you and the Indonesian party you wish to contact. You can also ask your bank or a trading company, law firm, consulting firm or embassy official to introduce you.

Build a Relationship Before Talking Business. Getting to know your counterpart is a key prelude to discussing a deal in Southeast Asia. Expect most of your first meeting to be taken up with general conversation. Sharing a meal helps you get to know your Indonesian contact, so does playing golf and going sightseeing. Each time you visit the market take time to update your counterparts on what's been happening and socialize with them before getting down to business.

Orientation to Time. Remember that Indonesia is a cluster of islands straddling the equator. The tropical climate combined with the low level of industrialization may explain why time has a different meaning there. While foreign visitors are always expected to be on time, local business people march to a different tick of the clock. So if you are kept waiting don't take offense. That's especially true in Jakarta where the cause of the delay could be a monumental traffic jam.

Of course the problem might be a different kind of jam, namely *jam karet,* meaning 'rubber time.' Time and schedules are flexible in the tropics. Like most of their neighbors in South and Southeast Asia, the Indonesians consider people and relationships more important than schedules and deadlines. For example the meeting before yours might have taken your counterpart an hour longer than expected, and it is considered very rude to break off one meeting in order to be on time for the next one.

Two practical tips regarding time and scheduling: Try to be punctual for your meetings and have plenty of reading material with you in case you have to wait for your local contact.

Hierarchy, Status and Showing Respect. The traditional culture accords high status to older people, especially older males. It is important to show appropriate respect by deferring to higher-ranking persons. Younger business visitors should defer to senior Indonesians, particularly when the latter are buyers or potential customers.

The way you dress can show either respect or disrespect to your counterpart. Because of the tropical climate men may find it uncomfortable to wear a suit. Nevertheless, do don a dark suit when meeting a high level government official. For meetings in the private sector a long-sleeved white shirt and tie with neat trousers is appropriate for meetings in the private sector. Women should wear a modest dress, lightweight suit or skirt and blouse.

At any business meeting you can expect to be served tea or a cold drink. No matter how thirsty you may be, wait until your host has taken a sip before drinking. To do otherwise would be a sign of disrespect or poor manners.

Maintaining Surface Harmony. Like other Southeast Asians, Indonesians are sensitive to slights and issues of face. For Western negotiators the easiest way to lose face and cause others loss of face is to display impatience, irritation or anger. Showing negative emotion disrupts the surface harmony of the meeting. Visitors are advised to maintain a calm exterior even if they are frustrated and boiling inside.

Verbal Communication. One important way Javanese maintain harmony during vigorous negotiations is to employ indirect, 'polite' language. There are at least a dozen ways of saying 'no' in Bahasa without actually saying it. Because your local counterpart is accustomed to circumlocutions and evasive language to avoid insulting others, he may take offense if you are overly frank and direct.

But beware of stereotyping in this complex culture. If you happen to be doing business with a Western-educated Javanese or an ethnic Batak of Sumatra, for example, you are likely to encounter a more direct approach to verbal communication.

It took me two or three visits to learn that Indonesians are embarrassed by elaborate expressions of gratitude. They seem to respond best to a simple 'thank you.'

Paraverbal Communication. Indonesians tend to speak rather softly and rarely interrupt another speaker. They may be startled by loud talk and are easily offended if interrupted in mid-sentence. Western visitors should avoid raising their voice or engaging in conversational overlap.

Some Indonesians laugh or giggle when they are nervous or embarrassed. Be careful not to join in the merriment until you know exactly what the laughter is all about.

Nonverbal Communication. Expect a gentle handshake accompanied by moderate eye contact when meeting someone for the first time. While Europeans for example shake hands each time they meet and depart, this is not necessary at subsequent meetings in Indonesia. When in doubt just do as your counterpart does. Except for the handshake Indonesians avoid physical contact with people they do not know well.

Intense eye contact such as would be appropriate in southern Europe or the Middle East is considered 'staring' in Southeast Asia and may make Indonesians uncomfortable. Also, if you wear sunglasses in Indonesia do remember to remove them when meeting a local person. Talking to someone from behind dark glasses is very rude in this society.

Because Indonesia is a Muslim culture the left hand is regarded as unclean. Avoid touching people, passing food or offering your business card with your left hand. It's okay to sign a document with your left hand if you are a southpaw but remember to give it to someone with your right hand.

Pointing at people or objects with your index finger is impolite. If you need to point, close your (right) fist and aim it thumb-first in the direction indicated. To call a waiter, simply raise your hand the way you did in school. Or you can extend your right arm and make a scooping motion with your hand.

Negotiating Protocol

Making a Sales Presentation. Take time to gauge the English-language capability of your audience before launching into your pitch. Use plenty of visuals and handouts, especially with materials having to do with numbers. Avoid anything smacking of 'hard sell.' Think in terms of *offering* your product or service rather than *selling* it.

Bargaining Range. Indonesians love to bargain. Since you are likely to run into unanticipated cost factors, remember to build some extra margin into your opening bid or quotation. With negotiations often dragging on for months or years your counterparts have a lot of time to keep chipping away at your initial position. Smart negotiators anticipate this and keep a good supply of bargaining chips in their back pocket.

Decision-Making Behavior. The decision-making process can take anywhere from four to six times as long in Jakarta or Bandung as it does in Frankfurt or Los Angeles. Remember to pack a large supply of patience when you go to do business in this part of the world.

Contracts. Indonesians tend to regard their relationship with you as far more important than the contract they signed. They usually prefer to sort out problems in face-to-face meetings rather than by calling a lawyer or by referring to the fine print in the written agreement. Of course you should get everything in writing to avoid later misunderstandings, but try to be sympathetic to your Indonesian partner's request to renegotiate some of the contract terms later.

Names and Titles. While many Javanese have only one name, people of the middle and upper classes often choose a family name. These surnames typically end in 'o' as in Sukarno, Suharto and Subroto. If you are introduced to a male with the single name Budi, for example, you should address him as "Mr. Budi." If he has a second name he becomes "Mr. _____."

Do not be surprised if your local counterparts call you by your given name preceded by Mr., Miss or Mrs. That's why "Mr. Bob" and "Mrs. Mary" are frequently heard appellations in Jakarta.

Gift Giving. Unlike many other Asian societies, Indonesia is not a gift-giving culture. If you do give someone a gift do not expect it to be unwrapped in your presence.

'Face' and Communication. This is a traditional, hierarchical, face-conscious society. Which means that visitors from more egalitarian, informal cultures may have trouble communicating with Indonesians.

Some tips regarding face:
— Avoid open confrontation at all costs.
— Avoid words or actions which might embarrass or shame someone. Never correct or criticize your Indonesian counterpart in front of other people.
— Higher status people never apologize directly to people of low status. Domestic servants or manual workers are likely to feel acutely embarrassed by a formal apology from a superior. A smile and perhaps a small gift accomplishes the same result without the embarrassment.
— No one wants to tell you bad news. If your local business partner delays telling you about a problem until it is too late to do anything about it, do not get upset. Remember that Indonesians are showing you respect by shielding you from bad news. You can solve this communication problem by developing a climate of trust with your local counterparts.

As a matter of fact, you will find that a close personal relationship is the basis for solving most business problems in Indonesia.

The Filipino Negotiator

The business culture of the Philippines is unique in Southeast Asia. Yes, Filipinos do share the basic values, attitudes and beliefs of their ASEAN neighbors. But 400 years of Spanish colonialism followed by nearly a century of strong U.S. influence have added other important features to the culture.

Business visitors find the Filipinos relationship-focused, hierarchical, and relaxed about punctuality and deadlines, as well as concerned about maintaining harmony and what Filipinos call "smooth interpersonal relations."

The Language of Business. While there are over 70 languages and dialects in the Philippines, the national language is Pilipino, based on Tagalog. One legacy of the U.S. presence is that most Filipinos engaged in international business speak fluent English. Visitors who use that language will have no more difficulty than they would in Singapore.

Those planning to set up an office or subsidiary should note however that it is now becoming difficult to find competent English-speaking middle managers and technicians. That is because so many of them have been recruited to work as expatriates abroad.

Making Initial Contact. As in other relationship-focused cultures, many Filipinos are reluctant to talk business with people they do not know -- especially foreigners who are trying to sell them something. Trade shows and official trade missions are good ways to meet prospective customers and partners. Another way is to have someone introduce you, preferably a person or organization who knows both you and the Filipino party you wish to contact. You can also ask your bank or a trading company, law firm, consulting firm or embassy official to introduce you.

Relationships. Getting to know your counterpart is a must for doing business here, as in other parts of Southeast Asia. Expect most of your first meeting to be taken up with general conversation. Sharing a meal helps you get to know your local counterpart, so does playing golf. Each time you re-visit the country, remember to take the time to update your Filipino partners on what's been happening and socialize with them before getting down to business again. Be conscious of the positive connotation of *pakikisma*, the Filipino term for togetherness and camaraderie. As in other Asian societies, the group is more important than the individual.

Orientation to Time. The tropical climate, the low level of industrialization and Manila traffic all conspire together to make punctuality problematic in this emerging Southeast Asian market. When you call for an appointment, your contact may jokingly ask, "Ah, do you mean Western time or Filipino time?" Despite the generally polychronic attitude towards time, business visitors from overseas are still expected to be fairly punctual for meetings.

Status, Self-Esteem and Showing Respect. As in other hierarchical societies, Filipinos accord high status to older people, especially older males. It is important to show appropriate respect to higher-ranking persons. Younger business visitors should defer to senior Filipinos, particularly when the latter are buyers or potential customers. As in the rest of Asia, the customer is king in the Philippines.

Like other Southeast Asians, Filipinos are sensitive to slights and issues of face. The traditional Filipino concern for face and self-esteem was reinforced by the Spanish obsession with honor and *amor-proprio*, meaning self-respect or self-esteem. Visiting business people should be sensitive to this concern when dealing with Filipinos of any rank or condition.

Maintaining Surface Harmony. Filipinos try hard to maintain smooth relations with others, even if things only look smooth on the surface. For Western negotiators the easiest way to lose face and cause others loss of face is to display impatience, irritation or anger. A display of negative emotion disrupts the surface harmony of the meeting. Negotiators should be careful to maintain a calm exterior even when frustrated or angry inside.

Verbal Communication. Indirectness is the rule. The ever-courteous Filipinos are so anxious to avoid offending others, they strenuously avoid using the rude word, 'no.' They prefer indirect, diplomatic language. There are many ways of saying 'no' in Pilipino without actually saying it. Because your local counterparts are accustomed to vague statements and evasive language to avoid insulting others, they may take offense if you are overly frank and direct.

Another reason for Filipino indirectness is their strong desire to avoid *hiya,* meaning shame or embarrassment. They strive to avoid bringing shame or embarrassment on themselves or others, and phrasing a statements in a roundabout way is a good way to reduce this risk.

Paraverbal Communication. Most Filipinos speak rather softly and rarely interrupt another speaker. They may be startled by loud talk and are easily offended if interrupted in mid-sentence. Expressive Western visitors should avoid raising their voices and try not to interrupt their local counterparts during business meetings.

Nonverbal Communication

Interpersonal Distance. Most of the time you can expect people to stand and sit at about an arm's length distance.

Touch Behavior. Except for the handshake and sometimes a light pat on the back, Filipinos tend to avoid physical contact with people they do not know well.

Gaze Behavior. Intense eye contact such as would be appropriate in southern Europe or the Middle East is considered "staring" in the Philippines and is likely to make local people uncomfortable. This is an interesting example of the persistence of cultural patterns. The Philippines spent four centuries as a Spanish colony administered from Mexico, and both Spaniards and Mexicans are accustomed to strong, direct eye contact. Nonetheless Filipinos still retain the Southeast East Asian preference for indirect gaze behavior.

Gestures. Pointing at people or objects with your index finger is impolite. If you ask directions on the street, rather than pointing local people may respond by shifting their eyes or pointing the chin in the direction indicated.

It is rude to beckon someone by crooking your index finger. To call a waiter, raise your hand or extend your right hand and wave it in a palm-down scooping motion.

Avoid standing with your hands on hips; this indicates anger, arrogance or a challenge.

Filipinos often greet each other by quickly raising and lowering their eyebrows. Accompanied by a smile, this gesture signifies a friendly 'hello.'

Two people of the same gender often hold hands in public; this usually indicates friendship.

Indicate the number 'two' by raising your little finger and ring finger rather than the index finger and middle finger as in some other cultures.

Business Protocol

Dress Code. The way you dress shows either respect or disrespect to your counterpart. For men, a business suit, white shirt with tie or the *barong tagalog* -- the formal Filipino shirt worn outside the trousers -- are all appropriate. Women should wear a dress, lightweight suit or skirt and blouse.

Meeting and Greeting. Expect a gentle handshake accompanied by moderate eye contact when meeting someone for the first time.

Name and Titles. Many Filipinos have Spanish-sounding given names such as Maria and family names like Cruz. These names were adopted during Spanish colonial rule and do not indicate Hispanic ancestry. Many upper-class Filipinos follow the Spanish custom of having two surnames, their father's followed by their mother's. If your Filipino counterpart invites you to use her or his nickname, do so and invite them to use yours in return. If you don't have a nickname, think about inventing one.

Titles are important in the Philippines. As in Latin America, professionals are often addressed by their family name preceded by their title, e.g. 'attorney de la Cruz' or 'engineer Martin.' People without professional titles are addressed with Mr., Mrs. or Miss followed by the surname. If the person has two family names, you need use only the first (father's).

Topics of Conversation. Good topics are family, food, culture, sports and Filipino history. Avoid discussing local politics, religion or corruption.

Gift Giving. Exchanging gifts plays an important role in relationship-building. *Utang na loob*, meaning debt of gratitude for favors or gifts, is an important component of the glue that holds this relationship-focused culture together. Filipinos do not usually open a gift in front of others.

Social Etiquette. If invited to a Filipino home, bring flowers or chocolates rather than alcohol as a hostess gift. A gift of wine or spirits would imply that your hosts may not have enough drinks for their guests. Note that when eating Filipinos often hold the fork in the left hand, using it to push food into the spoon which is held in the right hand.

When dining at someone's home, leave a bit of food on your plate. This assures your hosts they have fed you well. A clean plate signifies you haven't had enough to eat.

Remember that in the Philippines, over-indulgence in alcohol is considered ill-mannered behavior.

Interesting Local Specialties. Filipinos enjoy *bago'ong*, a salty, pungent paste made from fermented shrimp and used as a sauce and condiment. Visitors can impress their local hosts by partaking of this Southeast Asian specialty.

Your hosts may try to shock you with *balut*, an egg containing a fully-formed duck embryo. If you are not tempted by this purely Filipino delicacy, you can demonstrate your appreciation of local culture by declining with a smile rather than with an expression of disgust.

Negotiating Style

Making a Presentation. Use plenty of visuals and handouts, especially with materials having to do with numbers. Avoid anything smacking of 'hard sell.' Think in terms of offering your product or service rather than selling it.

Bargaining Range. Many Filipinos enjoy bargaining, so remember to build some extra margin into your opening bid or quotation. Smart negotiators keep a good supply of bargaining chips in their back pocket for use in the end game.

Decision-Making Behavior. Coming to a business decision is likely to take longer than in more deal-focused cultures. Patience is a key asset for negotiators in this part of the world.

A strong personal relationship accompanied by respect for local sensitivities is the proper basis for doing successful business in the Philippines.

Group B

Relationship-Focused – Formal – Monochronic – Reserved

The Japanese Negotiator

The Language of Business. These days more Japanese business people speak foreign languages, especially English. Nevertheless, because many of them read English better than they speak it, you should consider employing an interpreter. When working on a major deal, consider hiring your own interpreter rather than relying on your counterparts.

Relationship First. Developing rapport is an important and time-consuming part of the overall negotiating process. It is essential to get to know your counterparts before starting to discuss business. Socializing over drinks, meals and golf is a good way to build rapport.

Orientation to Time. Japanese value punctuality and strict adherence to schedules and expect the same of their foreign counterparts, especially potential suppliers.

Hierarchy, Status, and Respect. Younger, subordinate individuals are expected to defer to older, higher-ranking persons. Since few women have reached positions of authority in this traditional, hierarchical society, most men are not used to dealing with females on the basis of equality in a business context.

Further, in Japan the buyer automatically enjoys higher status than the seller in a commercial transaction, and buyers expect to be treated with great respect. Hence young foreigners, especially women, face a significant cultural obstacle when trying to sell to Japanese customers.

Here are four ways to overcome age and gender barriers with the Japanese:

- Get introduced by the eldest, most senior male colleague available. Status is transferrable.
- Learn how to show proper respect. Showing respect to others gains you respect.

- Establish your professional credentials, taking care not to appear arrogant. Expertise confers status.
- Many women are more skilled than males in reading body language. This ability is valuable when dealing with Japanese, who employ a good deal of subtle nonverbal communication.

Maintaining Surface Harmony. Japanese regard open displays of anger or impatience as infantile and offensive. They quickly lose respect for people who cannot retain a calm exterior under stress. Visiting negotiators are advised to avoid open confrontation at all cost.

Concern with 'Face'. Face has to do with self-respect, dignity, reputation. You can *lose face* by appearing childish or lacking in self-control, for example by losing your temper. You can cause your counterparts to lose face by expressing sharp disagreement, embarrassing them, criticizing them in public or by showing disrespect in other ways. Causing loss of face can completely disrupt a promising business negotiation.

You can give your counterpart face by using polite forms of address and observing local customs and traditions. Giving face is an effective way build a solid relationship. If you make a mistake you may be able to save your face with a humble apology. And you can save the other party's face for example by allowing him a graceful exit from a difficult negotiating position.

Formality and Rituals. To help maintain surface harmony and prevent loss of face, Japanese rely on ritualized codes of behavior. An example is the formalized exchange of business cards, the ritual of the *meishi* (see below). Japanese business men tend to dress and behave formally and are more comfortable with visitors who do likewise.

Communication Style

Reserved and formal while they are getting to know you. Less reliance on written and telephone communication, more emphasis on face-to-face meetings.

Indirect Verbal Communication. Japanese negotiators frequently employ indirect, vague, oblique language wherein the meaning is deliberately ambiguous and implicit rather than clear and explicit.

They tend to employ circumlocutions, understatement, silence, and evasive language to avoid offending the other party.

For instance, many Japanese consider it offensive to reply to a request with a blunt 'no'. So a negotiator might answer "We will do our best," or "That will be difficult" instead. The result of this politeness might be confusion on the part of the foreigner; surface harmony has been maintained at the cost of clarity.

Japanese distrust glibness. They use fewer words than people from more expressive cultures, relying more on paraverbal and nonverbal language.

Paraverbal Communication. Japanese tend to speak softly and hesitantly and employ frequent silences. They may pause at considerable length before answering a question or responding to a request and try to avoid interrupting the other party, since this would be extremely rude. A laugh or a giggle may signal nervousness or embarrassment rather than amusement. Visitors should avoid loud talking and always wait until their Japanese counterpart has finished speaking before starting to speak.

Nonverbal Communication. When meeting and greeting, expect a soft handshake. Avoid strong, direct eye contact, which may be misinterpreted as an attempt to intimidate or an indication of outright hostility. A smile may mask disapproval or anger. Body language is very restrained, formal, with small gestures. Avoid arm-waving and other vigorous gestures.

Japan is a low-contact culture. Expect very litle touching. Taboo gestures include arm-grabbing and backslapping.

Negotiation Style

Making a Presentation. Avoid opening with a joke or humorous anecdote. This would show lack of respect for the topic and for the audience. Speak clearly and simply. Avoid using double negatives and convoluted sentences, jargon, slang or unusual words.

Take care not to over-praise your product or company. Instead use testimonials or articles written about your firm. Use visual aids, especially for numbers, and provide copies of the presentation.

Decision-Making Behavior. Although things are changing, many Japanese companies still make decisions by consensus. This is a time-consuming process, another reason to be patient at the negotiating table.

Role of the Contract. The final written agreement is less important than the strength of the relationship with your counterpart. But put everything in writing anyway. The Japanese side may expect to rene-gotiate the contract if circumstances change. For some Japanese companies the contract is an expression of intent.

Some Westerners like to hand the other side a draft contract to be used as the outline for the negotiation and then discuss each item point by point. With the Japanese it is better to keep the draft to yourself. Look for areas of agreement before discussing the difficult items. And call in the lawyers only towards the end of the negotiating process, after basic agreement has been reached.

Business Protocol

Dress Code. Dark suit, white shirt, conservative tie for men. Conservative suit or dress for women.

Meeting and Greeting. Hand over your business card using both hands, holding it between thumb and forefinger with the side showing the Japanese printing facing up. Shake hands with a slight bow and state your name and your company's name. Receive your counterpart's card with both hands, study it for several seconds and then place it respectfully on the conference table in front of you or in your leather (not plastic) card holder. Expect a bow and a soft handshake. Avoid an excessively firm handshake or overly direct eye contact.

Forms of Address. Address your counterpart with his or her family name plus the suffix *san*, as in Watanabe-san. In Japan the family name comes first, followed by given names. But on business cards meant for foreigners they may reverse the order, so when in doubt ask which is the family name.

Gift Giving and Receiving. Exchanging gifts is an important part of the business culture, contributing to relationship building. Be pre-pared with appropriate gifts for your Japanese counterparts. A good choice is an expensive cognac, a good single malt whisky or a tasteful item which is typical of your city, region or country.

Note that the wrapping and presentation of the gift are more important than the contents. Have your gifts wrapped in Japan or by someone knowledgeable of Japanese customs. Present the gift to your partner with both hands. The recipient will probably put it aside and open it later. You should also receive a gift with both hands and open it later.

Wining and Dining. Entertaining and being entertained is an essential part of building a close relationship with your counterpart. In Japan you may wish to reciprocate with an invitation to a Western style restaurant serving for example French or Italian cuisine. In your homeland or in a third country, a restaurant offering local specialties is usually a good choice.

To show your commitment to Japanese customs, master the art of eating with chopsticks and toasting appropriately. For males, ritual drinking is a traditional way to get to know your counterpart. It is sometimes appropriate to drink heavily, even to get drunk. For some Japanese businessmen, drinking alcohol seems to dissolve the stiffness and formality you may encounter during business meetings.

Japanese tend to rely heavily on *tatemae* or surface communication, telling you what they think you want to hear. After a few drinks they may let their hair down and indulge in *honne* communication, telling you what they really think. So alcohol can be a good lubricant to a sticky negotiation.

Women are not expected to drink, and certainly not expected to get drunk. Not being able to join in the male drinking ritual could represent a slight handicap for women trying to do business with the Japanese.

Males who prefer not to drink alcohol can legitimately excuse themselves on grounds of illness or religious rules. They may however thereby miss out on some opportunities to deepen the relationship and to learn more about their Japanese partners.

Maintaining the Relationship. It is very important to stay in close contact with your Japanese customers and partners between visits, whether by telephone, fax, letter or email.

The Chinese Negotiator

China is a relatively homogeneous culture. The written language is the same throughout China, though the Chinese often speak the dialect of the region in which they have been raised. Therefore, while visiting negotiators will observe some differences between north and south, between the coastal and interior provinces, and especially between Hong Kong and the mainland, the following description basically holds true for the whole country.

The Language of Business. Though more and more Chinese negotiators speak English these days, it is wise to ask whether you will need an interpreter. When working on a major deal you may wish to hire your own interpreter rather than relying on one supplied by the Chinese side.

Use *Guanxi*. Chinese companies are uncomfortable talking business with strangers. Make initial contact at a trade show, on an official trade mission, or via an introduction from an intermediary. The latter should ideally be a respected person or organization known to both you and the Chinese party you wish to contact. If you do not have such a mutual friend, ask your government trade representatives, chamber of commerce, bank or trade association to introduce you.

Relationship First. In China, developing rapport is a critical part of the overall negotiating process. Get to know your counterparts well before starting to discuss business. Socializing over drinks and dinner is a good way to build rapport. In China, first you make a friend, then you make a deal.

Hierarchy, Formality, Status and Respect. Younger people defer to older, higher-ranking persons. Hence young export marketers for example must be careful to show respect to older, more senior Chinese buyers.

Maintaining Surface Harmony. Chinese regard open displays of anger or impatience as infantile, and lose respect for people who cannot retain a calm exterior under stress. Visiting negotiators are advised to stay cool and to avoid open confrontation at all cost. A false smile is preferable to an honest scowl.

Concern with 'Face'. Face has to do with self-respect, dignity, reputation. You can 'lose face' by appearing childish or lacking in self-control, for example, losing your temper. You can cause your counterparts to lose face by expressing sharp disagreement, embarrassing them, criticizing them in public or by showing disrespect. Causing serious loss of face can completely disrupt a promising business negotiation.

You can 'give' your counterpart face by using polite forms of address and observing local customs and traditions. Giving face is an effective way to build a solid relationship. If you make a mistake you may be able to 'save your face' with a humble apology. And you can save the other party's face for example by allowing him a graceful exit from a difficult negotiating position.

Verbal Communication. Especially in the north, Chinese are reserved and formal compared to people from more informal and expressive people such as Scandinavians, Americans and Australians. When discussing major issues they rely much more on face-to-face meetings than on written communications or phone calls. Chinese negotiators often employ indirect, vague, oblique language wherein the meaning is ambiguous rather than clear and explicit. They use evasive language not to mislead people but rather to avoid offending them.

For example, many Chinese consider it offensive to reply to a request with a blunt 'no'. Often a Chinese negotiator offers a polite evasion such as, "That will require further study" or "That will be difficult" instead. This kind of indirect, polite discourse sometimes confuses negotiators from cultures accustomed to more direct language.

Paraverbal Communication. Chinese, especially those from the northern part of the country, speak softly. They avoid interrupting other people, since this would be rude. It is important for visiting negotiators from more expressive cultures to avoid loud talking and to wait patiently until their Chinese counterpart has finished speaking before saying their piece. Another feature of Chinese paraverbal behavior is that a laugh or a giggle may signal stress, nervousness or embarrassment rather than amusement.

Nonverbal Communication

Eye Contact. Chinese may misinterpret a strong, direct gaze as an attempt to intimidate or even an indication of outright hostility.

Touch Behavior. China is a low-contact culture, with very little touching in a business situation.

Gestures. Touching thumb and forefinger together while raising the third, fourth and fifth fingers signals the number '3'. Since this gesture closely resembles the 'A-OK' sign, it can lead to confusion to visitors from other cultures. The Chinese use few gestures. Visitors should avoid arm-waving and wide gestures as well as arm-grabbing and backslapping. Striking the palm of one hand with the fist of the other is considered a vulgar gesture.

Orientation to Time. The Chinese value punctuality and adherence to schedules. They expect the same of their foreign counterparts, especially potential suppliers.

Business Protocol

Dress Code. Conservative suit, white shirt and tie for men; suit or dress for women.

Meeting and Greeting. Expect a soft handshake and moderate eye contact. Avoid greeting your counterpart with a bone-crushing handshake.

Forms of Address. Use the person's family name or organizational title: Mr. Li Er Peng is Mr. Li, not Mr. Peng. Avoid calling a Chinese by his given name unless specifically asked to do so.

Names and Titles. On business cards printed in Chinese the family name comes first, followed by two given names. But on cards printed in Western languages some Chinese reverse the order. When in doubt, ask which is the family name.

Business Cards. Have the text of your card printed in Chinese characters on one side. The exchange of cards is done using both hands while bowing your head slightly. When receiving your counterpart's card, take a moment to read it and then put the card away in a leather card case or place it on the conference table in front of you, across from the individual who gave it to you. Do not write on someone's name card in the presence of the giver.

Gift Giving. Exchanging gifts is a key part of the business culture, contributing to developing 'guanxi'. Be prepared with appropriate gifts for your counterparts. Expensive cognac is a good choice. Others are items typical of your state or region and tasteful logo gifts. Present the gift with both hands. The recipient will probably put it aside and open it after the meeting -- you should also receive a gift with both hands and open it later.

Wining and Dining. Entertaining and being entertained is an essential part of building a close relationship with your counterpart. In China you may be invited to one or more formal banquets, depending on the length of your stay. Have your local contact or your hotel help you reciprocate with an appropriate banquet before you leave China. Women are not expected to keep up with the rounds of banquet toasts and are definitely not expected to get drunk. Males who prefer not to drink alcohol can excuse themselves on the grounds of religious objection or ill health.

Hosting Chinese Visitors. A restaurant offering local specialties is usually a good choice. However, business visitors from China often prefer a good Chinese meal. To show your commitment to Chinese customs, master the fine arts of eating with chopsticks and toasting your counterparts appropriately.

Negotiating Behavior

Adapting Your Presentation. Avoid opening with a joke or humorous anecdote. This would show inappropriate informality. Take care not to over-praise your product or company. Instead, offer testimonials or articles written about your firm. In other words, let others praise your product and your firm. Likewise, avoid making negative comments about your competitors. Rather, you may want to pass along critical comments about your competitors made by respected third parties. It's better to let others criticize your competitors and their products.

Bargaining Range. Chinese negotiators often bargain vigorously and expect their counterparts to grant major concessions on price and terms during the course of the negotiation. They may measure their success at the bargaining table by how far they are able to move you away from your opening offer. So wise negotiators always build enough margin into their opening offer to leave room for bargaining.

Bargaining Style. Be prepared for bazaar haggling. Make any concession with great reluctance, and only on a conditional basis, demanding an equivalent concession in return.

Pressure Tactics. At a critical point in the negotiation you may spot your chief competitor seated in the reception area, waiting to meet your Chinese counterpart after your session. This is a great way to push you into a concession you didn't want to make.

Ploys and Counter-ploys. Although Chinese negotiators generally mask negative emotions, they may on occasion display anger as a tactic. Public sector negotiators sometimes plead the poverty of their country to obtain a lower price. They may also flatter you as an "old friend." Be aware that 'friends' are expected to help China by offering better terms.

Duration. Negotiating in China tends to be a long, time-consuming process requiring patience and a calm disposition. This is especially true when doing business with a government entity or a public sector company. Decisions take time. For example, it took Volkswagen nine years to negotiate an agreement to build an automobile factory in Shanghai.

Role of the Contract. Many Chinese negotiators regard the final written agreement as less important than the strength of the relationship with you and your company. That's fine for them, but be sure to get everything in writing anyway. The Chinese often expect to renegotiate the contract if circumstances change. Be prepared for this, and remember that renegotiation of terms can work for both sides. If they want to reinterpret a certain clause in their favor, consider agreeing on condition they accept amending an equally important clause in *your* favor.

Role of Legal Advisors. While you will of course dialog with your lawyers throughout the bargaining process, keep them somewhat in the background until towards the end of negotiations. Chinese tend to regard the presence of lawyers at the bargaining table as a sign of mistrust.

Maintaining the Relationship. Between personal visits, stay in regular contact with your counterparts. Deal-focused business people often overlook this vital step in enhancing the business relationship.

The Korean Negotiator

The business culture of Korea is unique within Northeast Asia. Korean negotiating behavior is similar in many respects to that of neighboring China and Japan, but differs in key ways. Perhaps the biggest difference is that Korean business people can be more direct and at times more confrontational than Chinese and (especially) Japanese negotiators.

Initial Contact. Always arrange for a formal introduction. Trying to directly contact a company or person you don't know rarely works. The best introducer is a respected person or organization of high status, someone known to both you and your Korean counterpart. Having the right connections is vital in Korea.

Relationships. Developing good rapport is essential to doing business successfully. Getting to know your counterparts well lays the groundwork for successful discussions. Maintaining smooth interpersonal relations is critical; extensive small talk as well as socializing over drinks and dinner and other entertainment are good ways to accomplish this.

Orientation to Time. Most Korean companies value punctuality and adherence to schedules. However, because of traffic congestion your local counterparts may sometimes arrive late for a meeting. It would be rude to show irritation over such an unavoidable delay. Some smaller firms take a more relaxed approach to punctuality.

Hierarchy, Status and Gender. Korean society is a steeply vertical one, with a strict hierarchy. Remember to show respect to people of high status, including the elderly and high-ranking company executives. Younger, subordinate individuals defer to older, higher-ranking persons.

Since few women have reached positions of authority in local companies, most Korean men are unaccustomed to dealing with females on the basis of equality in a business context. So women tend to face significant cultural obstacles when trying to do business with Koreans. Here are some steps for young business visitors – and businesswomen of any age – to take:

1. Arrange to be introduced (in person or by phone or correspondence) by the most senior male colleague available. In Korea, status is to a certain extent a transferable asset.
2. Following a proper introduction, present your business card which clearly shows your title and functions as well as any academic degrees and professional credentials. During the preliminary conversation, find occasion to refer to your rank, title, experience and professional qualifications. This should of course be done without any hint of arrogance or boastfulness. Credentials and expertise confer respect in this culture.
3. Any colleague or associate accompanying you should likewise make reference to your position, making it clear who is in charge. If you are the senior negotiator on your side and your subordinate is addressed by Korean counterparts, you should be the one to reply. Your subordinate should turn towards you and wait for you to speak.
4. Learn the verbal, paraverbal and nonverbal ways of showing proper respect to your senior Korean counterparts. Respectful behavior on your part makes it easier for them to treat you with proper respect.
5. Pay close attention to the paraverbal and nonverbal signals coming from the other side of the bargaining table. Women tend to be more skilled than most males in reading body language. Take advantage of this ability: it can be very useful with Koreans, who engage in a great deal of nonverbal communication. Furthermore, Korean negotiators respect foreigners who take the time and effort to correctly interpret their body language.

As more women enter the managerial ranks of Korean companies, female business visitors will find their task less daunting. One sign of change in this regard was the establishment of a MBA program for women in South Korea. Another sign was the establishment of a ministry of gender equality. So one of Asia's most male-dominated societies is evolving in the direction of equality for the female half of the population.

Maintaining Surface Harmony. Koreans are sensitive to perceived slights. Even if your local counterparts occasionally employ confrontational tactics, stay cool, do not over-react. Instead strive to maintain surface harmony at all times, even under provocation. Although Korean negotiators tend to be more confrontational than most Chinese and Japanese negotiators, maintaining surface harmony helps keep things moving in the desired direction.

Smooth interpersonal relations help you avoid disturbing a Korean's *kibun*. This term is usually translated into English as 'mood', but it is more complicated than that. Disturbing a Korean's 'kibun' is likely to sour his mood and make coming to agreement more difficult. Veterans of negotiating with Koreans agree that staying calm rather than displaying irritation or anger is the best way to get things done.

'Face'. Face is related to self-respect, dignity, reputation. Causing loss of face, even if unintentionally, can disrupt a promising business negotiation. It helps to use the proper forms of address with high-status persons and to observe local customs and traditions.

If you commit a minor faux pas, a simple apology usually works. If you should cause someone serious loss of face, the damage may be irreparable. But a high-status third party, such as the person or organization who introduced you, might be able to step in and smooth things over.

Verbal Communication. Most Koreans are skilled at controlling their emotions and hiding their true feelings. Whereas Germans for example are well-known around the world for their directness in communication, Koreans often resort to indirect, evasive language in order to reduce the risk of offending others. For example, to avoid offending the other party they rarely utter a blunt 'no'. Surface harmony and saving face take precedence over clarity of the message.

Koreans in turn expect their counterparts to avoid frank criticism or unnecessary brusqueness. Although Koreans are often more direct than the Japanese, they themselves are still very sensitive to perceived slights.

Nonverbal Communication

Koreans rely on a sort of 'sixth sense' to gauge the mood and reaction of other Koreans. This special sense involves reading paraverbal and nonverbal behavior. Most Koreans unconsciously expect foreigners to understand the subtle nuances of this silent language.

Koreans are more comfortable with silence than most Westerners. Expect significant pauses during meetings. Korean negotiators try to avoid interrupting the other party, since this would be considered rude. Visiting negotiators should likewise wait until their Korean counterpart has finished speaking before saying their piece.

You normally use only your right hand when passing something to a Korean. Exception: To show special respect, use both hands when presenting an object to a person of high status such as a customer – or use the right hand with the left hand supporting your right elbow.

Expect moderate eye contact. Most Koreans look into your eyes about half the time during a conversation. Avoid using a very direct, intense gaze, which would signal anger or hostility.

With Koreans, a smile often masks disapproval or even anger. Body language is restrained, formal, with very few gestures. Avoid arm-waving and other abrupt, vigorous gestures.

Interpersonal distance varies. On the street Koreans jostle one another regularly, even when there is plenty of space. In a business context, however, expect a medium-sized space bubble.

Korea is a relatively low-contact culture as regards foreigners. Expect very little touching.

Taboo behavior includes blowing one's nose at the dinner table. It is better to sniffle during the meal or better yet, leave the room and blow your nose out of earshot.

Business Protocol

Dress Code. Visitors should dress to show respect to their local counterparts. At the first meeting, a dark suit with white shirt and conservative tie is appropriate for men. Thereafter you can be guided by the dress of your local partners. Women business visitors should likewise dress conservatively.

Introductions. In Korea introductions are not made casually. Arrange for a formal introduction to your business contact.

Meeting and Greeting. Expect a bow and moderate eye contact, often followed by a handshake. Respond with a bow before exchanging name cards.

Forms of Address. Korean names normally consist of the family name first followed by two (occasionally one) given names. Refer to your counterpart by his family name, as in "Mr. Kim." To show respect to senior people, substitute his title for the "Mister." For example, "President Kim" or "Director Park." It is possible you will never use your local counterparts' given names.

Exchange of Business Cards. Exchanging name cards is very important. Receive your counterpart's card with both hands. Present your own card with the right hand or with the right hand supported at the elbow by your left hand. Study the other party's card, then put the card away in a quality leather card wallet. At a formal meeting, place it on the conference table in front of you and after the meeting put it respectfully away in your card wallet.

Gift Giving and Receiving. If you are meeting your counterpart at his office, consider bringing a gift if you have just arrived from abroad. If invited to a Korean's home, always bring a present.

Appropriate gifts include items typical of your own country or region as well as an expensive cognac or whiskey. Present the gift with both hands. The recipient will probably put it aside and open it later. You should also receive a gift with both hands and open it later.

Wining and Dining. Entertaining and being entertained is an essential part of building a close relationship with your Korean counterpart. For males, ritual drinking is a traditional way to get to know your counterpart. It is appropriate for men to drink heavily, even to get drunk. Alcohol often seems to dissolve the stiffness and formality often encountered during business meetings. Drinking can be a good lubricant to a sticky negotiation.

Women are not expected to drink, and are definitely not expected to get drunk. Not joining in the male drinking ritual could represent a handicap for women doing business in Korea. Males who prefer not to drink alcohol can excuse themselves on grounds of illness or religious rules. They may however miss out on some opportunities to deepen relationships and learn more about their Korean partners.

Negotiating Style

Making a Presentation. Avoid opening with a joke or humorous anecdote. This would show lack of respect for the topic and for the audience. Speak clearly and simply. Use visual aids as much as possible, especially where numbers are involved.

Determining Your Bargaining Range. When calculating your initial offer, allow some room for bargaining. That way you can give in gracefully when pressed for a concession, while of course demanding an equivalent concession in return.

Decision-Making. Bring patience with you to the bargaining table. Big decisions are made at the top of Korean companies, and chief executives are busy people.

Role of the Contract. To many Korean companies, the final written contract is often less important then the strength of the relationship between the two parties. For them, the legal agreement is akin to an expression of intent. Hence your counterparts may try to renegotiate at any time if circumstances should change. So it's wise to remember that renegotiation of terms can work both ways. If your Korean partners insist on changing a contract clause in their favor, an effective response is to require a change in another clause in your favor.

Resolving Disputes. Korean companies usually try to avoid litigation, depending instead on lengthy negotiations to resolve disagreements.

The Singaporean Negotiator

The Republic of Singapore is unique in the world marketplace. Flourishing on a lush tropical island just a stone's throw from the equator, this modern city-state stands out as the world's only industrialized economy well outside the temperate zone. The Republic's economic success is due to many factors, including hard work, frugality, effective government ... and air conditioning.

Those of us who have worked for years under conditions of tropical heat and maximum humidity can appreciate the impact of climate on productivity and the work ethic. So it's easy to see how the advent of cooled air played a supporting role in Singapore's rapid rise to wealth.

The Languages of Business. Another important factor in Singapore's success is its multilingual and multi-ethnic blend of Chinese (about 78%), Malays (15%) and Indians (6%). Most of the ethnic Chinese business people speak both Mandarin and English, the world's first- and second-most spoken languages respectively.

Fluency in Mandarin provides Singaporeans access to the booming China market, while competence in English makes doing business easy for exporters, importers and investors around the world. The Malay connection is useful in the neighboring markets of Malaysia and Indonesia, while Singapore's diverse Indian community eases entry to the India market. In brief, Singapore is a case study in how ethnic and linguistic diversity can contribute directly to a nation's economic success.

The Business Culture. English language facility is not the only reason visiting negotiators find it easy to do business in the Island Republic. Growing convergence in business customs and practices is another. While the national culture continues to emphasize traditional Asian values such as the importance of family, concern for 'face', and respect for authority, Singapore's *business* culture is quickly evolving towards an international style familiar to most globe-trotting executives.

Hundreds of European, U.S. and Asian companies have found that Singapore's geographic position plus the familiarity of language and business customs make it the ideal site for their Asia/Pacific headquarters. During the 1990s, high costs in Hong Kong and Tokyo drove dozens of companies to move their regional head offices to the Lion City. Some of them are now moving again, though, this time to Shanghai.

Making Contact. The rapidity of change in business behavior has opened something of a generation gap within the Singapore business community. Local entrepreneurs and managers in their 50s and 60s tend to do business in a more traditional, relationship-focused mode, while younger business people are usually more deal-focused.

With companies managed by younger executives, although an introduction never hurts, you can save time by making direct contact. With more traditional companies however the indirect approach via a third party is the route to go.

Verbal Communication: Although accustomed to speaking more directly than other Southeast Asians, Singaporeans still try to avoid answering questions or requests with a blunt 'no.'

- The word 'yes' might or might not mean your counterpart agrees with you. Unless spoken with emphasis it is often a way to avoid confrontation. Older Singaporeans dislike open conflict during a business meetings and will resort to verbal evasiveness to avoid giving offense.
- Avoid asking negative questions such as, "Isn't my shipment ready yet?" If a Singaporean replies "Yes,' he or she usually means "Yes, it is *not* ready," whereas most Westerners would take it to mean the shipment *is* ready to ship.
- Visitors sometimes perceive Singaporean Chinese as overly aggressive because of the way they ask questions. For instance, "You want this sample now or not?" may sound rude, but it simply means, "Would you like to have a sample now?"
- Singaporean English may vary in other ways. If your counterpart offers to "send" you to the airport, that means he will pick you up at your hotel himself and drive you there. If he is cruising the streets looking for an empty "parking lot,"he is seeking what Americans call a parking space.

Paraverbal Behavior: Most Singaporeans speak relatively softly. Loud talk is a sign of poor manners. Interrupting someone in mid-sentence is impolite.

Nonverbal Behavior

Expect a rather gentle handshake. Avoid responding with a bone-crushing grip. Men usually wait for a woman to offer her hand first.

Singaporeans sometimes smile to cover anxiety or embarrassment rather than to express amusement.

When seated, be careful not to cross your legs in such a way that the sole of your shoe is pointed at someone. Do not touch or move objects with your foot.

As in other parts of Southeast Asia, avoid beckoning someone with a crooked forefinger. The polite way is to extend your right arm palm down and make a scooping motion.

Business Protocol

You can generally get down to business without elaborate rituals and hours of small talk, and you can expect your Lion City counterpart to be fairly punctual for meetings as well.

Avoid using first names until your Singapore counterpart suggests it. This is especially important when dealing with older people.

Take care not to interrupt the other party in mid-sentence. Conversational overlap is considered rude here.

When dealing with government officials, remember that gift-giving is taboo, and that if they go to lunch with you they will insist on paying their share. Singapore officials have earned an enviable reputation for honesty and efficiency around the world.

Introductions. When introducing two people, state the name of the more important or more senior person first, e.g., "Chairman Lee, meet Mr. Jones."

Exchanging business cards (called 'name cards' in Southeast Asia). After the introductions the visitor presents his or her card first, preferably with both hands but never with the left. The card should be handled with respect, as it represents the person who gave it to you.

Do not toss it casually onto the conference table, put it in your back pocket, or write on it.

Good topics for conversation. Food, travel, sightseeing, history, business. Avoid discussing local politics, religion or sex.

Wining and Dining. Spouses are usually invited for dinner but not for lunch. Meals are a very important part of life in Singapore.

Negotiating Behavior. To conclude an important deal, expect to make two or more trips to Singapore over the course of several months. The pace of negotiations is slower than in more deal-focused business cultures. Visiting business people find Singaporeans polite but persistent negotiators.

Business Entertainment. Singaporeans are extremely hospitable, and the island's famous cuisine is as delicious as it is varied. Two of the most famous local specialties are pepper crab and durian, the latter an 'aromatic' delicacy regarded by Southeast Asians as the King of Fruits. Some mischievous Singaporeans tease visitors by pushing them to sniff the powerful odor of the durian. While the taste is quite bland, to most Westerners the scent is reminiscent of a clogged sewer, or worse.

My favorite food in Singapore remains fish-head curry. South China contributed the fish head, India the basic curry sauce, and Southeast Asia some of the spices. It is a fitting symbol of the unique Chinese-Malay-Indian potpourri that is Singapore today.

Group C

Relationship-Focused – Formal – Polychronic – Expressive

.

The Arab Negotiator

In defining the Arab world it is helpful to think in terms of four concentric circles. The large outer circle is **the Muslim world**, consisting of over 80 countries with majority Muslim populations.

Within that outer circle is **the Middle East**, comprising the Islamic cultures of West Asia and Africa, but also a number of non Arab Muslim nations such as Turkey, Iran, Pakistan and Afghanistan. The people of the latter countries speak languages other than Arabic and are also ethnically distinct from the inhabitants of the Arab world.

Next comes a third, smaller circle consisting of some 22 countries usually called **the Arab world,** members of the Arab League. Generally, a country considered itself part of the Arab world if (a) its inhabitants speak Arabic and (b) think of themselves as Arabs. So in effect you are an Arab if you speak the language and consider yourself one.

Then finally we come to the fourth, innermost circle, which is the main focus of this profile: the six Arab countries of the Gulf Cooperation Council or GCC. They are Bahrain, Kuwait, Oman, Qatar, Saudi Arabia (by far the most populous of the GCC) and the United Arab Emirates, or UAE. These are **the Gulf Arabs**.

We will look at the similarities among the six business cultures of the Gulf as well as at the differences. However here is a comparison of 2002 population figures for the six GCC countries, adapted from a report in *The Economist* of 23 March 2002:

Saudi Arabia	23,000,000
UAE	3,300,000
Oman	2,400,000
Kuwait	2,300,000
Qatar	720,000
Bahrain	650,000

Religion. The most obvious cultural commonality linking the Arabs of the Gulf is of course Islam. Even the several million foreign workers in the region are mostly Muslims from South and Southeast Asia –

although a surprising 25 percent of Saudi Arabia's 5.5 million foreign workers are Christians, Hindus and Buddhists.

Less obviously, Islam also represents a somewhat divisive factor within the region. That's because while most Gulf Arabs are Sunni Muslims, a significant minority belong to the Shia sect. Centuries of bitter strife divide these two groups.

Further, there is also the division between the puritanical Wahhabi sect, dominant in Saudi Arabia, and the more liberal brands of Islam found in some other Gulf countries. For example, the Saudis forbid alcohol and women are not allowed to drive a car. In fact, only the erstwhile Taliban regime of Afghanistan imposed a stricter version of Islam.

Saudi Arabia is also the only Gulf state which forbids the practice of religions other than Islam. The Saudi religious police, who drive around in distinctive white cars, frequently arrest foreign workers from developing countries for holding non-Muslim religious services. In contrast, although the Wahhabi sect is also dominant in Qatar, that smaller Arab country actually allows the construction of Christian churches.

Dubai, part of the UAE, and Bahrain are the most liberal societies of the GCC, while Kuwait, Oman and Qatar fall somewhere in between. One example of this cultural difference within the Gulf: Saudi customs officials routinely confiscate Christian Bibles and other non-Muslim religious writings at the border, but Oman today boasts a Hindu temple, Bahrain even a Jewish synagogue!

It is of vital importance for visitors doing business in the Gulf to be aware of the differences. Behavior permissible in one Gulf state can be cause for severe punishment in another. According to a report in *The Wall Street Journal* of 9 April 2002, for instance, several dozen foreigners are beheaded every year in Saudi Arabia for serious crimes, including sorcery.

Customs regarding appropriate male-female interaction is a frequent cause of problems for foreigners visiting the more conservative countries of the Gulf, where men must be very careful not to compromise a local woman's reputation. Males should not smile warmly at women, stand too close, or engage in more than superficial conversation.

For the majority of Westerners today religion is at most only one aspect of life. A small aspect for many, larger for others. But for the average inhabitant of the Gulf, whether Shia or Sunni, religion is truly a way of life. About 40 percent of Saudis are illiterate. For great numbers of Gulf Arabs, literate or not, Islamic values still exert a powerful influence on thoughts and behavior.

Finally, Westerners are well advised to avoid ascribing traditional Muslim values and beliefs to cultural backwardness. Your Arab counterparts are certain to take offense at any hint of such an attitude. In this context it would be wise to remember the German saying, "Andere Länder, andere Sitten." Or the equally relevant Danish proverb, "Skik følge eller land fly!"

Communicating with Arabs

We have seen some ways in which the Gulf Arabs differ culturally. Now let's look at another important commonality – the way Arabs communicate. Like culture and religion, culture and communication go hand in hand. We cannot do business of any kind without communicating, whether verbally or nonverbally.

The Language of Business. Today many Gulf Arabs involved in international business speak English fluently. Nevertheless, be prepared to employ an interpreter in case of need. If you are working on a major deal it may be wise to hire your own interpreter rather than relying on one supplied by your local contacts.

Making Contact. In most Arab countries it is customary to do business through a local agent. Your success will depend largely on your choice of agent and how you work with him. Look for someone with good contacts, with access to the right people and channels of distribution. While agent commissions vary, expect to pay around 5 to 8 percent.

The Importance of Personal Relationships. Developing strong personal relationships is the key to doing business with Arabs. The Arabic word for a network of contacts and personal relationships is *wasta*, a word similar in meaning to the Chinese *guanxi*. The similarity makes sense when we recall that geographers label 'the Middle East' more accurately as West Asia. And all over Asia, whether West or East, you need personal contacts to make things happen in business.

Verbal Language

Evasiveness, Indirectness. Arabs generally prefer not to say 'no' bluntly, believing it is more courteous to say unpleasant things in an indirect way. Furthermore, 'yes' may not actually mean yes unless said forcefully or repeated several times. Arab verbal communication is similar to that of East and Southeast Asians when it comes to indirectness, but closer to that of Latin Europeans in terms of expressiveness.

Emotional Expressiveness. Whether in Arabic or English, most Arabs speak in an emotionally expressive manner. This can be confusing for northern Europeans, especially Scandinavians, who typically communicate in a more reserved way. Arabs like to speak and write in a flowery, elaborate, repetitious mode, with frequent use of exaggeration, wild promises and dire threats. For most Arabs, anything really worth saying seems to be worth saying several times.

Nonverbal Language

Space Behavior. Like most Middle Easterners, Arabs of the same sex like to stand closer to each other than some foreigners are accustomed to. Try not to move away, since this would signal coldness to your local counterpart. On the other hand, men and women in the region maintain a respectfully wide interpersonal distance.

Touch Behavior. Coming from an expressive culture, Arabs engage in frequent touching among friends, but until they know someone well they usually confine physical touching to a gentle handshake. Back-slapping and elbow-grabbing are definitely out of place. However, the amount of physical contact between business acquaintances varies within the Arab world. Observe those around you and take your cue from your local counterparts.

Gaze Behavior. During a business or social discussion Arab men expect you to look them in the eye. If you frequently glance away it indicates lack of interest or worse, lack of respect. On the other hand, a woman visitor should avoid making direct eye contact on the street with a male, who would be likely to interpret strong eye contact as a sexual invitation.

Gestures. Visitors should avoid the thumbs-up sign, which is an obscene gesture in Arab countries.

Body Language Taboos. As in other Muslim cultures, the left hand is considered unclean. Always use your right hand only when eating or when passing something to an Arab. Offer your business card or a gift with your right hand, for example. And when seated, avoid showing the soles of your shoes or sandals: they are also unclean.

Younger, highly-educated Arabs sometimes scoff at such customs as old-fashioned. But you can be sure that most of these young people still follow these 'outmoded' traditions when with their parents and older relatives. Culture changes, but slowly.

Orientation to Time

Punctuality. Arabs tend to look at time differently than people from monochronic cultures. People and relationships are far more important than calendars and clocks. So your counterpart may keep you waiting while he deals with unscheduled visitors and family emergencies. He may be late for any number of pressing reasons.

Meeting Interruptions. Once your meeting starts you may find it frequently interrupted by phone calls, papers to sign, and drop-in visits by old friends and relatives.

Deadlines. It is unwise to push hard for something to be done by a specific date. You will do better to build some flexibility into your schedule so that a delay of a few days or weeks will not cause you a serious problem. Patience is an important virtue in the Gulf.

Hierarchy, Status and Honor

Ascribed Status. An Arab's status is determined primarily by his or her social class, family background, and age.

Gender and Business. Saudis and many other Arabs are not used to seeing women in business. For this reason they may have difficulty relating to female executives. Two tips for women wishing to do business in the Arab world:

1. Be introduced by an older, high-ranking male. The status of his age and gender can rub off on you.
2. Gradually establish your professional or technical credentials, without appearing cocky or boastful. Your expertise will confer status.

Honor and the Family. An Arab's honor, dignity and reputation are precious to him and must be protected at all cost. Loyalty to the family is paramount. The family comes before the individual.

Business Protocol and Etiquette

Scheduling. Avoid the month of Ramadan, which is a movable feast falling on different dates each year according to the Western calendar. Because meetings often start late and run long, it is advisable to schedule only one meeting per day in Saudi Arabia and most other Gulf countries.

Dress Code. Men wear a jacket and tie for business meetings. Good quality accessories such as your watch, pens and briefcase enhance status. Women wear loose-fitting, modest clothing with a high neckline and sleeves to the elbows or longer. Skirts should be preferably of ankle length; avoid pants and pantsuits. Keep a scarf at hand in case of need for covering the head.

Meeting and Greeting. Expect a gentle handshake with intense eye contact. You will be offered tea or coffee. This is an important feature of Arab hospitality; it is impolite not to accept.

Forms of Address. Saudi men commonly have three names: a given name, a middle name (often a patronymic) and a family name. Address your Arab counterpart by his title or honorific plus the first of his three names. Thus Dr. Hassan bin Abdul-Aziz Khalid would be addressed as Dr. Hassan. Expect to be addressed in the same way, so Robert White would be "Mr. Robert."

Titles are important and widely used, more so in Arabic than in English. "Sheikh" (pronounced "shake") is a title of respect for a wealthy, influential or elderly man. Address government ministers as "Your Excellency." Find out whatever titles a person may have and use them. Ask your local contact to write out the names of the people you will be meeting and help you with the pronunciation.

Exchanging Business Cards: Present your business card with your right (clean) hand only. Receive your counterpart's card in the same way.

Meeting Etiquette. Some Arab businessmen serve coffee as a non-verbal signal that the meeting is about to end, sometimes lighting incense at this point as well.

Gift Giving: Gifts are welcome but not expected. Choose something for which your own country is well-known, but avoid giving alcohol or other items forbidden to Muslims. Be careful about admiring any of your counterpart's possessions. He might present you with the object of your admiration and feel insulted if you decline.

Business Entertaining: Your Arab hosts will probably do all the entertaining while you are in their country. If invited to dinner at a businessman's home you need not bring a gift. Expect to eat a great deal as a way of showing your appreciation. Your host will press you to eat more you than really want to. Eat as much as you can. When you have reached your limit, you may have to decline further helpings three times, emphatically, in order to make the point.

Hosting Arab Guests. Be aware of the foods (all pork products and sometimes shellfish) and drinks which are prohibited to Muslims, but do not be totally surprised if an occasional Arab visitor enjoys a drink of alcohol when abroad. Keep pushing your guests to eat and drink. Traditional Arabs wait until they are asked the third time before accepting food; with Western-educated Arabs this procedure may not be necessary,

Exchanging Favors. The exchange of favors is a cornerstone of any relationship with Arabs. If you are asked for a favor, do it if you can. If you think you may not be able or willing to do it, reply that you will do your best. Your Arab friend will understand if circumstances later make it impossible to fulfill his request, and will much appreciate the fact that you agreed to try to help.

Negotiating Behavior

Bargaining Range. Saudi negotiators tend to be enthusiastic bargainers and may expect their counterparts to grant major concessions on price and terms during the course of the negotiation. Some Arabs measure their success at the bargaining table by how far they are able to move you away from your opening offer. They think of negotiating as a challenging contest, a competitive sport. Hence it is wise to build plenty of margin into your initial offer so as to leave room for maneuver during the lengthy negotiating process.

Making Concessions. Be prepared for some serious bazaar haggling. Take care to make each concession with great reluctance and only on a strict "if ... then," conditional basis. Always demand something equivalent in return for each concession in price, terms or other issues.

Decision Making. Negotiating in the Arab world tends to proceed at a leisurely pace. It would be a tactical error to press hard for a quick decision. Go with the flow. Decisions take time, so adjust your expectations accordingly.

Contracts. Get everything in writing to avoid future misunderstandings.

Maintaining the Relationship. It is very important to stay in contact with your Arab customers and partners between visits via phone, email or fax.

Throughout the Arab world, **wasta** *is the key to business success.*

The Egyptian Negotiator

With well over 60 million inhabitants, Egypt is easily the Arab world's most populous nation. Some 90 percent of the people are Sunni Muslims; the main religious minority is Coptic Christian. The official language is Arabic, and the Cairo dialect is in fact the most widely-understood spoken version of the language throughout the Arab world. Most Egyptians involved in international business speak English or French, or both.

Religion. For most Westerners these days religion is just a part of life, a small part for some, larger for others. But for the average Egyptian, whether Muslim or Copt, religion is truly a way of life. Religious beliefs in this society have a powerful influence on people's thoughts and actions.

For example, "Insha'allah" – literally "If God wills" – is used to indicate that it is God, not man, who really decides what is going to happen in the future. And "bukra, Insha'allah" means "tomorrow, God willing." Europeans and Americans often misinterpret this usage as a way of avoiding responsibility for getting things done on time, whereas millions of Egyptians honestly believe that "Man proposes, but God disposes."

Business visitors to this Muslim culture will greatly increase their chances for success if they invest time learning about Islam and the history of Egypt.

Verbal Communication

Some foreign visitors are confused by the Egyptian tendency to engage in conversational overlap, that is, starting to talk before another speaker has finished. If you find yourself being interrupted, just remember that no offense is intended. Conversational overlap is normal in this expressive culture.

Emotional Expressiveness. Egyptians speak and write in a long-winded, flowery, repetitious manner with frequent use of exaggeration, wild promises and dire threats. Anything worth saying seems to be worth saying more than once. They are proud of their verbal proficiency.

Indirectness. Egyptians often avoid saying 'no' in a straightforward, blunt manner, believing it is more courteous to say unpleasant things in an indirect, roundabout way. And 'yes' may not actually mean yes unless said forcefully or repeated several times. Verbal communication is similar to that of southern Europeans in terms of expressiveness, but closer to that of East and Southeast Asians in terms of indirectness.

Key Words and Phrases. Another revealing expression often heard is "Ma'alish," translated as "It doesn't matter," or "Never mind," or "No problem." This expression irritates some business visitors, who may feel that whatever it is really does matter, or really is a problem!

Verbal Taboos. Visitors should carefully avoid profanity, off-color jokes and references to sex, religion, politics or current events in the Middle East. Furthermore, it is better not to mention death, illness or natural calamities. In this culture words have quasi-magical power – many local people believe that speaking of dying, disease or disasters brings bad luck.

Nonverbal Communication

Interpersonal Distance. The body language of Egyptians is as expressive as their verbal language. In hotel lobbies in Alexandria and Cairo I have seen visiting Western businessmen step back involuntarily when their local counterparts walk up to greet them. While this is an understandable reaction, many Egyptians misinterpret such a reaction as a signal that you dislike or distrust them.

Egyptian men are most comfortable with a small "space bubble" of about half an arm's length in a business situation, but Egyptian males and females actually stand further apart than is the custom in most of Europe, North America and East Asia. Visitors from these parts of the world need to remember that in Egypt, same-sex spacing is closer while opposite-sex distance is wider.

Touch Behavior. Egyptians engage in frequent touching among friends, but until they know someone well they confine physical touching to the handshake. American back-slapping and elbow-grabbing are definitely out of place.

Eye Contact. During a business or social discussion Egyptian men expect you to look them in the eye while you are conversing with them. If you frequently glance away it indicates lack of interest in the discussion, or worse, lack of respect for them. On the other hand, a woman visitor should avoid making direct eye contact on the street with an Egyptian male, who would be likely to interpret such gaze behavior as a sexual invitation.

Gestures. Visitors familiar with Greek and Italian hand gestures might be confused when they see an Egyptian holding out his right hand with the tips of the fingers touching the thumb. In Italy this is a way of asking "What do you mean?" In Greece it signifies "That's perfect!" But in Egypt it means "Be patient," which in this culture is excellent advice indeed!

Left Hand Taboo. As in other Islamic societies, the left hand is considered unclean. Always use your only right hand when eating or when passing something to an Egyptian. Offer your business card with your right hand, for example. And when seated, avoid showing the soles of your shoes or sandals; they are also unclean.

Younger, highly-educated Egyptians sometimes scoff at this and other taboos as old-fashioned customs. But most of these young people still follow these 'outmoded' traditions when with their parents and older relatives.

Formality, Hierarchies and Respect. It is important in Egypt to address counterparts with their professional and academic titles, and to show respect to older and higher-ranking people.

Time and Scheduling. Here in this relaxed-time culture visitors will find a non-level playing field. Egyptian businessmen and government officials are often late for meetings, whereas visitors are expected to be on time. Remember, patience is a virtue. If you are kept waiting in Cairo it may be because your counterpart was held up in traffic. Cairo seems to be in permanent gridlock, so locals hold meetings in their cars these days.

On the other hand, your local counterpart's previous meeting may have run on longer than expected. Egyptians find it impolite to end a meeting abruptly just because they have another one scheduled. Or perhaps the person you are supposed to meet was called upon to help a friend or relative out of a jam. In this culture people are more important than clocks, schedules and agendas. Whatever the reason for being kept waiting, it's important to avoid displaying open irritation or impatience.

For example, I have seen monochronic Western visitors in the reception area glance repeatedly at their watches, drum their fingers on the table, and make snide comments to their associates. If you are in Egypt as a buyer, you may be forgiven for such rude behavior. But if your mission is to sell something, to promote a project, or to negotiate a joint-venture agreement, the appropriate response to tardiness is to grin and bear it. In this culture it is offensive to become visibly upset at having to wait for someone – especially if that someone is a customer.

Interrupted Meetings. Once the meeting begins you may notice another key difference in meeting behavior. It is rare to have a private tete-a-tete in this market. The more senior the person you are trying to talk to, the more distractions you are likely to encounter. Do not expect your counterpart to hold incoming phone calls. In Egypt it is rude to turn away drop-in visitors or to refuse to take a phone call.

It took me several visits to understand the rules of these 'open meetings.' Now I just sit back and relax each time my counterpart picks up the phone or waves an interloper into the room when I'm in mid-sentence. I try to remember that another time it may be *my* urgent phone call which will get through even though the busy official has an office full of visitors. I've also learned to schedule just one or two meetings a day in Cairo or Alexandria so I don't fall behind schedule.

Business Protocol

On a positive note, most Egyptians are warm, friendly and hospitable. Return their friendliness by always accepting their offer of tea, coffee or cold drink. Take at least a sip even if you are not thirsty. The drink is really a symbol of Egyptian hospitality, to refuse a cup is to spurn that hospitality.

Likewise, when your local business contacts come to your office or hotel meeting room, be sure to offer them something to drink. Failure to do so indicates coldness or lack of interest.

Dress Code. The appropriate business dress for men is a suit and tie during the winter, shirt and neat pants in the summer. A tie and jacket is in order for meetings with senior government and public sector officials. Women visitors should wear a simple, elegant Western suit or dress and carry a scarf to cover their hair when called for, such as on a visit to a mosque.

For casual wear neither sex should wear shorts. Women should take care not to appear in revealing apparel such as halter tops, sleeveless blouses and short skirts.

Small Talk. As is the case with most other Mediterranean cultures, it is vital to get to know your counterpart before starting to discuss business. Chatting about nonbusiness matters while sipping coffee or tea is a good way to break the ice. Good topics of conversation are Egyptian history, travel, food and monuments.

On the other hand, stay away from Middle Eastern politics. In fact, avoid politics in general unless your local counterpart raises the issue. While it is permissible to talk about families, avoid asking about your male counterpart's wife or daughters.

Names and Titles. Address most people with the appropriate honorific or title, e.g. Mr., Mrs., Madame, Doctor, Professor – followed by the first name. So it would be "Madam Leila" or "Dr. Hisham" until you are asked to drop the formality. People with Western first names are likely to be Christians, those with Islamic names such as Mohamed or Mahmud are Muslims. Address high government officials and senior diplomats as "Your Excellency."

Meeting and Greeting. When introduced, men shake hands with both men and women and women shake hands with other women. But avoid a bone-crushing grip: Egyptians are accustomed to a gentle handshake.

Entertaining. Entertaining and being entertained is an essential part of building a close relationship with your counterpart. If invited to dinner at an Egyptian's home, expect to eat a great deal as a way of showing your appreciation. Your host will probably press you to eat more you than really want to. Eat as much as you can. When you have reached your limit, you may have to decline a further helping three times, emphatically, in order to make the point.

Similarly, when hosting Egyptians you should keep urging them to eat and drink. Remember the Rule of Three. People are expected to refuse something that is offered two times to be polite; only the third refusal is to be taken seriously. Remember also that over 90% of Egyptians are Muslims, so avoid offering alcoholic beverages and pork products.

Even if your Egyptian counterpart enjoyed a glass of wine or whisky on a visit to your country, back in Egypt he may want to present himself as a teetotaler.

It is appropriate to show appreciation for the fine food when dining in someone's home, but avoid overdoing the compliments. To Egyptians, the food is less important than the opportunity to relax and interact with friends. Furthermore, in middle- and upper-class homes most of the food is prepared by servants. So thank your hostess enthusiastically for a lovely evening, of which the food was only a part.

Gift Giving. Gifts are welcome but not expected. Choose something for which your country is well-known, but avoid giving alcohol or other items forbidden to Muslims. Good ideas are quality 'coffee table' books or illustrated calendars showing scenes from your home country or region. If invited to someone's home for a meal, bring a cake or high quality chocolates. Flowers are for weddings and to cheer up sick people. Always present the gift with both hands or with the right hand only, never with the left (unclean) hand.

Negotiating Style. Egyptian negotiators tend to be enthusiastic bargainers, often expecting their counterparts to grant major concessions on price and terms during the course of the negotiation. Some local businessmen measure their success at the bargaining table by how far they are able to move you away from your opening offer.

They often seem to think of negotiating as a challenging contest, a competitive sport. Hence it is wise to build some margin into your initial offer so as to leave room for maneuver during the lengthy bargaining process.

Be prepared for some bazaar haggling. Take care to make each concession with great reluctance and only on a conditional basis, demanding something equivalent in return for each concession.

Negotiating in Egypt tends to proceed at a leisurely pace. It would be a tactical error to press hard for a quick decision.

The Turkish Negotiator

With one foot in Europe and the other in the Middle East, the Republic of Turkey forms a geographic and cultural bridge between West and East. For people from outside the region, learning to do business with the Turks is useful preparation for negotiating throughout the eastern Mediterranean and the Arab world.

With a population of over 60 million, Turkey is an attractive market itself in addition to being a gateway to the markets of the Middle East and Central Asia. The business centers are Istanbul and (to a lesser extent) Izmir; the political capital is Ankara.

Religion. Although 90 percent of the population are Sunni Muslims, there is no official religion. Turkey is unique in the Muslim world in that the Republic has remained secular since it was founded under Kemal Ataturk in 1923. A fundamentalist Islamic minority exists, but the current government intends to keep it on the sidelines in order to promote Turkey's eventual entrance into the European Union.

Making Contact. Avoid June, July and August when many Turks will be away on vacation, and check for local holidays. In Turkey both religious and non-religious holidays are celebrated.

A deep strain of economic nationalism runs through officialdom. Courts are slow and tend to side with local companies against outsiders. Mid-level bureaucrats find ways to obstruct foreign investment even though top government officials court international investors. Most successful foreign companies in this market work with local partners who are able to overcome the tough legal and bureaucratic barriers to investment and doing business in Turkey.

One way to find the right partner is to attend trade fairs in Istanbul or elsewhere. Another approach is to join an official trade delegation organized by your government, chamber of commerce or industry association.

Business Communication

Language of Business. The official language is Turkish, which is a non-Indo-European language but written in the Latin alphabet.

These days many younger Turks involved in international business speak English, German or French. However, for the first meeting it is a good idea to ask whether you should arrange for an interpreter. Your local contact may bring someone to translate, but this person may not be a competent linguist. Your country's embassy in Istanbul or your hotel should be able to recommend a reputable individual or translation bureau.

Verbal Language. This is a relationship-oriented culture. When negotiating with older Turkish counterparts, expect a good deal of small talk before getting down to business. You can also expect a certain amount of polite indirectness.

Nonverbal Communication

Interpersonal Space. As in most Mediterranean cultures, Turks tend to stand and sit closer to other people than northern Europeans, North Americans and East Asians are accustomed to.

Eye Contact. Maintain good eye contact during business meetings. A steady gaze signals interest and sincerity whereas to many Turks, weak eye contact indicates dishonesty.

Gestures. Turks may signal 'yes' with a slight downward tilt of the head, 'no' by raising the eyebrows and tilting the head upwards while making a "tsk! tsk!" sound with the tongue against the front teeth. Some people finger their 'worry beads' as a nervous habit.

To attract a person's attention Turks wave their hand up and down with the palm facing out. To signal "come here" or "follow me" they make a scooping morion with the fingers curled downward.

Body Language Taboos. When seated with legs crossed it is rude to direct the sole of your shoe towards someone. It is therefore better to keep both feet on the floor during meetings. When meeting with older Turks, avoid touching people or passing objects with your left (unclean) hand. When conversing with someone face to face it is impolite to stand with hands on hips or with your arms crossed. Avoid pointing at people with the index finger.

It is rude to blow one's nose during meal times; in case of need, leave the room or turn away from the table and blow as silently as possible. Also, placing the thumb between the first two fingers in Turkey is an obscene gesture, similar in meaning to showing the middle finger in many other cultures around the world.

Hierarchies, Status and Gender

Turks are strongly family-oriented. Older people are treated with great respect. Corporate cultures are strictly hierarchical. In family businesses the senior male usually makes the final decision, consulting other family members as needed.

Foreign business women rarely encounter difficulties doing business in Turkey, where educated women hold responsible positions in some companies. Outside of business situations women do not converse with a man until formally introduced.

Time and Scheduling

Punctuality. Unusually for a Middle Eastern business culture, Turks are relatively punctual for meetings. They expect visitors to be on time as well. Even more unusually, dinner parties also start on time, though it is acceptable to be about 15 minutes late for a large cocktail party.

Business Protocol and Etiquette

Dress Code. Men should wear a conservative suit or sport coat with tie, although in hot weather a long-sleeved white shirt and tie without jacket is acceptable. Female visitors should wear a suit or modest dress with heels and carry a scarf to cover their hair when called for, such as on a visit to a mosque. For casual wear neither sex should wear shorts.

Women should take care not to appear in revealing apparel such as halter tops, sleeveless blouses or short skirts. Remove your shoes before entering a mosque as well as many Turkish homes.

Meeting and Greeting. Shake hands using a firm but not crushing grip with everyone at every meeting, whether business or social. Start with the older people present. Expect no other physical touching: this is a low-contact culture.

Forms of Address. At the initial meeting, refer to doctors, lawyers and professors by their title alone, e.g. "Doktor" or "Avukat." For those without professional titles, address them by their first name followed by the honorific "bey" for males – e.g. "Ahmet Bey" – and "hanim" for women. In written communication, address male counterparts with "Bay" plus the family name, women with "Bayan" plus the family name.

Small Talk. It is important to get to know your counterpart before starting to discuss business. Chatting about non-business matters while sipping coffee or tea is a good way to break the ice. Turks don't talk much about the weather. Good topics of conversation are Turkish history, food, monuments, travel, sports and family.

But stay away from local politics as well as such topics as the Kurdish issue, Cyprus, the European Union and Bosnia. Avoid politics in general unless your local counterpart raises the issue.

Business Entertainment. Turks are friendly, hospitable people. Return their friendliness by always accepting their offer of tea or coffee. Take at least a sip even if you are not thirsty. The drink is really a symbol of hospitality; to refuse a cup is to spurn that hospitality. Likewise, if your local counterparts come to your office or hotel, be sure to offer them something to drink.

Your local counterparts will probably insist on hosting you at all meals while in Turkey. When you invite your Turkish partners for lunch or dinner, take the waiter aside in advance to arrange payment. Otherwise your guests are likely to fight you for the check.

Gifts. Good business gifts are desk accessories, pens or good quality logo items. For hostess gifts, candy, cakes or flowers are welcome. Your hostess will probably not open the gift when you present it. Bring wine or spirits only if you know your hosts drink.

Negotiating Behavior

Turkish business people tend to be enthusiastic bargainers, expecting the other side to grant important concessions during the negotiating session. Some seem to measure their success at the bargaining table by how far they are able to move you away from your opening offer. Hence it may be wise to anticipate this behavior by building some margin into your initial offer so as to leave room for maneuver during the bargaining process.

Make any concession with reluctance and only on a conditional basis, requiring something equivalent in return for each concession in price, terms or other issues.

As in other parts of the Middle East, expect negotiations to take time. Trying to accelerate the process by prodding or pushing is likely to be counterproductive. In general, negotiating with the government or public sector requires more patience than with private sector companies. Decisions are usually made at the top of the organization.

Detailed contracts are important but may be difficult to enforce, since Turkish courts commonly side with the local party.

The Greek Negotiator

There are two keys to doing successful business in Greece. The first is having the right contacts, the second is developing close relationships with potential business partners. But how are you supposed to get started if you don't have the right contacts to begin with?

Getting Started. One proven method of making initial contact is to attend trade shows where you can meet potential customers, distributors, agents or partners. Although Greeks do not like doing business with strangers, trade fairs provide an acceptable way to get in touch with them. Another effective option, when available, is to join an official trade mission organized by your government, chamber of commerce or private organizations.

If neither an exhibition nor a trade mission fits your schedule, the third option is to arrange for an intermediary to introduce you to Greek prospects. For instance, a mutual friend, business associate, bank, chamber of commerce or trade association can make a call on your behalf or write you a letter of introduction. And remember that golf buddy who works for a company with an office in Athens? Why not ask him to arrange an introduction.

Business people lacking existing contacts really need to employ one of these contact strategies, because cold calls do not work well in Greece.

Building Relationships. Having made initial contact, the next step is to build a personal relationship, a process which takes time and patience. Fortunately you can usually expect your Greek counterpart to either speak English or provide a fluent English speaker for the meeting.

However, savvy visitors do not expect to talk a lot of business at the first meeting. This is the time to relax, sip coffee and get to know each other a little. Ask questions about Greek food, wine, sightseeing attractions and the like, and respond with similar information about your own country. How will you know when to start talking business?

That's easy. Your counterparts will signal their readiness by asking detailed questions about your company and your product or service.

Sharing a meal is a great way to learn about each other, to develop a relationship, and Greeks are generous hosts. Forget about power breakfasts, though, think lunch instead. In Athens most business people get to the office early, say between 7:00 and 7:30, and except for a mid-morning break work straight through until around 3:00 or 3:30. An invitation to lunch means you are making good progress in getting to know your local counterpart.

Wining and Dining. Dinner time is usually around 9:00 pm or later. Greeks normally entertain business visitors in restaurants, so if you are honored with an invitation to dinner at home, be sure to accept. In such cases suitable hostess gifts are chocolates, pastries or fine cognac. A potted plant also makes an excellent gift, but remember that it should be wrapped when you present it to your hostess.

During the meal expect your host to insist that you sample everything and take second helpings. Be sure to keep both wrists on the table -- Greeks would wonder what you're doing with that hand in your lap. To signal that you have really had enough to eat, place your napkin on the table. It is polite to stay until at least 11:00 pm.

When it is your turn to host a lunch or dinner it is a good idea to ask your Greek partners to select the restaurant. And be sure to urge them repeatedly to eat and drink. Whereas Europeans and North Americans may feel uncomfortable with such pushing, in the Near East this comes across as the ultimate in good manners.

Wining and dining is an important feature of building a close relationship in Mediterranean cultures. Your counterpart wants to get to know you personally as well as from a business point of view, which is why face-to-face contact is so important. In the more task-focused markets of northern Europe you can conduct a lot of business by fax, email and telephone. But in Greece, a strongly relationship-focused culture, you need to visit your customers and business partners more frequently.

Nonverbal Communication

Interpersonal Space. A subtle problem in nonverbal communication is caused by the north/south difference in European space behavior. Northern Europeans move around with a larger 'space bubble' than southern Europeans. For example, most Germans and Scandinavians feel comfortable at an arm's length distance from other people in a business or social setting.

Greeks display friendliness by standing or sitting much closer. If you unconsciously step back, Greeks may read retreat as a sign of unfriendliness, while the unprepared visitor tends to see them as pushy and aggressive.

Eye Contact. Another source of misunderstanding is gaze behavior. When negotiating with Greeks, maintain strong eye contact whenever you are speaking or being spoken to. Letting your gaze wander during a discussion is rude, indicating lack of interest on your part.

Gestures and Facial Expressions. Greeks tend to speak loudly and communicate with lots of facial expression and gestures. Unfortunately, business visitors sometimes misunderstand the local body language. For example, to signify 'no' many Greeks tip their head back without saying a word, a movement which foreigners may misinterpret as a nod of the head meaning 'yes'. Lifting one's eyebrows is another nonverbal way of saying no. Should you hear a word which sounds like 'nay', be aware that it could be the Greek word for yes!

Hellenes also sometimes misinterpret foreigners' body language. As an example, the familiar "thumbs up" sign is an obscene sexual gesture in northern Greece. And a friendly wave with palm showing and fingers extended is a serious nonverbal insult to a Greek.

Business Protocol

Dress Code. Doing business in Greece calls for a certain level of formality. Men should wear a suit and tie, women a dress or suit, even if your local counterpart is dressed more casually. During the hot summer months men will be invited to doff jackets and loosen ties and women can wear lighter-weight business attire.

Meeting and Greeting. As in the rest of Europe, address Greeks by their family name until they suggest moving to a first-name basis. However, in contrast with many other European cultures you can normally dispense with formal academic and professional titles.

Male visitors being introduced to a Greek male should give a very firm handshake and look the other party in the eye. Women tend to use a lighter handshake. Shake hands whenever you meet and again when you take leave.

Punctuality. While locals often turn up half an hour or so late, visitors are expected to be on time. Nor should you be offended if your meeting is frequently interrupted with phone calls and casual drop-ins. Greeks are clever enough to conduct several meetings simultaneously and are quick to pick up the thread of your conversation after each interruption.

Emotionally Expressive Communication Style. Speaking of interruptions, like other Mediterraneans most Greeks are masters of what academics call conversational overlap. By the time you are halfway through your statement, a Greek has already figured out what you are going to say next. So he exuberantly breaks in to agree, disagree or change the subject.

While many North Americans and northern Europeans find this behavior rude, it is simply an example of the outgoing, expressive Hellenic communication style. I have attended important negotiation sessions in Athens and Thessaloniki which quickly deteriorated into chaotic shouting matches, yet just as quickly got back on track with both sides calmly taking turns in the conversation. Perhaps eight years of living and doing business in the Mediterranean region accustomed me to this expressive conversational style.

Women in Business. Some older Greek executives have trouble relating to female business visitors. Here are three practical tips to help women overcome the gender barrier:

1. Get introduced by an older, high-ranking male.
2. Be an expert in your line of business. Expertise gives you status, even in male-dominated business cultures.
3. Learn the nuances of how to communicate respect. For example, greet the oldest person in a group first, pay him special attention throughout the meeting, and when hosting a meal keep urging him to eat.

Negotiating Tips

Budget plenty of time and patience. The negotiating process may take longer than you expect, and decision-making also takes time. Avoid showing irritation or impatience.

Greeks enjoy vigorous bargaining, sometimes to the point of bazaar haggling. They are usually reluctant to accept an initial quotation as final. Therefore it is wise to build some bargaining room into your opening offer so as to leave room for concessions.

Any concession you make should be granted with a show of great reluctance, even pain. And be sure to make any concession conditional. That is, demand a quid pro quo each time.

Try to keep smiling, even in the face of occasional confrontational tactics.

The Brazilian Negotiator

Language of Business. The national language is Portuguese. Only a minority of Brazilian business people speak fluent English. Visitors who speak Spanish should know that using that language implies to some Brazilians that Spanish is a more important language than Portuguese. Inquire about the possible need for an interpreter before your visit.

Initial Contact. In Brazil local contacts are essential. Potential buyers do not react well to a direct, 'cold' approach. Attend a trade show or join a trade mission to meet interested parties. You can also arrange for a chamber of commerce, trade association, government agency, bank or business associate to introduce you to Brazilian companies.

Your first written correspondence should be in Portuguese, stating that if possible you would prefer to correspond in English from then on. Request an appointment about two weeks in advance. Expect to meet in a office rather than in a restaurant or bar. Schedule only two meetings per day, one between 10:00 and 11:30 am and the second starting at 3 pm.

Don't expect to get down to business quickly. Brazilians need time to get to know you.

Relationships. Expect to invest a considerable amount of time developing good rapport and a pleasant, relaxed relationship before discussing business. Establishing an atmosphere of trust is a precondition to a successful business relationship. Good topics for small talk are football (soccer), Brazilian history, literature and places to visit as well as information about your home town and region. You will probably need two or three visits to the country before you can expect to do serious business. Like other Latins, Brazilians value deep, long-lasting relationships.

Orientation to Time. In the southern part of Brazil business people increasingly value firm schedules and punctuality, particularly in Sao Paulo, the commercial capital of the country, but the clock ticks at a different speed for the fun-loving Cariocas of Rio. There you might find yourself waiting an hour or more for your local counterpart. However, business visitors are expected to be punctual.

Hierarchy, Status and Respect. In Brazil one's status depends more on social class, education and family background than on personal achievement. Business visitors can enhance their status by displaying a lively interest in intellectual pursuits, dressing elegantly, and staying in top hotels.

Expressive Communication Style. A warm and friendly people, Brazilians tend to be talkative, nonverbally expressive and open about showing emotion in public. Don't be offended if you are sometimes interrupted in mid-sentence: conversational overlap is not rude in Brazil. Do however avoid direct confrontation during negotiations.

Nonverbal Behavior. Men and women shake hands warmly when introduced and again when departing. Male visitors should expect to shake hands with another male for a considerable length of time. Take care not to withdraw your hand prematurely.

Brazil is a high-contact culture. After they get to know each other, two men will shake hands and touch each other on the elbow or forearm, perhaps slap each other on the back or shoulder. Male friends will exchange the *abraço* or embrace while women friends brush cheeks with a kissing motion of the lips.

In another sign of friendliness Brazilians stand very close to each other when talking and maintain strong eye contact with the person they are conversing with. Both sexes use frequent gestures. Avoid using the 'A-OK' sign, a very rude gesture in Brazil. On the other hand the 'fig' sign, considered vulgar in some other Latin American countries, signifies good luck. This gesture involves clenching the fist with the thumb pointing upwards between the index and middle fingers.

Business Customs and Protocol. Although Brazilians interact fairly informally, business visitors do need to take note of certain customs.

Dress Code. Male executives tend to wear fashionable three-piece suits. Office workers wear the two-piece version. Male visitors should note that proper business attire always includes long-sleeved shirts, even in hot weather. Brazilian men make fun of male visitors wearing short-sleeved dress shirts. Women in business wear elegant suits or dresses as well as blouses and skirts. Blouses and jackets may have short sleeves. Both sexes should avoid wearing green and yellow, the colors of the Brazilian flag.

Meeting and Greeting. Address your male counterpart as *Senhor* plus the family name. For women it is *Senhora* and her family name. Medical doctors, lawyers and all university graduates are addressed as *Doutor* (Doctor). Expect to move to a first-name basis fairly soon, but wait until the Brazilian party starts using your given name.

Conversational Overlap. Expect frequent interruptions during business meetings, especially in government offices. This is not regarded as rude or improper behavior.

Wining and Dining. Women drink wine, spirits and liqueurs; beer is considered a man's drink. Brazilians normally eat a light breakfast between 7:00 and 9:00 am and a substantial lunch between noon and 2:00 pm. Dinner usually starts after 7:00 pm but dinner parties don't normally get underway until after 10:00 pm.

Table Manners. Avoid using the side of your fork to cut anything and do not pick up food of any kind with your hands. Although they are a very expressive people, Brazilians do not like a lot of conversation during meals. Wait until coffee is served before talking business.

Gift Giving. Good gifts to bring from abroad for men are music tapes and small electronic gadgets such as quality calculators. For women, perfume. If invited to dinner at home bring chocolates, champagne or a container of fresh strawberries. Avoid purple flowers, which are associated with funerals.

Women in Business. Female business visitors who dress and act professionally encounter no great barriers to getting things done in Brazil. Unwanted male attention should be politely but firmly ignored.

Exchanging Favors. Brazilians frequently ask friends and business acquaintances for small and large favors and expect these requests to be granted. Be careful of asking favors of Brazilians, however. They might very well agree to do what you ask even if they would much rather not, since refusing you would be rude.

Negotiating Style. Brazilians are widely known as tough bargainers, not afraid to turn down offers rather bluntly. Such frankness is however not intended to be rude or confrontational. They simply want you to know where they stand. Budget enough time for a lengthy negotiating process and include a substantial margin in your opening offer so as to leave room for concessions. Expect very few silences during these bargaining sessions: Brazilians seem to talk constantly.

Wise negotiators include plenty of time for socializing during these drawn-out discussions. If you wish to entertain a high-level executive, ask his secretary to recommend a restaurant. It is important to host your counterpart only at elegant, prestigious establishments. Similarly, business visitors should only stay in top hotels while in Brazil.

The Mexican Negotiator

Language of Business. Fluency in Spanish is a great asset to doing business, though today more Mexican businessmen speak English. This is especially the case in Monterrey, along the northern border, and to a lesser extent in Mexico City and Guadalajara. It would be wise to look into the possible need for an interpreter before your visit. Remember to have your company and product literature professionally translated into Spanish before arriving in Mexico.

Making Contact. A local connection is very important. Avoid a direct, 'cold' approach to a prospective business partner. Instead plan to attend a trade show or join a trade mission to meet interested parties, or arrange for a chamber of commerce, trade association, government agency or bank to introduce you to Mexican firms.

Start at the top: approach the most senior person in the company. Your first letter or fax should be in Spanish, but specify that if possible you would prefer to correspond in English from then on. Request an appointment about two weeks in advance; let the Mexican party decide the time and place to meet.

Build a Relationship before Talking Business. Budget enough time to get to know your counterpart before starting to talk business. Good topics for small talk are Mexican art and literature as well as your home country You will need lots of "face time." Two or three meetings may be needed to establish trust, after which serious business discussions can begin.

Mexicans value deep, long-lasting relationships. Personal contacts and relationships are major factors in business success. You need *palanca* – pull, 'clout', a connection – to get things done quickly. It's who you know that counts.

Indirect Verbal Language. They often communicate in an indirect way. For example, during a negotiation they may avoid a direct answer to a question. You may need to rephrase the question or ask it in a different way.

Formality, Hierarchy and Status. Mexicans value formality more than most North Americans and Scandinavians. Until you get to know your local counterpart use his title and family name, e.g. *Doctor* Morales, *Director* Reyes, *Profesor* Santana. Later you can switch to just the title without the family name. For example, use *Licenciado* (*Licenciada* for a woman) to refer to someone with a university degree. Do not use first names until the Mexcian party suggests it. And remember that the person's 'middle' name is part of his or her family name.

Orientation to Time. Although things are changing in the northern part of the country, do not expect absolute punctuality in Mexico. Local business people may be half an hour to an hour late without causing offense. Visitors however should always be punctual. Avoid scheduling multiple meetings in any one day. One meeting at 10:00 am and another in the late afternoon is about right. If someone gives you a meeting time and adds *a la gringa,* expect them to be roughly on time. On the other hand, *a la mexicana* would indicate a more relaxed approach to scheduling.

Emotionally Expressive. Mexicans communicate expressively, both verbally and nonverbally. For example, during a lively discussion they may start talking before you have quite finished. This is not considered rude behavior.

Nonverbal Behavior

Interpersonal Distance. Like other Latins, Mexicans tend to stand and sit closer to others than northern Europeans and North Americans are accustomed to.

Touch Behavior. Expect very frequent hand and arm gestures.

Eye Contact. Maintain steady eye contact with the person you are conversing with. In Mexico, "the eyes are the windows of the soul." A good steady gaze suggests honesty, an averted gaze may indicate the opposite.

Gestures. It is impolite to appear in public with your hands in your pockets. Putting hands on hips signifies a challenge or threat to others. If someone shakes their hand from side to side with forefinger extended, they are saying 'no.' In contrast, the "thumbs up" sign indicates 'yes' or approval of what has just been referred to.

Business Protocol

Meeting and Greeting. Shake hands with men both when meeting and departing, using a moderate grip. Avoid further physical contact until you know the person well. Give women a slight bow and wait for them to extend their hand. Even if you don't speak Spanish, learning the principal greetings will be appreciated. *Buenos dias, buenas tardes* and *buenas noches* mean good morning, good afternoon and good evening or good night respectively.

Meeting Protocol. During meetings expect frequent interruptions: phone calls as well as visitors dropping in without an appointment. Be aware that these interruptions are not considered impolite. Rather, Mexicans would consider it rude to turn away drop-in visitors or to refuse to take phone calls. Refer to an office secretary as "Senorita" whether she is young or not and whether she is single or married. On your second trip to Mexico, bring small gifts such as perfume for the secretaries of important people. If you are a male, tell her your wife bought it for her.

Gift Giving. Good business gifts are premium cognacs and Scotches, cocktail table books, desk clocks and gold pens or lighters. Remember that silver objects are only for tourists. Give gold items to your business contacts.

Women in Business. Women business visitors may not be treated with the same respect they are used to at home, since Mexican men are not used to dealing with female executives. Women are advised to dress conservatively and to behave professionally at all times.

Wining and Dining. It is important to entertain your local counterparts only at top restaurants. Suggest several and let your guests choose the one they prefer. Breakfast and lunch are good opportunities to talk business, while dinner should be reserved strictly for socializing. Breakfast can be as early as 8:00 am, lunch normally starts around 2:00 pm and dinner begins after 9:00 pm. Be careful to reciprocate all meal invitations.

If accompanied by your spouse it is OK to invite your counterpart's spouse. Foreign business women should always include the wives of their Mexican male customers or contacts in any dinner invitation. When entertaining male guests women should also make prior arrangements with the headwaiter for payment, since otherwise Mexican men will absolutely insist on picking up the check.

Negotiating Behavior

Bargaining Range. Consider putting some extra padding into your opening offer. The negotiating process can be long and vigorous, and Mexicans tend to be hard bargainers.

Deadlines. They may also be optimistic with deadlines and schedules, so it's wise to mentally add a few days or weeks to any target date you are given. Establish a number of 'milestones' to monitor your counterparts' progress in meeting delivery dates. That is, fix certain dates on which you will check with them to gauge their adherence to schedule.

Decision-Making. Always take time to think over any proposal your counterparts make. Quick acceptance seems to make the Mexican side think they have conceded too much. Tell them you need time to consider the idea.

Our daughter-in-law Maria has been involved for some time with Maxican cross-border operations in the company she works for. Here are her comments.

Cross-Border Operations:

By Maria Giangrasso Gesteland

Just a stone's throw from Texas, New Mexico, Arizona and California, the Mexican border towns provide incentives for investments. Many multinational corporations decide to construct manufacturing sites on the Mexican side of the U.S. border in order to take advantage of favorable labor costs and proximity to the world's largest consumer economy. Although there are several ways for companies to set up operations on the border, the most common option is the maquiladora.

A maquiladora is a Mexican manufacturing company operating under a special customs agreement, allowing the company to temporarily import machinery, equipment, and materials, in addition to the parts and components needed for assembly or manufacturing on a duty free basis. At this writing the finished goods produced in a maquiladora must be for export. The laws are changing and soon finished goods will be able to be sold in the Mexican market as well.

For a firm that is not ready to take the risk of opening a maquiladora operation the option of working under a shelter organization is available. A shelter organization provides a maquila, the building and the labor, does the border transfers, assumes the overhead and takes care of insurance and incidentals for a flat fee. The manufacturer supplies the materials and components from which the finished goods will be produced, plant equipment, and the technical know how for production. The two largest and most respected shelter organizations are Intermex and American Industries.

Economic development organizations along the border join together to create incentives and relationships to encourage industrial development in the region. Anyone interested in further exploration can contact the various Economic Development groups located on the U.S. side of any of the major border towns. They are eager to help develop the industrial and legal contacts the investor needs to be successful.

Group D

**Relationship-Focused – Formal
– Polychronic – Variably Expressive**

The Russian Negotiator

Since the business culture of a country tends to reflect its general culture, how much has today's Russian negotiating behavior changed from that of the former Soviet Union? Well, for one thing, today's *biznesmyen* quite likely know the rules of the game in the outside world.

However, visiting negotiators find that Russian business culture continues to exhibit features which set it apart from others. This is hardly surprising given the fact that over the centuries Russia developed in isolation from the countries of western and central Europe.

Consider the centuries of brutal Tatar (Central Asian) rule, which lasted from 1240 to about 1480. Further, consider that under czarism and the Russian Orthodox church Russia experienced neither the Reformation, the Renaissance, nor the Enlightenment – the three cultural revolutions which combined to make modern Europeans think and act the way they do today.

While western Europe and parts of central Europe were developing political democracy, the rule of law, and free-market economies, in Russia the peasant collectivism of the *mir* was reinforced by 70 years of Soviet collective farms. Totalitarian Party rule lasted until a decade or so ago.

Then add in the current environment of political chaos, crime and corruption, and it's easy to see why Russia remains a challenging place to do business despite the recent changes. Chaos, crime and corruption -- along with capricious regulations and bureaucratic red tape -- continue to present barriers to trade. But as the world's largest (11 time zones) and fifth most populous (about 150 million people) country, Russia remains a tempting market for those who know how to overcome the barriers.

Personal Relationships. Connections or *blat* play a key role in doing business with Russians. As is the case in other relationship-focused markets around the world, you need personal relationships to get things done. It's who you know that counts. The Chinese and other

East Asians call these vital relationships *guanxi*, the Latin Americans *palanca*, the Egyptians *wastah*, the South Slavs *veza*.

Most business in Russia is done face-to-face. Frequent visits to the market and frequent phone calls are essential. This again is true of the RF business cultures of Asia, the Middle East, Africa, Latin America, and much of eastern Europe.

Vodka seems to lubricate the rapport-building process. A strong liver is as important to visiting negotiators as a good brain.

And while written contracts are as important as anywhere else in today's global marketplace, be prepared for your Russian counterparts to try to renegotiate the agreement not long after it was signed.

Direct, Low-Context Communication. Russia's version of relationship-focus does however differ from most other RF cultures in an important respect: verbal communication. Unlike East and Southeast Asians for example, Russian negotiators tend to be direct, even blunt, saying pretty much what they mean and meaning what they say.

This is in contrast to the majority of relationship-oriented cultures, where people commonly use indirect, high-context communication. The Russian combination of an RF approach to business with fairly direct, low-context communication behavior is somewhat of a rarity. Among the other business cultures exhibiting this feature are France, the Catalan region of Spain, parts of Chile, to some extent Venezuela and northern Mexico, and parts of east-central Europe.

Formality, Status and Hierarchies. Here again we have a special case. Russians belong to the more formal wing of Europeans, closer to the Germans and French than to the informal Scandinavians. And as we know, formal cultures are also hierarchical – see Japan and France, for example – just as informal cultures are also egalitarian, as in Australia and Scandinavia.

But while Russian culture is formal and hierarchical, at the same time a key value is *uravnilovka*, egalitarianism. Russians deeply resent it when others have more than they do. In the old joke, God gives Ivan the peasant a wish: he can ask for anything he wants. "Well, Mr. God," says Ivan, "You know my neighbor owns a cow."

"So I suppose you want two cows then?" God replies.

"Oh no, God," says Ivan, "What I want is for my neighbor's cow to die."

'Uravnilovka' is related to Scandinavian egalitarianism, which looks askance at people who seem to rise above the rest. A similar value is expressed in the Australian saying, "The tall poppy gets cut down." So we have an apparent contradiction: egalitarian values coexisting with formal, hierarchical behavior. But such cultural contradictions are common in the real world. Look at the USA, where egalitarian ideals coexist with hierarchical attitudes in large organizations.

Russian formality shows up in the way people dress and in their meeting and greeting rituals; hierarchies are evident in the top-down approach to management as well as in the relative scarcity of women in positions of authority. Visitors are expected to observe a certain degree of formality in dress and in public behavior. The latter is especially important at the first meeting with Russian counterparts.

Hierarchical attitudes affect business visitors in two ways. First, while visiting female executives will be treated with delightful Old World gallantry, they can also expect to be patronized. Few women have reached positions of authority in Russian business organizations, so the men are not used to interacting with women on anything approaching a basis of equality.

Second, both male and female visitors will note that all important decisions are reserved for the top man in the organization. Typical of strongly hierarchical societies, this characteristic slows progress and can bring about long delays in negotiations. In Russia it is even more important than in most other business cultures to make sure one is negotiating with the real decision-maker.

Polychronic Time Behavior. Russian managers admit that while they are usually unconcerned with punctuality, "We try hard to be on time when meeting with foreigners!" Most visitors from time-conscious, monochronic cultures report little evidence of these efforts to be on time.

Meetings often start an hour or more late, run on well beyond the anticipated ending time, and are frequently interrupted. Russian top executives seem to find it normal to conduct three or four different conversations simultaneously, some face-to-face and others on one or more telephones.

Here are some practical tips for time-conscious business visitors:
– Schedule no more than two meetings per day;
– As far as possible, try to ignore the interruptions and distractions.
– Remember: In Russia patience is more important than punctuality.

Emotionally Reserved/Expressive Communication. While it is generally possible to classify cultures as either Reserved (Finns, Japanese, Thais) or Expressive (southern Europeans, Latin Americans, Mediterranean people), Russian negotiators frequently display both types of behavior.

At the first meeting, expect a quiet, restrained manner; at subsequent sessions be prepared for more demonstrative behavior. Be ready for emotional outbursts and displays of temper at critical points in the discussions. If this behavior startles negotiators from East and Southeast Asia, they should remember the Chinese proverb, "Enter village, follow customs." When entering Russia, expect emotional expressiveness.

Paraverbal and Nonverbal Behavior. Negotiation is really a specialized form of communication and unfortunately, differences in the way people communicate often cause misunderstandings in the bargaining process. So let's look at Russian paraverbal and nonverbal communication:

Voice volume. Moderate. Visitors should avoid loud, boisterous conversation in public.

Interpersonal distance. From close to medium -- 12 to 18 inches (20 to 30 cm).

Touch behavior. Among friends, frequent touching, bear hugs and cheek-kissing.

Eye contact. Direct gaze across the negotiating table.

Taboo gestures. For some Russians the 'A-OK' thumb-and-forefinger sign is obscene. Standing with hands in one's pockets is rude.

Business Protocol and Etiquette

Dress code. Conservative. In winter, adopt the layered look. Expect to check your overcoat in most public buildings.

Meeting and greeting. Shake hands and state your name. Formulas such as "how are you?" are unnecessary.

Forms of address. When introduced, use title plus last name, not first names. Later you might move to using the first name plus patronymic, but wait until your counterpart suggests it.

Exchanging cards. Bring plenty of cards which show your organizational title and any advanced degrees. Do not be surprised if your Russian counterpart does not have a card.

Topics of conversation. Avoid discussions of war, politics and religion. And remember, Russians tend to be sensitive about their country's recent loss of superpower status.

Business gifts. Quality pens, books, music CDs, solar-powered calculators, liquor, card wallets, gift soaps, T-shirts.

Business entertaining. It is an honor to be invited to a Russian home: be sure to accept. However, most business entertaining is done at restaurants.

Drinking. Russians seem to have a high tolerance for alcohol. Few foreigners succeed in staying with the locals drink for drink. To limit your intake, drink only when someone proposes a toast. If there are many toasts, switch to sipping. Be prepared to drink at least one or two small vodkas.

Russian Negotiating Style

Making your presentation. Especially at the first meeting, avoid starting off with a joke. Show that you are taking business seriously. Pack your presentation with facts and technical details.

Local sensitivities. Avoid statements such as, "We are planning a really 'aggressive' marketing campaign." The word 'aggressive' has a negative connotation in Russian. Also avoid proposing a 'compromise' during the negotiation – many Russians regard a compromise as something morally wrong. Instead, suggest meeting each other halfway, or make your proposal conditional on an equivalent concession from your counterparts.

Bargaining style. Be ready for hardball tactics -- a tough, sometimes confrontational approach, occasionally punctuated with table-pounding, temper tantrums, emotional outbursts, brinkmanship, loud threats and walkouts. With some Russian negotiators these components of the 'Soviet' style of bargaining have survived into the post-Soviet era. Counter these tactics by staying calm. More often, your counterparts will simply try to out-wait you, exploiting your presumed impatience. Counter this with patience, patience and more patience.

Resolving disputes. Insist on a clause calling for arbitration in a third country. Sweden is a popular choice.

The Polish Negotiator

Polish business people often exhibit features of both the relationship-focused and deal-focused approaches to business. For example, it is important to have the right contacts and to build strong relationships, but at the same time Polish negotiators tend to be verbally direct. That is a fairly unusual combination of cultural traits.

Furthermore, most Polish business people are formal and moderately polychronic. Their communication behavior is likely to be reserved at the first meeting, then considerably more expressive as they get to know you.

Geography and history provide important clues to this country's business culture. Positioned as it is between Germany and Russia, Poland has for centuries been influenced by both East and West.

Poles were less influenced by decades of communist rule than some of their neighbors. There are two main reasons for this difference. First, the strength and popularity of the Roman Catholic church. Second, the prevalence of private agriculture: collective farms played a smaller role in Poland than in most other countries on the eastern side of the old Iron Curtain.

Relationships. As with most markets outside northwestern Europe, North America and Australia/New Zealand, it is vital to have the right connections in Poland. Who you know counts for a great deal. That said, visitors will observe a trend: Polish business people are becoming more deal-focused, i.e., more like the Germans, Scandinavians and Americans, while still retaining elements of the RF approach. In other words, like the French and Russians, Poles can be classed as either moderately relationship-focused or moderately deal-focused.

Verbal Directness. At the bargaining table in Poland you will experience verbal directness rather than polite circumlocutions most of the time. The Polish combination of a relationship-oriented approach to business along with low-context communication is relatively uncommon in the global marketplace. Other examples are the Russians, the French, and the Spaniards from Catalonia.

Formality, Status and Hierarchies. Poles are more formal than Danes, Swedes, Australians or North Americans, something like the Germans and French, for instance. The formality is evident in the way people dress and in their meeting and greeting rituals. Hierarchies are evident in the top-down approach to management and in the relative scarcity of women business managers.

Women can expect to be treated by their older male counterparts with Continental gallantry. Among some men of the older generation, hand-kissing is as prevalent as it used to be in Vienna. But on the other hand, women negotiators may find they are being patronized. Few women have reached positions of authority in business, so many men are not used to interacting with women on a basis of equality.

Polychronic Time Behavior. Younger Polish business people are aware of the importance of punctuality, schedules and deadlines. They admit with some embarrassment that visitors are often kept waiting. Expect meetings to start 15 to 20 minutes late, to run on beyond the anticipated ending time, and to be interrupted from to time.

Variable Expressiveness. At the first meeting, expect a reserved manner; thereafter be prepared for more demonstrative behavior. Poles do not always hide the fact that they are irritated, frustrated or angry.

Paraverbal and Nonverbal Behavior

Voice Volume. Moderate. Avoid raising your voice during negotiations as well as in public.

Interpersonal Distance. Medium – 15 to 25 inches (25 to 40 cm).

Touch Behavior. This a low-contact culture in a business setting. Except for the handshake, expect little or no touching in a business situation: closer to the German style than the French.

Eye Contact. Direct gaze across the negotiating table: less intense than in the Middle East and southern Europe, but more direct than is common in East and Southeast Asia.

Business Protocol and Etiquette

Dress Code. Conservative suits and ties for men, dresses for women.

Meeting and Greeting. Shake hands, make eye contact and state your name. Formulas such as "how are you?" are unnecessary. Shake hands again when leaving the meeting. It is polite for men to wait for a Polish woman to extend her hand. Male visitors are not expected to kiss a woman's hand; instead, a slight bow may accompany the handshake.

Forms of Address. When introduced, address your counterparts by their professional or academic title plus family name. Only relatives and close friends address each other by first names.

Exchanging Cards. Your cards should show your organizational title and any advanced degrees.

Topics of Conversation. Most Poles regard their country as part of Central Europe rather than Eastern Europe. Referring to Poland as part of East-Central Europe is acceptable.

Business Gifts. At the first meeting, a bottle of imported spirits such as scotch or cognac is appropriate, but not vodka: good vodka is readily available locally.

Social Gifts. Bring flowers when invited to someone's home for a meal. While the florist will usually give you good advice, remember to bring an uneven number and avoid both red roses and chrysanthemums -- the former imply romantic intentions, the latter are for funerals. Other good gifts are imported wine, chocolates, coffee, perfume and cigarettes.

Business Entertaining. It is an honor to be invited to a Polish home: be sure to accept. However, most business entertaining is done at restaurants.

Wining and Dining. As in many other East Central European countries, Poles tend to take breakfast between 7:00 and 8:00 am, then work straight through the day without a lunch break. So they eat lunch ('obiad') around 3:00 or 4:00 pm. This is the main meal of the day. If invited to a business lunch, expect to eat between 4:00 and 5:00 pm. The evening meal is usually a light repast around 8:30 pm or so.

Negotiating Behavior

Making a Presentation: To show you are serious, avoid starting off with a joke at the first meeting. As you would in Germany, load your presentation with background information, facts and technical details.

Bargaining style: Wise negotiators keep some bargaining chips in reserve until the endgame. Your opening bid should be realistic but at the same time should include room for maneuver.

Decision Making: The negotiating process usually takes longer when dealing with the government or public sector than when doing business with the private sector.

The Romanian Negotiator

Next to Albania, Romania experienced the most oppressive post-war Communist rule of any Eastern European country. Business visitors will encounter the residual effects of a failed centralized economy for years to come, as the society slowly recovers. Patience is advised.

Romania falls into the southeast quadrant of the north/south and east/west fault lines which divide European business cultures. The country's business behavior reflects Romania's geographic location in eastern European, while its people's communication style reflects the influence of Latin Europe to the south.

The Language of Business. Like their Hungarian neighbors, Romanians speak a non-Slavic language. Romanian is a romance language distantly related to French, Italian, Spanish and Portuguese as well as to the Romansch or Ladino of eastern Switzerland. Partly for that reason French remains an important language of business, although younger people are increasingly choosing English as their second language. German is also increasingly used for business.

Relationship-Oriented Market. As in the rest of East Central Europe, cold calls do not work well in Romania. It's vital to have the right connections. Especially at the beginning of a business relationship, expect to discuss important business issues face-to-face or on the telephone, rather than via fax or e-mail. Budget plenty of time for getting to know your counterparts before getting down to business.

Verbal Indirectness. Romanians often prefer a roundabout way of saying things, rejecting northern European and North American directness. Negotiators will get better results if they avoid asking too many direct questions, instead probing gently for the information they need while gradually building a pleasant relationship with their Romanian counterparts.

Formality, Status and Hierarchies. Romanians interact more formally than Danes, Australians or North Americans. Formality is evident in the way they dress as well as in local meeting and greeting rituals. Hierarchies are evident in the top-down approach to management and in the relative scarcity of women business managers.

Visiting female executives are likely to be treated by senior male counterparts with traditional Continental gallantry. Among some males of the older generation, hand-kissing is as prevalent as it used to be in Vienna. On the other hand, women negotiators may feel they are being patronized. Few women have reached positions of authority in business, so men are not used to relating to women on the basis of equality.

Polychronic Time Behavior. Meetings often start 30 to 60 minutes late and last beyond the anticipated ending time, but visitors are expected to be punctual.

Expressive Paraverbal and Nonverbal Behavior

Interpersonal Distance. Romanians stand and sit closer together than northerners, so be ready for the same interpersonal distance you find in Greece -- about half an arm's length.

Touch Behavior. Be prepared for much more touching than in the other countries of East-Central Europe. This is a high-contact culture, with (among friends) lots of hugging and kissing.

Eye Contact. Steady, considerably more focused than the gaze behavior negotiators encounter in East and Southeast Asia.

Gestures. The broad and frequent Italian-style hand and arm gestures may startle some visitors from the reserved cultures of East and Southeast Asia.

Business Protocol and Etiquette

Making an Appointment. Your letter will be given more attention if written in English rather than Romanian. Write two to three weeks before the desired meeting date and then follow up by fax, telephone or e-mail.

Dress Code. Conservative suits and ties for men, dresses or suits and heels for women.

Meeting and Greeting. Shake hands, make eye contact and state your name. If you meet the same person again later that day, shake hands again. In fact, expect to shake hands every time you meet. Shake hands again when leaving a meeting. Wait for a Romanian woman to extend her hand. Male visitors are not expected to kiss a woman's hand; instead, bow slightly when shaking her hand.

Forms of Address. When introduced, address your counterparts by their professional or academic title plus surname. Only relatives and close friends address each other by given name.

Exchanging Cards. Your cards should show your organizational title and any advanced degrees.

Topics of Conversation. Sports, travel, films, books, fashion and food. Avoid personal questions about someone's family or job.

Business Gifts. Inexpensive gifts are given to celebrate the signing of an agreement or perhaps for the Christmas holidays. Tasteful logo gifts such as pens or lighters are acceptable.

Social Gifts. Bring wrapped bouquets of flowers when invited to a private home for a meal.

Wining and Dining. People usually take breakfast around 7:00 am, lunch about noon and dinner at 7:00 or 7:30 pm. Lunch is generally the main meal of the day.

Toasting. This is the custom at both formal and informal meals. Touch glasses, nod and say, "To your health" or "Good luck."

Negotiating Behavior

Making a Presentation. Avoid starting off with a joke at the first meeting. Use plenty of visuals and clearly-written handouts. Include background information, facts and technical details.

Bargaining Style. Romanians are tough negotiators. Keep some bargaining chips in reserve until the end game. Your opening bid should be realistic but should also definitely include some room for maneuver.

Dishonest Practices. Take precautions to avoid being cheated. Romania is the second-poorest country in Europe after Albania and has just started on the long road to developing a free market economy.

Facilitation Payments. Some low-level officials expect a 'tip' for handling routine applications and other paperwork. A pack or carton of Kent cigarettes used to be the preferred currency for such transactions. Consult with your local contacts on this delicate issue.

Decision Making. Count on the negotiating process taking longer than it would in Western Europe or North America.

The Slovak Negotiator

Geography and history explain a good deal about the business culture of Slovakia. A branch of the West Slavs, closely related to but less numerous than the Czechs, the Slovaks were colonized by Hungarians under the Austro-Hungarian Empire. After the breakup of that empire in the aftermath of World War I, they were dominated by the Czechs in Czechoslovakia and then for a few years became a puppet state of Nazi Germany.

As part of the new Czechoslovakia after the Second World War, Slovaks soon found themselves under Soviet domination, a condition which lasted until the fall of the Iron Curtain. The "Velvet Revolution" of 1993 finally brought them independence from the Czechs – but not prosperity.

Viewed from western Europe, Czechs and Slovaks appear to be sister cultures. Seen from Prague, the Slovaks are *little* sisters, but Slovaks think of themselves more as cousins of their prosperous western neighbors. The Czech Republic is the western-most Slavic country. It shares borders with both Germany and Austria and is strongly influenced by German culture. In fact, other Slavs often call Czechs "the Germans of East Central Europe."

One result of German cultural influence is that the Czechs are the most task-oriented, deal-focused, and time-conscious business people in East Central Europe today. They are relatively willing to talk business with strangers and quick to get down to business.

Slovaks on the other hand are more relationship-oriented and less open to business approaches from strangers. They need time to get to know new potential business partners. While Czech society is urban, industrialized, and largely secular, that of the Slovaks is rural, agricultural, strongly Roman Catholic, and traditional.

Relationships. In Slovakia visiting negotiators rarely encounter the northern European and North American attitude of "Time is money, let's get down to business!" at meetings. Small talk is important, as it is for example in relationship-oriented Italy. It takes time to build trust: centuries of political and economic domination by non-Slovaks will not be forgotten quickly.

Language of Business. While the national language is Slovak, younger business people are likely to speak English or German, sometimes both. It's still a good idea to ask your local counterparts whether an interpreter will be needed because senior managers often do not speak foreign languages. Although the Czech and Slovak languages are mutually intelligible, using a Czech person as interpreter may not be a good idea since it might offend some Slovaks.

Verbal Communication. Slovak negotiators typically speak less directly than northern Europeans and North Americans. They may be reluctant to reply to your proposal with a blunt no, often preferring a vaguely-worded response. Similarly, if they respond with a weak 'yes' it probably indicates lack of interest. If in doubt, keep probing with polite questions until you are sure you understand what they mean to say.

In English-speaking cultures people often add "how are you?" after saying "hello," even when meeting people for the first time. This is simply a greeting ritual; no response other than "I'm fine, how are you?" is expected. However, Slovaks, in common with many other Europeans, do not routinely ask strangers how they are feeling. Your local counterpart may be surprised by such a question unless you already know each other. On the other hand, once a relationship is established it is quite proper to inquire about someone's health.

Formality, Status and Hierarchies. Slovaks tend to be more formal than North Americans, Scandinavians and younger Brits. The level of formality is more akin to that of the French, Germans and Italians. Business formality is expressed in meeting-and-greeting rituals as well as in the way people dress. Hierarchical values show up in the top-down approach to management and in the rarity of women business managers. Visiting female executives are likely to encounter rather traditional attitudes towards gender roles.

Polychronic Time Behavior. Whereas foreign visitors are expected to be on time for meetings, local counterparts may not always be punctual. Slovaks tend to be less time-conscious than their Czech cousins, much less so than most German business people. Also, negotiations often last longer than they would in Sweden, the US, UK, or Germany. Wary after decades of isolation from the global marketplace, Slovaks need time to size up potential foreign business partners before coming to a decision.

Reserved Communication. Slovak negotiators tend to be less demonstrative than Italians but a bit more expressive than northern Europeans. Social interaction can be quite lively once the two sides get to know each other.

Paraverbal and Nonverbal Behavior. Differences in the way people communicate can cause misunderstandings in the bargaining process. Slovaks normally prefer a non-confrontational, low-key approach to negotiations. Visitors need to read nonverbal signals to understand what is going on. For example, if your local counterparts suddenly become quiet or avoid eye contact at the bargaining table, you know you have stepped on their toes. To get back on track, smile and make a light-hearted remark – perhaps a self-deprecatory one.

Other tips:
- Keep your voice down. Slovaks are put off by loud voices, histrionics and table pounding.
- Maintain an interpersonal distance of between 15 to 25 inches (25 to 40 cm).
- Avoid physical touching except for the handshake.
- Expect moderate eye contact. You will encounter a direct gaze across the negotiating table, though less intense than in the Middle East and Italy.

Business Protocol and Etiquette. Make appointments by telephone, fax or email about two weeks in advance. Corresponding in English is acceptable, although taking the trouble to have your letter translated into Slovak will impress your prospective customer or business partner. Best times for business meetings: between 9:00 am and noon and from 1:00 to 3:00 pm (13:00 to 15:00).

Dress code. Dark suits and ties for men, conservative dresses or suits for women.

Meeting and greeting. In a business situation, say hello, make direct eye contact and state your full name. Formulas such as 'how are you?' are unnecessary. Shake hands again when leaving the meeting. In social settings the verbal greeting often suffices; handshakes are optional. Whereas in many cultures men wait for women to extend their hand, in Slovakia the man often offers his hand to a woman first.

Forms of address. When introduced, address your counterparts by their professional or academic title plus family name. Only relatives and close friends address each other by first names.

Exchanging business cards. Your cards should show your organizational title and any advanced degrees.

Topics of conversation. Remember that Slovaks consider their country part of Central Europe rather than of Eastern Europe. Referring to Slovakia as part of East Central Europe is acceptable. Avoid references to politics in general and to the Communist era in particular. Good topics are soccer, ice hockey, hiking, biking and all kinds of music.

Gift Giving. While not expected, gifts of moderate value are welcome. Bring a bottle of good scotch or cognac or small items such a quality pen or cigarette lighter. Imported wine or liquor is the best choice when invited to someone's home for a meal. A bouquet of flowers may be considered inappropriate by some Slovaks – flowers tend to carry a romantic connotation.

Negotiating Behavior. Expect slow, methodical progress. Your opening offer should be fairly realistic: the 'high-low' tactic common in many business cultures may cause the Slovaks to mistrust you. Patience and a soft-sell approach will get you the best results.

Group E

**Moderately Deal-Focused – Formal
– Variably Monochronic – Expressive**

The French Negotiator

The French business culture is in a class by itself. In origin a hybrid of Teutonic influences from the north of Europe and Latin infusions from the south, France's negotiating style is unique.

For example, while the French are relationship-focused they are at the same time a nation of true individualists. Moreover, though they dislike getting straight to the point and often employ indirect, high-context communication, they are also quick to argue, and will bluntly disagree with you across the bargaining table. And despite the fact that the word 'egalitarian' is derived from *egalité*, France remains one of Europe's most hierarchical societies today.

In other words, French business executives tend to be relationship-focused, high-context, highly status-conscious individualists; a rather unusual combination of cultural traits. While of course no two Gallic negotiators operate exactly alike, the following profile should help prepare you for your next business meeting in France.

Language of Business. It is definitely French, despite the fact that so many business people there speak English well. While foreign buyers can get by with English or German, export marketers are usually expected to speak French. Parisians especially seem to find it physically painful to hear their language spoken poorly. Written correspondence should likewise be in French and the key parts of your product literature should be translated as well.

Good interpreters are easy to find in Paris or Lyon, but marketers who do not speak the language are likely to find themselves at a disadvantage. Despite the local sensitivity to the language, do try to use your French even if you make mistakes or have a foreign accent. You will be given credit for trying.

Making the Initial Contact. Connections count heavily in this market. Trade shows and official trade promotion missions are good ways to make initial contact. The alternative is to arrange for a formal introduction to potential customers, distributors or partners. Ask your country's embassy to introduce you. Other useful intermediaries are chambers of commerce, trade associations and international banks, law and accounting firms. But don't overlook that golf buddy or neighbor of yours whose company has a big office in Paris!

Your letter requesting a meeting should be in flawless business French. As in other hierarchical cultures, it is wise to start at the top. Address the letter to the President/Directeur General and if you are a senior person in your company, request a meeting with him.

Importance of Relationships. France is a country of personal networks. You get things done more quickly by working through inside contacts than by 'going through channels.'

The French want to know a good deal about you before discussing business, but building rapport involves less small talk than in some other relationship-oriented cultures. Displaying knowledge of French history, literature, art and philosophy is a good way to build rapport. Discussing French cuisine and wine over a meal is another good way.

Orientation to Time. Visitors are expected to be roughly on time for business meetings, particularly if they are selling. Outside of Paris and Lyon however, it is not unusual for your local counterpart to appear a few minutes late. Nor do meetings always follow a fixed agenda as they commonly do across the border in Germany. Instead you may experience free-form discussions with everyone present having his say.

Hierarchy and Status. Level of education along with family background and wealth determine status in France. Graduates of the select Grandes Ecoles hold high positions in government and industry. Three out of four top managers of the 200 largest French companies come from wealthy families, whereas in Germany the figure is one out of four and in the U.S. one out of ten.

French bosses tend to run their companies in an authoritarian style. Managers are expected to be highly competent and to know the answer to virtually every question that arises. They are often reluctant to delegate authority. Fraternization with the rank and file is not common. The traditional French management style contrasts sharply with the Scandinavian model, with its flat structure and egalitarian approach.

Communication Style. The French are verbally and nonverbally expressive. They love to argue, often engaging in spirited debate during business meetings. Negotiators from less confrontational cultures such as East Asia should not mistake this love of debate for hostility.

Verbal Communication. While they relish verbal conflict the French dislike getting straight to the point. They tend to favor subtle, indirect language and like to present their point of view with Cartesian logic, elegant phrasing and verbal flourishes. This is one reason Gallic business people prefer to negotiate in French: their verbal pyrotechnics are mostly lost when expressed in another language.

Nonverbal Communication. Among friends and relatives the French display high-contact behavior, including in public. A study of comparative touch behavior at cafes in Paris and London showed that within the space of an hour French couples touched each other over one hundred times while the British couples did not touch each other at all.

Always shake hands both when meeting and when leaving someone. The French use many more hand and arm gestures than Asians and Anglo-Saxons. The thumb-and-forefinger circle signifies 'zero' in France. To indicate "A-OK" they flash the thumbs-up sign instead. Taboos include standing or speaking with hands in one's pockets and slapping the palm of one hand over a closed fist.

Negotiating Style

Your Presentation. Avoid hard-sell tactics, hyperbole and flippant humor. Prepare a sober presentation with a logical sequence of arguments. If you encounter forceful disagreement on some points be prepared to respond with factual counter-arguments. Vigorous disagreement with specific issues does not necessarily signal lack of interest in your overall proposal.

Bargaining Style. Be prepared for long, relatively unstructured negotiating sessions punctuated frequently with verbal confrontation. Your counterpart may also attack the thought process behind your bargaining position. The French pride themselves on their logical thinking and often seem to relish faulting the logic of others.

Decision Making. Although the senior member of the French team is likely to make most of the decisions, that does not mean those decisions will be made quickly. Expect decision-making to take longer than in Anglo-Saxon countries.

Business Protocol and Etiquette

Dress Code. As might be expected in a hierarchical, status-conscious society, the French dress and behave formally in a business setting. And being French they dress with style, panache and elegance. Male business visitors should wear a dark suit; women should choose tasteful, somewhat conservative clothing and accessories.

Meeting and Greeting. Handshake with moderate pressure and steady eye contact. Among males the older or higher status person should initiate the handshake. A woman of any rank can decide whether or not to offer her hand.

Forms of Address. With local counterparts you don't know, the greeting is *monsieur, madame* or *mademoiselle* without the person's name, as in *"Bonjour, monsieur!"* Always use the *vous* (formal) pronoun rather than the informal *tu*. As a foreigner, once you have built a relationship it is possible that your French opposite number may suggest using first names. Do wait for the local person to take this step however. And remember to continue using *vous* even when on a first-name basis.

Women in Business. Because relatively few women have reached high positions in French companies, female business visitors may occasionally feel somewhat out of place. Businesswomen should dress and act professionally at all times and should avoid negotiating behavior that could be interpreted as overly aggressive.

Wining and Dining. Entertaining and being entertained is an important way to build rapport. According to a recent study, two out of three French business people regularly lunch in restaurants, while more than eight out of ten of their Dutch and British colleagues wolf a sandwich at their desks. And while almost half of the Brits and Germans surveyed felt business lunches were a waste of time, 70% of the French think they are an important part of doing business.

There is a certain ceremonial aspect to dining in France. Many Western ideas of proper table manners originated in France, so visitors are advised to observe some key rules of etiquette.

Breakfast usually consists of coffee and a roll, but the American custom of the "power breakfast" is being adopted by an increasing number of Frenchmen.

Business lunches often last two to three hours over at least that many glasses of wine. In some cultures it is a sign of generosity to fill a wine glass to the brim, but in France, as elsewhere in Europe and in North America, when pouring wine for your neighbor at table remember to fill the glass only two-thirds full. Avoid discussing business at least until dessert is served unless your host broaches the subject earlier.

Invitations to **Dinner at Home** are more common in the provinces than in Paris. Always accept such an invitation, and plan to arrive about 15 minutes after the appointed time.

What should you bring the hostess? Flowers may not be your best choice: Your hostess may not appreciate having to search for the right size vase in the midst of all her other duties. And then you would have to remember to bring an uneven number (but never 13!), to avoid chrysanthemums (funerals only), red roses (they signify you are having an affair with your hostess) and yellow flowers (they imply your host is having an affair with someone else).

Nor is wine a better choice. A bottle of undistinguished plonk brands you as ignorant or cheap, while with the good stuff you risk insulting your host by insinuating that his cellar is inadequate. The best solution therefore is usually a box of the very best chocolates you can find.

Wait at the door until the host or hostess invites you in. Men should not take off their jacket unless encouraged to do so by the host. Wait for your host or hostess to start eating. If you are accustomed to keeping one hand in your lap, leave this custom behind. Your table companions are liable to roll their eyes and ask each other what you are doing under the table.

When the salad arrives, do not cut your lettuce with a knife. Instead fold it into small pieces with your fork. Peel the fruit with a knife and eat it with a fork. It is impolite to take two servings of cheese, and extremely gauche to slice the tip from a wedge of cheese.

The Belgian Negotiator

Although it is a small country tucked away in the northwestern corner of the Continent, Belgium is in many respects a microcosm of Europe. It reflects within its borders the north/south division of the Old World. Half of the 10 million Belgians speak Flemish, a language of the Germanic north, while a third speak French: the premier language of the Latin south. Meanwhile English has become a very important third language spoken by most Belgian business people, especially those in Brussels.

Business visitors from outside of Europe find that learning Belgian business customs and practices will help them conduct successful negotiations in many other markets of Western Europe.

Languages of Business. The Flemish/French linguistic division has helped promote English as the neutral medium of international business communication in Belgium. While English-speaking negotiators are unlikely to need an interpreter these days, it is still courteous to offer to bring one to the first meeting. Visiting negotiators who speak French should consider speaking English when doing business in the northern part of the country, to avoid irritating Flemish speakers.

Making the Initial Contact. Major banks, trade associations and the Belgian Chamber of Commerce can be helpful in making business contacts. It is a good idea to make the first contact by a letter written in formal, correct business English. Follow up with a phone call requesting an appointment. Avoid business visits in July or August, the most popular months for family vacations, as well as during Holy Week and the Christmas holiday season.

Meeting Protocol. Businessmen should wear a dark suit and tie with well-polished shoes. The tie should not be removed even in hot weather. Stylish dresses or skirts and blouses are the appropriate attire for businesswomen.

When introduced, shake hands with a quick motion and light pressure while speaking your name clearly and repeating the other person's name. Shake hands again when it is time to leave. It is polite for men to wait for a woman to offer her hand when being introduced to her. At business meetings it is common courtesy to shake hands with everyone, both when arriving and when departing. It is customary to include secretaries in this ritual.

In contrast to the practice in many other European cultures, in Belgium it is usually unnecessary to use professional titles. However, do address Belgians by Mr., Mrs. or Miss plus the surname. It would be inappropriate to call a new business acquaintance by his or her first name. If you are from an informal culture, your counterpart may suggest a shift to first names after you have known each other for a few months.

Good topics for conversation are the history, art and special attractions of the city or region you are visiting. It is a good idea to do some relevant background reading before you arrive. Belgians also like to talk about European sports, particularly bicycle racing and football (soccer). They especially appreciate questions and comments about Belgian cuisine and beer, both of which rank among the very best in Europe.

Topics to Avoid. The French/Flemish linguistic division and local politics.

Verbal Communication. Belgian negotiators tend to use direct, straightforward language. If they disagree with you can count on them to say so clearly rather than couching their disagreement in elaborate diplomatic verbiage. While perhaps less abrupt than the Dutch, they do value frankness.

Paraverbal Communication. Most Belgians speak more softly than Americans and Latins. They also avoid conversational overlap, so negotiators from emotionally expressive cultures should take care to wait for their local counterparts to finish talking before speaking their piece.

Nonverbal Communication

- Within Europe the peoples of the Latin south are typically less reserved and more demonstrative than their northern cousins. This distinction holds true within Belgium, where the Flemish-speaking northerners are more taciturn and less expressive than the French-speaking Walloons.
- As in the rest of Europe, handshaking is a very important ritual. Remember to shake hands both when greeting people and when saying goodbye, meanwhile maintaining good eye contact. Physical contact beyond the handshake should be avoided.
- Visitors coming north from business meetings in Italy or the Mediterranean region will notice that Belgians generally stand and sit somewhat further apart from each other while talking than southern Europeans. The common interpersonal distance in Belgium is an arm's length -- about the same distance most northern Europeans are accustomed to.
- Slouching, talking with hands in one's pockets or chewing gum in public are all considered impolite. Men rise when women enter the room and step aside for women to enter a room first.
- One important taboo concerning body language: Belgians find it rude to point with one's forefinger.

The Use of Time. Belgian negotiators tend to be monochronic in their use of time: They value punctuality and avoid interrupting business meetings. This attitude contrasts with the polychronic approach in parts of southern Europe, where minutes and seconds are less important and where your meeting may be interrupted frequently by phone calls, secretaries bringing in documents to be signed, drop-in visitors and the like.

In Belgium you are expected to be on time for meetings and you can normally expect your negotiation to proceed on schedule, much as it would in Germany or Switzerland.

Decision-Making. You can expect your Belgian counterparts to move things along a bit slower than would be the case in the U.S. but much faster than for example in the Middle East, Latin America or South Asia. Avoid giving the impression of impatience.

Business Gifts. An excellent choice would be the latest book related to the branch of business you and your counterpart are engaged in.

Business Entertainment. Because most Belgians prefer to spend evenings with their families, you are more likely to meet your local customer or partner for lunch rather than dinner. But expect little conversation about business since in this part of the world mealtimes are really for relaxing and getting to know your local counterpart.

Visiting businesswomen may meet resistance when trying to pay for lunch. To avoid argument, make payment arrangements with the headwaiter in advance or make it clear that the meal is a company expense.

It would be unusual to be invited to a Belgian home for dinner, though somewhat more common in the Flemish-speaking region.

Social Etiquette. If you are invited for dinner, bring flowers or candy. Stand until the hostess is seated and also wait for her to start eating. Avoid talking about business unless your hosts raise the issue first.

Belgian cuisine ranks among the world's very best. Local specialties include 'French' fries and waffles as well as fine chocolates. Food and drink make excellent topics for dinnertime conversation.

Business hours in Brussels are from 8:30 am until noon and then from 2:00 until 6:00 pm, Monday through Friday.

The Italian Negotiator

"When in Rome, Do as the Romans Do?" As someone who lived and worked for over eight years in Italy, a variation on the old chestnut makes more sense to me: "When in Rome, observe how the Romans are doing things ... and then act appropriately." For example, let's say your Roman counterpart shows up half an hour late for a major meeting, offering a big smile but no excuse. Should you match his casual attitude towards punctuality at your next get-together?

Orientation to Time. Certainly not, especially if you are the seller. All over the world today the customer is king If you come from a clock-worshiping culture such as North America, turning up late would show disrespect for your prospective buyer. And Italians tend to be very sensitive to issues of *rispetto* and *honore*.

Instead, the appropriate reaction to tardiness is to open your briefcase and tackle some of that paperwork that's been piling up on you. Convert waiting time to working time. Your Roman business associate almost certainly means no offense by showing up a little late. It's just that time seems to take on a different meaning as you move south in Europe.

The Importance of Face to Face Contact. Italians strongly prefer to conduct important business face-to-face rather than by phone, fax or e-mail. Whether buying, selling or negotiating a joint venture, you will get better results by honoring this preference.

Relationships. While Americans and many northern Europeans expect to get right down to business, Italians want to get to know you first. They prefer to build a personal relationship before getting down to the nitty gritty.

Nor are we talking about just a few minutes of small talk here. In Italy it takes longer to get to know your counterpart, though a plate of pasta and a couple of glasses of wine can accelerate the process. Wining and dining is a key part of the business scene in this part of the world. So take your time, don't rush things. It's usually fun to "do as the locals do."

Paraverbal Communication. A business discussion in Rome or Naples frequently evolves into what appears to be a verbal free-for-all. Italians are exuberant, enthusiastic talkers. They are also quick thinkers who can figure out what you are going to say long before you have finished saying it. So they often jump in with their response while you are still talking.

In Italy, when chairing a meeting between locals and northern Europeans or North Americans I sometimes had to restrain our Italian business partners, because many northerners find it rude to be interrupted in mid-sentence. If you were to respond by trying to out-shout the locals, things quickly get out of hand.

Nonverbal Communication

Interpersonal Distance. When there are only two passengers in an Italian elevator they stand close to each other. In fact in both social and business situations Italians like to stand relatively close to others, which can be disconcerting for visitors with big space bubbles. As friendly, expressive people they do not feel comfortable at arm's length.

Touch Behavior. Italians are a tactile people. While visiting negotiators will observe that Italians engage in frequent physical contact, outsiders should not initiate the hugging and kissing. Wait for your local counterpart and then respond in a way that seems comfortable. Visitors from more reserved cultures such as northern Europe and East Asia should realize that frequent touching reflects Latin expressiveness and warmth, and prepare themselves accordingly. A person who shrinks from physical contact is liable to be labeled as cold, unfriendly or arrogant.

Gaze Behavior. Another example of contrasting behavior is the use of eye contact. In Italy, direct eye contact shows we are interested in what the other person is saying while lack of steady eye contact indicates lack of interest. It is polite to maintain steady eye contact across the conference table when negotiating with Italians.

Gestures. Whole books have been written on Italian body language. Fortunately, Italian negotiators usually tend to restrain themselves when conducting business with foreign counterparts. It is not true that an Italian with his hands tied behind his back is mute!

Business Protocol and Etiquette

Dress Code. Italian business men and women dress with style and elegance, setting great store by the concept of *la bella figura*. Milan and Florence are among the fashion capitals of Europe. One's outward appearance reflects one's inner values. So we show proper respect for our business counterparts by dressing appropriately.

Forms of Address. Some informal Scandinavians and North Americans are mislead by the warmth and friendliness of Italians into moving too quickly to a first-name basis. In a business setting it is customary to start off using any applicable academic title or honorific, followed by the person's last name. So if Giorgio Bianchi has a university degree, address him as *Dottor* Bianchi. An engineer would be *Ingeniere*, your lawyer *Avvocato,* and a respected local bigwig might be called *Commendatore.* When should you start calling Italian business acquaintances by their first names? Right after they invite you to do so.

'Campanilismo': Local Patriotism. One complication of trying to decide which local customs to adopt is that you will encounter major cultural variations within the peninsula. You will hear people say, "There are 57 million people in this country, but not a single Italian." That obvious exaggeration points up the fact that many inhabitants think of themselves first of as Florentines, Milanese, Venetians, Romans, Calabresi, Sicilians, et cetera, and secondarily as Italians.

The Spanish Negotiator

The second largest European country in terms of area, Spain is also a land of sharp regional contrasts. That means that while the national business culture of Spain is relationship-focused, formal, polychronic and moderately expressive, visitors can expect regional variations. For foreigners, the most important of these variations are usually those between Castile and Catalonia, represented by Madrid and Barcelona respectively.

Regional Differences. *Madrileños* refer to the people of Catalonia as "the Germans of Spain." The businessmen of Barcelona, the largest European city which is not a capital city, are often described by other Spaniards as hard-working, aloof, frugal, lacking a sense of humor, and dressing so as to appear less wealthy than they are. They are also regarded as "more European" than their Castilian counterparts.

In response Catalonians often stereotype Madrileños as work-shy, bureaucratic, phony, arrogant people who dress to look wealthier than they are. For foreigners however the key difference between the two regions is the language difference: Castilian Spanish versus Catalan.

Language of Business. Business visitors who do not speak Spanish will find that many younger Spaniards can communicate effectively in English, while older people are more likely to speak French.

Relationships. Having the right personal contact, *enchufe,* is more important than in the more deal-focused markets of northern Europe. This is especially true of Castilians, whereas such connections are somewhat less important in Catalonia. Face-to-face personal contact in business is important in Spain, as it is in the other Latin countries of Europe.

Indirect Verbal Communication. Compared to northern Europeans, Spaniards often prefer high-context, roundabout language, and tend to avoid responding with a blunt 'no'. Here again the Catalonians depart somewhat from the mainstream culture. They are considered quite direct, even gruff, by other Spaniards.

Formality, Status and Respect. Honor and respect are very important for Spanish people. Age confers status. Few women reach top positions in local companies. Formality in forms of address is a way of showing appropriate respect. Visitors should address older people and professionals by their family name plus title, e.g. *Señor* Garcia. With others, *Don* or *Doña* plus the first name would be appropriate, e.g. Don Antonio.

A Fluid-Time Culture. Although the word *mañana* literally means 'tomorrow,' in practice it refers to some time in the indefinite future. Latin Europe in general and Spain in particular are mañana cultures: polychronic, to use the technical term. Punctuality is not a key concern, especially in the southern part of the country. Visiting negotiators need to bring a generous supply of patience.

Emotionally Expressive. Although less demonstrative than most French or Italians, the Spanish tend to be more expressive than the more reserved British, Dutch, Germans or Scandinavians. This is true of both paraverbal and nonverbal communication. But again, Catalonians are considered less expressive than Castilians and other Spaniards.

Paraverbal Communication. The expressive Spanish tend to speak loudly in comparison to more reserved northern Europeans. Spirited communicators, they also frequently engage in conversational overlap: interrupting each other as well as their foreign counterparts in mid-sentence during business meetings.

For example, researchers taped a series of negotiations between Swedish and Spanish companies and found that the Spaniards interrupted the Swedes five times for each time the Swedes interrupted the Spanish. While conversational overlap is normal in Latin cultures, it is considered rude in northern Europe.

Nonverbal Communication

Interpersonal Distance. While northern Europeans tend to maintain an arm's length distance between each other in a business context, Spaniards value a smaller space bubble.

Touch Behavior. As with other expressive cultures, the Spanish indulge in frequent physical contact with people they know well. Visitors from more reserved societies should wait for their local counterparts to initiate most forms of physical contact, except for the handshake.

Gaze Behavior. Expect strong eye contact: Spaniards like to 'read' each other's eyes. Visiting negotiators from East and Southeast Asia should not misinterpret this behavior as aggressive.

Business Protocol

Dress Code. The dress code is relatively formal: suit and tie for the men, fashionable business attire for women.

Meeting and Greeting. Expect a firm handshake with steady eye contact. Be sure to look your local counterpart directly in the eye when being introduced.

Gift Giving. Giving gifts is not as important a part of the Spanish business culture as it is in many other relationship-focused markets, such as those of Asia.

Wining and Dining. In terms of business entertaining, power breakfasts are more common in Barcelona than Madrid. Business lunches run over two hours in Barcelona, three or more in Madrid.

While many Castilians prefer not to talk business at dinner, Catalonians regard it as quite acceptable. Madrileños begin thinking about dinner around 10:30 or 11:00 pm whereas in Barcelona you will probably meet for drinks around 8:30 and go to dinner about 9:30.

Negotiating Style. Like the Italians, Spanish negotiators often rely more on quick thinking and spontaneity during a bargaining session than on the painstaking preparation and planning typically favored by Germans and Swiss. Because they rely on thorough discussion of the issues at the conference table, negotiating sessions are often lengthy affairs. Visitors should come prepared for vigorous give-and-take and a certain amount of bazaar haggling.

The Hungarian Negotiator

Visitors who have done business in other major European markets will find many Hungarian business customs and practices similar to those of Western and Central Europe. However, you will also find that in its particular mix of traits, Hungary's business culture is one of a kind.

To wit, the Hungarian cultural blend is one of relationship-focus, indirectness in communication and negotiations, formality and hierarchical relations in business interaction, and a high degree of emotional expressiveness. These characteristics are common enough in southern Europe, though not among Hungary's neighbors.

What makes Hungarian business behavior special is that time behavior is monochronic: punctuality is valued, as is adherence to schedules and deadlines. We normally associate such time-consciousness more with northerners (e.g., the Germans and Swiss) than with southern Europeans. In this sense Hungarians are more akin to the Milanese or Catalans than say the Romans or Neapolitans.

From Central Asia to Central Europe. Not surprisingly, geography and history are keys to understanding the Hungarians today. On the map Hungary appears as a non-Slavic wedge separating the southern Slavs (Bulgarians and the peoples of the former Yugoslavia) from those of the north: the Czechs, Slovaks and Poles. As a non-Slavic people surrounded mostly by Slavs, Hungarians sometimes feel like outsiders.

Ethnically most Hungarians are descendants of the warlike Magyars who pushed into Europe a thousand years ago from their original homeland in Central Asia. Thus their language is not an Indo-European tongue but rather part of the Finno-Ugric group, distantly related to the languages spoken by other ancient settlers from Central Asia: the Finns, Estonians and Lapps.

Invaded by the Mongols in 1241, Hungary was also occupied for 150 years by the Turks after losing the decisive battle of Mohacs in 1526. The embattled Hungarians were defeated again in 1849 by the Austrians and Russians, then somehow also managed to end up on the losing side in both World Wars. Centuries of defeats and invasions may explain a tendency to pessimism and cynicism.

Industrialization came late to Hungary, as was the case with the rest of East Central Europe except for the Czech lands. That's why values derived from the landowning nobility and gentry persisted well into the 20th Century, rather than being displaced by a middle-class mindset. In this, Hungarian cultural values resemble those of the Poles rather than for example those of the Czechs.

As with the Polish 'szlachta', the Hungarian nobility and gentry accounted for between 5 and 10 percent of the total population: an unusually large proportion. The persistence of rural, feudal values may account for the formality and hierarchical behavior still found in Hungary today. This contrasts with the Czechs, for example, whose values reflect a more urbanized, middle-class, industrial society. There, industry and commerce were eclipsing agriculture as early as the 1930s, when Hungary was still in a pre-industrial phase of development.

Although Poles and Hungarians share a number of cultural features, they do differ somewhat in terms of religious affiliation. Almost all Poles are Roman Catholics, whereas some 20 percent of Hungarians are Protestants: Calvinists and Lutherans. So when it comes to religion, Hungary again forms a bridge, this time between Catholic Poland and the more Protestant Czech Republic.

Language of Business. Aware that Magyar is hardly a world language, most Hungarian business people today speak either English or German, often both. You can write them for an appointment in either of those languages. But before arriving for a meeting it's a good idea to ask whether you should arrange for an interpreter. Whereas most Hungarian firms employ translators, they don't always have skilled interpreters on board.

Despite the fact that Magyar is a non-European tongue, the language issue is not as big a problem as one might expect. While conducting a seminar on cross-cultural business behavior recently in Pecs, in southern Hungary, I found that each of the participants was fluent in four languages and several could speak five.

Relationships. As with most markets outside northwestern Europe, North America and Australia/New Zealand, it is vital to have the right connections in Hungary. "Who you know" counts for a great deal.

This contrasts with the situation in deal-focused cultures such as that of Germany, where such contacts are always helpful but rarely essential.

Critical business issues need to be discussed face-to-face in Hungary; frequent visits and phone calls are required. Globe-trotting business people will recognize these practices from other relationship-oriented markets, such as those found in most of Asia, the Middle East, Africa, Latin America and much of Eastern Europe. As in Asian markets, you can also expect lengthy, rapport-building preliminary small talk before getting down to business.

Verbal Indirectness. As in most other relationship-focused cultures, when negotiating business in Hungary you will often experience verbal indirectness and polite evasions. Hungarians prefer to avoid rude words such as 'no'. Verbal indirectness is part of what U.S. anthropologist Edward T. Hall calls 'high-context' communication. Low-context people tend to speak directly, frankly, even bluntly. The meaning of what they are saying can be found mostly in the words they are using. In contrast, high-context people prefer to use vague, indirect language, where much of the meaning is found in the context surrounding the words.

High-context Arab, Japanese or Chinese negotiators phrase things indirectly in order not to offend people, couching negative responses in vague, roundabout language for the sake of being polite. Most Hungarian negotiators lean a bit towards this Asian indirectness, which sometimes confuses their counterparts from the low-context cultures of northern Europe and North America.

We will leave it to anthropologists to speculate whether Hungarian indirectness can be traced back to their distant origins in Central Asia. (Maybe not; most Finns are direct.) For visiting business people from low-context cultures, the important thing is to know what to expect.

Formality, Status and Hierarchies. Hungarians are more formal than Scandinavians, Australians or North Americans, more like the Spanish and Germans, for instance. Formality is expressed in the way people dress and in their meeting and greeting rituals. Hierarchies are evident in the top-down approach to management and in the relative scarcity of women business managers.

As in Poland, businesswomen visiting Hungary can expect to be treated by their older male counterparts with Old World charm and gallantry. Among many men of the older generation, hand-kissing is as prevalent as it used to be in Vienna. But on the other hand, some women report feelings of being patronized. Since few Hungarian women have reached positions of authority in business, men may often be unaccustomed to interacting with their female associates on the basis of equality.

Both male and female visitors will note that important decisions are reserved for the top man in the organization. Typical of hierarchical societies, this trait can slow progress and cause delays in negotiations.

Monochronic Time. Most Hungarians value punctuality, schedules and deadlines. They are usually on time for meetings, sometimes even five minutes early, and seldom keep visitors waiting. Visitors are expected to match this behavior.

Emotional Expressiveness. Whereas most Finns, Japanese and Thais for example tend to be reserved, most Italians, Greeks and Latin Americans are more outgoing and expressive. Visitors will find Hungarians closer to the expressive end of the scale.

At the first meeting you can expect a relatively reserved manner, but once the ice is broken Hungarians become more demonstrative. Germans and Austrians for example used to describe them as "fiery, explosive, unpredictable." Expect your counterparts to speak for effect, indulging in exaggeration, overstatement, even bombast. Unlike their immediate Central European neighbors, the verbal behavior of Hungarians is sometimes reminiscent of the Middle East and Latin America.

Paraverbal and Nonverbal Behavior

Because negotiation is actually a specialized form of communication, differences in the way people communicate often cause misunderstandings in the bargaining process. Which is why business visitors should know the basics of Hungarian paraverbal and nonverbal communication. Of course, as with any business culture you will find plenty of individual variation.

Voice volume. Moderate. Avoid raising your voice and pounding the table during negotiations.

Interpersonal distance. Medium -- 15 to 25 inches (25 to 40 cm).

Touch behavior. A moderately high-contact culture socially, when it comes to business touching it is more restrained. Good male friends make cheek-to-cheek contact (first left, then right) while shaking hands when they haven't seen each other for a while. But in a business situation, expect little or no touching except for the handshake.

Eye contact. Direct gaze across the negotiating table: less intense than in the Middle East and southern Europe but much more direct than in East and Southeast Asia.

Business Protocol and Etiquette

Dress Code. Men wear conservative suits and ties; women wear dresses or suits.

Meeting and Greeting. Shake hands, make eye contact and state your name. Shake hands again when leaving the meeting. Wait for a Hungarian woman to extend her hand. Male visitors are not expected to kiss a woman's hand; instead, a slight bow may accompany the handshake.

Forms of Address. When introduced, address your counterparts by their professional or academic title plus family name. Only relatives and close friends address each other by first names.

Exchanging Cards. Your cards should show your organizational title and any advanced degrees. Expect to exchange cards with each business person you meet.

Topics of Conversation. Hungarians regard their country as part of Central Europe rather than of Eastern Europe. The term East-Central Europe is also acceptable. Sports and music as well as Hungarian food and wine are safer topics than politics and religion.

Gift Giving. Business gifts are not expected. Bring imported liquor (not wine), chocolates or a bouquet of flowers when invited to someone's home for a meal. Present the bouquet in its wrapping, remembering to bring an uneven number and avoiding both red roses and chrysanthemums (the former imply romantic intentions, the latter are for funerals).

Business Entertaining. It is a rare honor to be invited to a Hungarian home; be sure to accept. Most business entertaining is done at restaurants.

Wining and Dining. Breakfast is served between 8:00 and 9:00, lunch from 1:00 to 2:00 and the evening meal around 7:00 or 8:00. "Power breakfasts" are not common. Business is also not usually discussed at dinner, which is reserved for relaxing and getting to know one another. You may discuss business over lunch if your local counterparts agree.

Table Manners. Wish everyone at the table "good appetite" before the meal begins. Wait for your host or hostess to start eating. Like all Europeans, Hungarians keep the fork in their left hand rather than switching from left hand to right as Americans do.

Social Etiquette. A man is expected to walk to the left of a woman or of an honored guest of either gender.

Negotiating Style

Your Presentation. To show you are serious, avoid starting off with a joke at the first meeting. As you would in Germany, load your presentation with background information, facts and technical details.

Bargaining Style. Most Hungarian business people seem to enjoy bargaining. Wise negotiators keep a few bargaining chips in reserve until the endgame. Your opening bid should be realistic but at the same time should include enough room for maneuver.

Decision-Making. As in many other cultures, the negotiating process usually takes longer when dealing with the government than when doing business with the private sector.

Group F

Moderately Deal-Focused – Formal – Variably Monochronic – Reserved

Negotiating in the Baltic States

Any country's business culture and bargaining style reflect the underlying values, attitudes and beliefs of the society. Cultural changes take place more slowly and gradually than political and economic changes.

Visiting negotiators familiar with the major European business cultures often comment that the three Baltic states are a microcosm of Europe. As might be expected, the business behavior of Estonians, Latvians and Lithuanians corresponds generally to that of their northern European neighbors: the Scandinavians, Germans, Poles and Russians.

However, first-time visitors may be less prepared for the fact that the Baltic business cultures also reflect the north-south divide of the European continent. Estonians, northernmost of the three, are relatively individualistic, deal-focused, direct in the way they communicate across the bargaining table, and also the most reticent and reserved of the Baltic peoples. These are familiar northern European traits.

The Estonians' reserve and verbal directness as well as their task-focused approach to the business at hand remind many visitors of Swedish negotiators. Perhaps even more so the Finns, to whom the Estonians are in fact ethnically and linguistically related.

At the other extreme, Lithuania is the southernmost of three Baltic lands. Sometimes called 'the Latins of the Baltic region', the Catholic Lithuanians are more group-oriented and relationship-focused than the Estonians. They also tend to be indirect in their communication behavior as well as expressive and outgoing. These are of course familiar to us as southern European characteristics.

The Lutheran Latvians, as befits their geographical location between the other two and the long history of German cultural influence, are in an intermediate position in terms of their business behavior. They are moderately deal-focused, indirect and demonstrative compared to Estonians, but somewhat more direct and more reserved than their Lithuanian cousins to the south.

In other words, expect northern European-type negotiating behavior in the Baltic states, but be prepared for significant intra-regional differences.

Languages of Business. The Latvian and Lithuanian languages belong to the Indo-European language family; Estonian is part of the Finno-Ugric language group, related to Finnish. English-speaking business visitors to Riga and Vilnius will find more of their counterparts speaking English than was the case a few years ago. In general, visitors are more likely to find fluent English-speakers in Latvia than in Lithuania.

German, Russian and Polish are other languages commonly understood in the two countries. But despite the strong Nordic influence in Latvia, few Latvians speak a Scandinavian language. When making appointments, inquire about the need for an interpreter. Your Baltic counterpart will normally be quite willing to arrange for linguistic support should it be necessary.

Business Approach. Compared to relationship-focused Asians, Arabs and Latin Americans, most Latvians and Lithuanians are deal-focused. That is, in Vilnius and especially in Riga you can expect to get down to business fairly quickly. Small talk and preliminaries are not as drawn-out as in southern Europe or the Mediterranean region. Business discussions tend to move along point by point in a linear fashion as in Germany, rather than take off in unexpected directions as often happens in France.

On the other hand, making direct contact with prospective customers and business partners is less effective than in the more strongly deal-focused cultures of North America and northern Europe. Marketers from abroad will have better luck if they have a good referral or introduction, even better luck if they meet prospects at a trade show or on an organized trade mission.

Formality, Status, Hierarchies and Respect. Danish visitors remark that their Baltic counter-parts dress and act more formally than most Scandinavians. Reflective of their hierarchical cultures, Latvians and Lithuanians conduct business in a more formal manner than Americans and the egalitarian Canadians, Australians and Scandinavians. It is important to show a certain degree of respect to older and senior persons.

Punctuality and Scheduling. Business meetings generally start on time; visitors are expected to be punctual. As opposed to more polychronic societies, meetings in Lithuania and Latvia tend not to be interrupted. This is another facet of business behavior which is more Germanic than Latin. Schedules and deadlines are generally adhered to -- of course, always within the limitations imposed by the underdeveloped infrastructure which is characteristic of both countries. As in Scandinavia, if you are invited to someone's home for dinner be sure to arrive on time: no more than five or ten minutes late.

Negotiating Behavior

- Negotiating an agreement is likely to take longer than it would in Western Europe or North America. It takes time to build a climate of trust.
- Finding the right local representative or distributor is the main key to achieving satisfactory results. Having patience is another important key.
- Expect older Latvians and Lithuanians to show the influence of decades of Soviet influence. Many younger Balts are less bureaucratic, more open and more deal-focused.
- Visitors should stay cool, avoid table-pounding and open displays of temper.
- Be prepared for occasional hardball tactics, e.g. brinksmanship. Perhaps due to Soviet tutelage, Balts sometimes try to use an artificial deadline to put pressure on foreign counterparts. The most effective counter is to this tactic is to insist on a *quid pro quo* of equal value for whatever concession your counterparts are pressing for.
- When you do reach agreement, expect it to be formalized in a detailed contract. Take the time to review the document carefully before signing, and insist that the English-language version be the binding one.

Paraverbal and Nonverbal Communication

Voice volume. Like Scandinavians, most Balts speak relatively softly in business situations.

Silence. Long pauses during discussions are found more commonly in Estonia than in Latvia and Lithuania.

Conversational overlap. Interrupting another speaker in mid-sentence is considered rude behavior, especially in Estonia and Latvia. Wait until your counterpart has finished talking before speaking up.

Interpersonal space. Expect the typical northern European-sized space bubble, about an arm's length between people in a business situation, whether standing or seated.

Touch behavior. Little physical touching in a business situation. Expect somewhat more expressiveness after a relationship has been established.

Eye contact. It is polite to maintain a steady (but not intense, "in-your-face") gaze across the conference table, much as one would in Germany or Scandinavia.

Gestures. Especially in Latvia and Estonia, expect controlled facial expressions and few gestures. Avoid hands in pockets while conversing. Chewing gum in public is considered impolite in all three Baltic states.

Women Negotiators. Women business visitors normally encounter few problems in the Baltic markets. To avoid possible misunderstandings, women should avoid behavior which could be construed as flirtatious.

Some older Latvian and Lithuanian men may not be accustomed to negotiating with business women on an equal basis. To ensure being treated with the appropriate level of respect:

Inform your Baltic counterparts of your title and level of responsibility before you arrive for the first meeting.

When you are introduced, make sure your business card clearly states your position.

Find opportunities during the preliminary conversation for you and your associates to further explain your status.

Business Protocol and Etiquette

Dress Code. Neat and conservative. For men, business suit, white or pastel solid-color shirt with a subdued tie. For women, an elegant suit or dress.

Meeting and Greeting. When meeting male counterparts, men should state their name clearly and shake hands firmly, then exchange business cards. Shake hands again when leaving. Men should wait for women to offer their hand. Female business visitors who feel comfortable shaking hands should feel free to do so. For both sexes: Bring plenty of business cards; give one to each person attending the meeting.

Forms of Address. Expect to use your counterpart's family name and professional title, if any. Avoid use of first names until your Baltic counterpart clearly invites you to do so.

Gift Giving. Business gifts are welcome but not expected. If invited to someone's home, bring flowers in an odd number, and remember to unwrap the bouquet before offering it to your hostess. Other good choices are imported wine, cognac or good chocolates.

Wining and Dining. Business entertainment normally takes place outside the home, at lunch or dinner. A few younger Baltic businessmen may feel comfortable talking business over breakfast.

Group G

Deal-Focused – Moderately Formal – Monochronic – Reserved

The British Negotiator

In view of the significant regional differences within Great Britain, it's important to note that this profile focuses on the negotiating behavior of business people in England. For the sake of variety we will use 'Britain' and 'England' as well as 'British' and 'English' interchangeably.

Visiting negotiators from Asia, the Mediterranean region, Africa and Latin America can expect to do business with deal-focused, individualistic, direct, reserved, monochronic counterparts. But German, Swiss and Scandinavian visitors instead find the English moderately relationship-focused, indirect, hierarchical and mildly polychronic. In contrast, U.S. negotiators see the Brits as reserved, formal, class-conscious and relaxed about time and scheduling.

All of these conflicting descriptions are correct. British negotiators do tend to be direct, deal-focused and time-obsessed compared to most Latins, Arabs and Asians. At the same time however, they are also more indirect, relationship-oriented and relaxed about time than northern Europeans, as well as more formal and reserved than Americans.

Language of Business. Few Britishers today speak another language well enough to handle a serious business negotiation. Visitors not fluent in English should consider hiring an interpreter.

Making Contact. Famously a land of "old school ties" and the "old boys' network," Britain is a market where referrals, recommendations and testimonials are extremely useful. If you do not have such connections, address your letter to the owner of a small company or to the Chairman or Managing Director of a larger firm. My advice is to phone the executive's secretary before writing to get the correct name and exact title of the addressee. Trade shows, trade missions and chamber of commerce introductions are good ways to get in touch with potential customers and partners.

Write in English with basic information about your company and your product, adding that you will contact them soon to set up an appointment. Follow this with a phone call requesting a meeting two or three weeks hence. Your British counterpart will suggest the time and place.

Moderately Deal-Focused. Brits usually want to chat with a new business contact at some length before getting down to business. Visitors are well advised to wait for their local counterpart to initiate the business part of the meeting. The English need to get to know their overseas counterparts a bit before talking business. In contrast, some Germans, Swiss, Scandinavians, and Americans become impatient with what they regard as unnecessarily long preliminary conversations.

Orientation to Time. The pace of business life in London is somewhat leisurely relative to that of Hong Kong or New York. And while visitors are expected to be on time, locals are often a few minutes late for meetings. Still, the British are definitely clock-obsessed compared with most Latins, Arabs and Africans as well as the majority of South and Southeast Asians.

Formality, Hierarchies and Status Differences. Status in England is largely determined by one's regional origin, social class, family background and accent. This contrasts with the situation in the U.S., for example, where personal achievement is regarded as more important than one's class or family tree. It also differs from Australia and the Nordic countries, where people are uncomfortable with obvious status differences. The existence of relatively large status distinctions explains the formality in social interaction noted by Australian, American and Scandinavian visitors. While Americans for example like to switch almost immediately to the use of given names in business meetings, the English usually prefer to stay with Mr. or Mrs. until at least the second or third meeting.

That said, visitors find that younger English business people are becoming less formal. Today it is increasingly common to hear a Brit introduce himself as "Bob" or herself as "Mary" in a telephone conversation. And, as elsewhere, the rapidly growing use of electronic mail acts to 'informalize' the communication process.

Communication Style. In common with their German, Dutch and Scandinavian neighbors, the English are reserved rather than expressive or demonstrative in the way they communicate. This is evident in their use of understatement, large space bubble, low-contact body language, restrained gestures, and in their preference for always keeping a "stiff upper lip."

The British may appear somewhat more expressive and extroverted than the Japanese, but they come across as reserved and introverted compared with the Latins of Europe and the Americas.

Verbal Communication. Negotiators from the high-context cultures of East Asia, the Arab world, and Latin America are sometimes offended by what they regard as overly direct language, especially in northern England. But on the other hand, Dutch, German and Swedish visitors may be puzzled by the vague, indirect, roundabout language they encounter. Fact is, the British occupy an in-between position among the world's cultures when it comes to verbal directness.

Part of visitors' confusion stems from class differences. Many upperclass Brits seem to value vague, oblique language, while others speak more directly. Visiting negotiators should be mentally prepared to encounter either verbal style.

Paraverbal Communication. British negotiators rarely interrupt their counterparts across the bargaining table. They are also less likely to raise their voice than are negotiators from more expressive societies such as those in southern Europe and Latin America.

Nonverbal Communication

The Handshake. When meeting and greeting, a light handshake is common. The British normally do not shake hands with colleagues upon meeting in the morning and again when leaving the office, as is common practice in some Continental cultures.

Spatial Behavior. The normal interpersonal distance in a business context is about an arm's length. The British tend to stand and sit further apart than Arabs and Latins. Moreover, two Englishmen in conversation will often stand at a 90-degree angle to each other, rather than facing each other directly as two Italians or two Arabs usually do.

Direct, face-to-face conversation seems to make some Brits uncomfortable.

Gaze Behavior. Eye contact tends to be less direct than in emotionally expressive cultures such as Italy and Brazil. A very direct gaze may be interpreted as rude and intrusive.

Touch Behavior. This is a low-contact culture. Except for the handshake, most English people avoid touching others in public. For example, the American custom of back-slapping, elbow-grabbing and arm-around-the-shoulder is considered slightly vulgar.

Gestures. As is the case with other reserved cultures, the British use relatively few hand and arm gestures. When flashing the two-finger 'peace' sign, make sure your palm is facing outward. With palm inward this is an obscene gesture. Avoid pointing with your index finger; instead indicate direction with a nod of your head.

Business Protocol

Dress Code. Men wear a dark suit, plain shirt, conservative tie and polished black shoes. Avoid striped ties: they can be seen as imitating prestigious British regimental ties. The black shoes should be of the laced type rather than loafers, which are considered too casual. Natural fibers are considered more acceptable than synthetics. Women should likewise dress conservatively, avoiding garish colors and too much jewelry.

Meeting and Greeting. While men exchange light handshakes, some women chose not to offer their hand. Men should always wait for the woman to extend her hand.

Forms of Address. Use Mr, Mrs., Miss or Ms. until your counterpart suggests switching to given names. Medical doctors, dentists and clergy expect to be addressed with their titles, but a male surgeon is plain Mister. Visitors accustomed to saying "Yes sir" and "No sir" as a sign of respect to older or senior people should avoid this practice in Britain.

Business Gifts. This is not a gift-giving culture. It's better to invite your counterparts to dinner.

Social Etiquette

Hostess Gifts. If invited to an English home, bring chocolates, liquor, champagne or flowers. Avoid white lilies (only for funerals) and red roses (unless you wish to signal a romantic interest). Be sure to send along a handwritten thank-you note the next day. During the meal keep both hands on the table but both elbows off the table.

Wining and Dining. Pub lunches are customary for business entertainment while dinners tend to be more of a social event. Avoid talking business unless your British counterpart clearly initiates such a discussion.

Pub Etiquette. Patrons take turn ordering drinks. When ordering drinks at the bar, catch the publican's eye and say, "Another pint, please!" rather than shouting or silently holding up your glass for a refill. In fact, 'please' and 'thank you' are very important words throughout Britain.

Negotiating Style

Your Presentation. Accustomed to understatement, British buyers are turned off by hype and exaggerated claims. Presentations should be straight-forward and factual. Humor is acceptable, but visitors from abroad should remember that it rarely translates well. The safest humor in England is of the self-deprecatory variety.

Bargaining Range. English negotiators have been doing business all over the world for hundreds of years. They may put a wide safety margin in their opening position so as to leave room for substantial concessions during the bargaining process. This practice may put off negotiators from Germany and Sweden, where this 'high-low' tactic is frowned upon.

Decision-Making. Some "time is money" Americans may find the British process too time-consuming, but for the rest of the world's business cultures it is quite normal.

Role of the Contract. Expect emphasis on the legal aspects and the fine points of the written agreement. Should a dispute or disagreement arise later the British tend to rely on the terms of the contract and could become suspicious if their counterpart invokes non-contract issues such as the importance of the long-term relationship.

The Irish Negotiator
(Eire: Republic of Ireland)

Visitors used to doing business in Britain will find the similarities in business behavior in the Republic of Ireland more numerous than the differences. However, the differences are big enough to get in the way unless we are prepared.

Relationships. Americans used to cold calls and "one-call closings" may be surprised by the much greater amount of relationship-building they will need to do business successfully in Ireland. Here are some proven ways for deal-focused people to build effective relationships in this market:

- Expect to socialize before, during, and after sit-down bargaining sessions.
- Important issues should always be handled in face-to-face meetings rather than over the phone or by written communication.
- Whenever a significant amount of time (a month or more) has elapsed since the last face-to-face get-together, the visitors should start the session with plenty of social chit-chat on subjects of mutual interest. This should be followed by references to what has happened since the last meeting.
- When making new contacts, consider arranging to be introduced by an influential third party. If someone on your team has an 'Irish connection' – close or distant relatives – this will facilitate the trust-building process.
- It is very important for visitors to avoid anything which might be interpreted as showing off. Like Australians, the Irish warm to people who come across as modest and unassuming.

Formality and Social Hierarchies. In general the Irish are much less class-conscious than the British. Most people use first names in a social setting, but when meeting Irish business people for the first time it's a good idea to let them suggest moving to first names. It is appropriate to use professional and academic titles such as Professor or Doctor, although as in Britain surgeons only rate "Mr."

Orientation to Time. The pace of life in Ireland is a bit slower than in Germany or the U.S., even in Dublin. Schedules and deadlines may not be rigidly adhered to, and your counterparts may be late for appointments, but the Irish still expect foreign visitors to be on time for business meetings.

Communication Behavior. Visitors find their Irish counterparts somewhat reserved at first, although more gregarious and expressive than the British. People in Ireland usually loosen up rather quickly over a few pints of Guinness – one more reason to spend time in pubs!

The Irish tend to be less direct than Scandinavians or Americans, often avoiding a blunt 'yes' or 'no' in response to a question. Directness seems to be equated with rudeness, especially among Irish people born and raised outside of the capital city. Dubliners are somewhat more direct in speech and writing.

Business Protocol

Meeting and Greeting. A firm handshake with good eye contact is the norm. Shake hands when you are introduced, when you meet and when you take leave of people you don't know well, and when you meet a friend you haven't seen for quite a while.

Touch Behavior. This is a low-contact culture. Except for the handshake, most Irish people avoid touching others in public. The American custom of back-slapping, elbow-grabbing and arm-around-the-shoulder is out of place unless the contact is initiated by your Irish counterparts.

Gestures. Expect few hand and arm gestures. When flashing the two-finger 'peace' sign, make sure your palm is facing outward. With palm inward this becomes an obscene gesture.

Dress Code. Business people generally dress less formally than in the UK or in most parts of the continent. However, visitors are well advised to dress conservatively for the first meeting with new counterparts.

Business Gifts. While this is not a gift-giving culture, small gifts such as pens, books, desk accessories and ties may be exchanged at the successful conclusion of negotiations.

Social Etiquette

Queue Behavior. As you would in Britain, always take your place in lines.

Hostess Gifts. If invited to an Irish home for a meal, bring a small gift such as chocolates, liquor, champagne or flowers. An invitation to 'tea' can mean either just that, but it can also mean a full meal. If in doubt, ask. Remember to send a thank-you note.

Pub Etiquette. Pub lunches are customary for business entertainment. Patrons take turns ordering drinks. Keep track of rounds, pay for yours when it's your turn. People who pay for extra rounds are seen as show-offs. Refusing a drink is a major insult. Traditional Irishmen expect women to order a glass (half a pint) rather than a pint of beer. Toasts: "Cheers" is good. "Slainte" (SLAHN-chah), good luck, is more formal.

Negotiating Behavior

Your Presentation. Irish business people are turned off by hype and exaggerated claims. Presentations should be straightforward and factual. Humor is acceptable, but remember that jokes and humor translate poorly across cultures. The safest humor in Ireland is of the self-deprecatory variety.

Bargaining Range. Beware of putting too wide a safety margin in your opening position. This tactic may convince the Irish you are the wrong business partner.

Overcoming Negotiating Obstacles. Be relaxed, friendly and as humble as possible. The Irish have a very long memory for perceived slights and for what they regard as unfair dealings in the past. The best way to overcome this tough obstacle is to (a) build strong, trusting relationships and to (b) structure the new deal so as to offer plenty of WIN to the Irish side.

Decision-Making. Americans may find the Irish negotiating process time-consuming, but in relation to the rest of the world's business cultures it is quite normal.

The Danish Negotiator

The Danish business culture is deal-focused, more so than the British, a bit less than the Germans, distinctly less than Americans. Danish negotiators also tend to be moderately informal, monochronic, and relatively reserved.

Deal Focus. Business visitors can anticipate certain negotiating behaviors. You can contact a Danish company directly to make an appointment rather than going through an intermediary. Having the right contacts and personal connections can be helpful, but is less important in Denmark than in the classically relationship-oriented cultures of Asia, Latin America and the Middle East.

If you are offering the right product or service at the right price and quality, a deal can usually be closed in less time than is the case in RF markets. For example, when our Global Management consultancy helped a U.S. manufacturer crack the Japanese market, it took two and a half years from the first (indirect) contact for us to land the first order. At about the same time we aided another American company in the same industry get started in Denmark. In that case we were able to contact potential importers directly, and the first contract was signed just six weeks later.

At the first meeting Danes usually get down to business after a few minutes of small talk. They get to know their counterparts while talking business, whereas in RF cultures such as China and the Arab world the visitor must take more time to build rapport first.

Danes are direct. They normally say what they mean and mean what they say; in RF cultures people often favor vague, indirect, oblique language so as to avoid offending one's counterparts.

Informal, Egalitarian. Visitors find the Danes very egalitarian and hence relatively informal in contrast to business behavior in more formal, hierarchical cultures. It is not necessary to show special deference or overt respect to people of high status. Danes address each other informally, usually employing the familiar pronoun 'du' and first names even when meeting counterparts for the first time. In most firms they also often dress relatively informally for business meetings.

Visitors encounter relatively few etiquette rituals in Denmark, whereas people in more formal, hierarchical societies value rituals as ways to ease interaction between strangers and to show appropriate respect to high-status persons.

Danes tend to be governed to some extent by the Nordic egalitarian code of conduct called *Jantelov*. This 'Law of Jante' ordains that no one should set himself or herself up as better, smarter or richer than anyone else.

Monochronic Time. Business cultures differ markedly in the way they use time. Denmark is a rigid-time culture as opposed to the fluid-time cultures of the Mediterranean region, the Middle East, South and Southeast Asia and most of Latin America. Edward T. Hall classified cultures as monochronic (rigid-time) and polychronic (fluid-time).

Meetings usually begin on time. Business visitors are rarely kept waiting. Schedules and deadlines are firm. Negotiations are rarely interrupted. Most Danes consider it rude if meetings are frequently interrupted by phone calls or other intrusions.

Emotionally Reserved Communication Style

Danes tend to be relatively restrained in their style of paraverbal and nonverbal communication compared with emotionally expressive Latin Europeans, Latin Americans, and many North Americans. This cultural characteristic can lead to confusion during international negotiations with more expressive counterparts.

Many Danes are so self-effacing and modest, they often mumble their name when introducing themselves. Moreover they typically understate their achievements and make a lot of self-deprecating remarks.

Indeed, it would be fair to say that modesty is a national characteristic of Danes – who may in turn be put off by the breezy self-confidence and self-promotion they see in people from certain other cultures. Foreign visitors will make a far more favorable first impression by letting the Danes find out for themselves how smart they are.

Paraverbal Language. Danes are relatively soft-spoken compared with people from more expressive cultures, though not so soft-spoken as for example the Japanese. Some Latins and Arabs misinterpret the restrained speech as lack of interest in the discussion. Visitors are unlikely to experience the long gaps in conversation often encountered in more reserved cultures such as Finland and Japan.

While in southern Europe and South America conversational overlap is accepted practice, Danes consider interrupting people rude behavior.

Nonverbal Language. Most Danes stand at an arm's length distance from conversational partners in business gatherings. In contrast, expressive Latins and Arabs step in closer, causing discomfort and stress to any Danes who are unaware of this difference.

Latins and Mediterranean peoples engage in much more physical contact than the reserved, low-contact Danes. Visitors from high-contact cultures may interpret Danish reserve as coldness or arrogance.

Danes normally engage in moderate gaze behavior while Arabs and Latins favor strong eye contact across the bargaining table. The Japanese, most Chinese and most Southeast Asians on the other hand avoid a direct gaze, which is perceived as rude, hostile, perhaps even threatening. Many Chinese and Southeast Asians characterize direct eye contact as 'fierce' gaze behavior.

Whereas the expressive Latins employ numerous vigorous hand and arm gestures and facial expressions during negotiations, most Danes employ a more restrained body language.

Business Protocol

Dress Code. Danish business people tend to dress relatively informally at the office, although this varies from one company to another. Male business visitors can perhaps be a bit more relaxed than when are meeting their German, French or British counterparts, but should still wear suit or jacket and tie to the first meeting. Women negotiators should wear a suit or dress.

Meeting and Greeting. Expect a firm handshake and steady, moderate eye contact. Business cards are normally exchanged with one hand. Address your counterparts with their surname until they suggest moving to first names, which often happens fairly early in the business relationship.

Wining and Dining. Most Danes are friendly, generous hosts. Business entertaining is done at lunch or dinner, rarely over breakfast. Among other things, Denmark is famous for *smørrebrød,* a selection of delicious open-faced sandwiches, often washed down with good local beer.

Gift Giving. Business gifts are less common here than in relationship-focused cultures. Bring a quality logo gift, an item your country is famous for, or a good book about your home country. If invited for dinner at home, bring wine or flowers. Flowers should be presented wrapped.

Negotiating Behavior

Business Presentations. Danish managers tend to be irritated by "hard sell" tactics. They react better to a well-documented, straightforward approach with no exaggerated claims.

Bargaining Style. Many Danes dislike that common international negotiating tactic, the 'high-low' gambit – starting off with a highly inflated initial offer. Business visitors fresh from negotiating in the Middle East, China or Brazil where negotiators expect this tactic will do better opening with a more realistic offer in Denmark.

Equally irritating to Danes is the use of artificial deadlines as a pressure tactic. "You've got to make your decision this week! Next Monday we are putting through an across-the-board price increase. Sorry about that ..."

The Contract. Danish companies regard the written agreement as definitive and refer to it whenever subsequent disagreements arise. In contrast, many people from RF cultures regard the contract as renegotiable. Chinese negotiators for example may depend on the relationship rather than the contract to solve eventual problems and disputes.

The Norwegian Negotiator

Visitors from northern Europe and North America find it easy to do business in Norway, partly because so many Norwegians today speak English and partly because the business practices are familiar. In contrast, visitors from most of Asia, Africa and Latin America may be puzzled by some differences in day-to-day business behavior in Norway.

Language of Business. Most Norwegians speak and read English fluently; many speak German or French as well. Visitors negotiators who do not command English will have no problem arranging for a competent interpreter in the major cities.

Making Contact. Although references and introductions are useful anywhere, you can also contact Norwegians companies directly to make an appointment. Intermediaries are less important than in the relationship-focused business cultures of Asia, Latin America, and the Middle East.

At the initial meeting Norwegians are usually ready to talk business after only a few minutes of small talk. Chit-chat and general conversation do not represent an important part of doing business in this culture. Norwegians get to know their counterparts while talking business, whereas in relationship-focused cultures visitors must take more time to build rapport.

Verbal Directness. Norwegians are used to frank, straight-forward language. This is in contrast to the indirect, roundabout language common in much of Asia, Latin America and the Middle East. On the other hand, most Norwegians are somewhat less direct than Germans. For instance, when not really interested in a particular deal, they may be reluctant to say that bluntly. In this they resemble many British negotiators.

Informality. Business visitors find Norwegians very egalitarian and less formal than people from more hierarchical cultures. For example, they are informal compared to Germans, although somewhat more formal than many Danes. It is okay for visitors to introduce themselves to their counterparts rather than waiting to be formally introduced by a secretary.

Although Norwegians usually address each other rather informally, first names are less commonly used than in the U.S. Wait for your local counterpart to suggest switching to first names. Expect fewer protocol rituals than in more formal, hierarchical societies.

Punctuality and Schedules. Business meetings start on time in Norway. If you going to be a few minutes late, call your counterpart to explain the problem and advise your new arrival time. It is polite for visitors to suggest a probable ending time for the first meeting, if possible. This allows your counterparts to plan their day. Meetings are rarely interrupted by phone calls or other intrusions.

Schedules and deadlines are firm. Norwegians quickly lose interest in dealing with business partners who fail to meet their obligations in a timely manner.

A note about social punctuality would be in order here. My wife, Hopi, and I lived in Singapore during the early 1990s. When we were invited along with several other couples to a seven o'clock dinner at the home of the Norwegian ambassador, all but one couple arrived a few minutes before seven. The guests stood around outside chatting with each other until exactly 7:00 pm, when one of the Scandinavian guests rang the bell. A few minutes later dinner was served, and by the time the tardy couple arrived, dinner was half over. You can be sure those two embarrassed people arrived right on the dot the next time they were invited to a Norwegian home for dinner!

Emotionally Reserved Communication Style

Although a warm and friendly people, most Norwegians are restrained in their paraverbal and nonverbal communication compared to expressive Latin Europeans and Latin Americans, as well as to many North Americans. Latins and Arabs for example sometimes misinterpret Nordic reticence as lack of interest in the discussion.

Paraverbal Communication. Norwegians tend to be soft-spoken and taciturn compared with Southern Europeans, though not compared to the Japanese. On the other hand, business visitors will not experience the long gaps in conversation encountered in even more-reserved cultures such as Finland and Japan. While in Latin Europe and South America it is acceptable to interrupt another speaker at meetings, in Norway this is regarded as rude behavior.

Nonverbal Communication. As is the case in other reserved cultures, Norwegians tend to stand at an arm's length distance from conversational partners in business gatherings. In contrast, expressive Latins and Arabs may step in much closer, causing discomfort and stress to locals who are unaware of this cultural difference.

Expect little touching in a business situation except for the handshake. Avoid arm-grabbing and backslapping. Visitors from expressive, high-contact cultures should not misinterpret Nordic reserve as coldness or arrogance.

At the bargaining table Norwegians normally employ moderate gaze behavior, i.e. alternately looking their counterparts in the eye and then looking away. This may confuse Arabs and Latins, who are accustomed to strong, steady eye contact. The obverse is that Norwegian gaze behavior may confuse the Japanese and many Southeast Asians. Negotiators from these cultures are used to soft, indirect eye contact and might equate the Scandinavian gaze with staring, which is perceived as rude or hostile.

While emotionally expressive Latins employ numerous vigorous hand and arm gestures and facial expressions during negotiations, Norwegians use few gestures. As in some other European and Latin American cultures, the 'A-OK' thumb-and-forefinger circle gesture is considered rude.

Business Protocol and Etiquette

Appointments. Office hours are normally from 8:00 or 9:00 am to 4:00 pm Monday through Friday. Summer hours are from 8:00 am to 3:00 pm. Avoid July and August, the week before and the week after Christmas, and the week before Easter as well as May 17 and 18. Be aware that if a public holiday falls on a Thursday, Norwegians are likely to take Friday off. They also like to leave the office promptly at closing time.

Dress Code. Male business visitors can be a bit more relaxed than when meeting German, French or Spanish counterparts, but should still wear a suit or jacket and tie to the first meeting. Women negotiators may wear a suit, dress or dressy pants.

Meeting and Greeting. Despite that Nordic reserve, expect a warm, friendly welcome. The greeting will be accompanied by a firm, brief handshake and steady, moderate eye contact. Shake hands with each person present and again when leaving. Some Norwegians may regard the American greeting, "How are you?" as a personal question which requires a detailed response. Better are impersonal expressions such as "Good morning" or "Good afternoon."

The Name Game. When introduced for the first time, address your counterpart by his or her full name. Americans and Australians need to remember to stay with surnames and titles until their Norwegian counterparts suggest moving to first names. Male visitors should not be surprised if they are addressed by their surname alone. While "Good morning, Smith" would be considered rude in North America, it is quite acceptable in Norway.

Titles. Professional titles such as Doctor and Professor are used, followed by the family name, whereas business titles such as 'Director' are not used. It is appropriate to address government officials with their titles.

Conversation. Norwegians appreciate modesty and a certain degree of humility. They consider flaunting wealth or success to be in poor taste. Be sure to avoid comments which could be taken as boastful or self-promoting. Good topics of conversation include hobbies, politics, travel and sports, especially winter sports such as skiing. Avoid criticism of peoples or cultures: Norwegians value tolerance and charity. Also to be avoided are comments about the high cost of living in Norway; your local counterparts are tired of hearing about it.

Gift Giving. Except for Christmas presents and tasteful logo items, this is not a gift-giving business culture. However, upon successful completion of negotiations, a bottle of quality cognac or whiskey will be welcome. Make sure your gift is neatly wrapped in quality paper.

Business Entertaining. Norwegians very often invite visitors out for meals. Business entertaining is done at lunch or dinner, rarely over breakfast. If the meeting takes place in the late morning, you may invite your local counterpart for lunch. However, be ready to yield graciously to an invitation from the Norwegian side. Here, the person who invites pays the bill.

To catch the waiter's attention, raise your hand with the index finger extended. It is okay to discuss business during lunch. At a business dinner it is polite to wait for the host to bring up business matters.

It is perfectly acceptable for a female business visitor to invite a male counterpart to dinner, and she normally will have no problem paying the bill. A woman alone will also feel comfortable in a restaurant or bar.

Formal Toasting. Usually the host makes a short speech and proposes the first toast. Guests look into the eyes of the person being toasted, give a slight nod and say 'Skål'. Before putting your glass down, look into the person's eyes again and nod. Both women and men may offer toasts. Guests may toast the hostess by saying 'Takk' (thank you).

Social Etiquette. It is not uncommon for visitors to be invited home for a meal. Dinner is commonly eaten between 5:00 and 6:00 pm. Be on time. If you are going to be more than a few minutes late, call.

Guests should wait at the door until invited to enter. It is polite to remain standing until the hostess is seated and to start eating only after the host invited everyone to begin. It is customary to thank the hostess by saying, 'Takk for maten'. Guests from some East Asian cultures should remember that it impolite to leave soon after dinner. Expect to leave around 10:00 pm in the winter, about 11:00 pm in the summer. Unless your hosts are smokers, do not light up in a Norwegian home or office without asking permission.

It is polite to bring chocolates, pastries, wine, liquor or flowers. Avoid lilies, carnations and all white flowers, which are more appropriate for funerals. Present the gift to the lady of the house, who is likely to open it upon receipt.

Negotiating Behavior

Sales Presentation. Scandinavian business people tend to be irritated by "hard sell" tactics. They react better to a well-documented, straightforward approach without hype or exaggerated claims.

Humor. In contrast to some other northern European cultures such as Germany, humor is quite acceptable during presentations. Jokes and casual conversation mix well with serious business discussions. But remember that because it is strongly culture-specific, humor often does not translate well. Self-deprecating humor is perhaps the least likely to offend.

Bargaining Style. Avoid the negotiating tactic known as the 'high-low' gambit: starting off with a highly inflated initial offer and then offering price reductions. Business visitors accustomed to doing business in cultures where this tactic is popular, will be more successful in Norway opening with a realistic offer.

Using artificial deadlines as a pressure tactic is also likely to backfire. Far worse however would be to offer, directly or indirectly, any kind of inducement which could be taken as a bribe. Norway and its Scandinavian neighbors consistently rank at the top of any list of corruption-free business cultures – one more reason why visitors find Norway a pleasant place to do business.

The Contract. The written agreement is regarded as definitive when subsequent business disagreements arise. Norwegians may react negatively if an international counterpart relies on the strength of the relationship between the two sides to renegotiate terms after the contract has been signed, an approach employed by some East Asian firms. Norwegians may also be irritated by negotiators who insist on having a lawyer sit with them at the bargaining table. It is better to keep legal advisors in the background until it's time to finalize the agreement.

The Swedish Negotiator

Twice as large in population as their Nordic neighbors, Sweden boasts a strong engineering industry led by big companies such as Ericsson, Volvo and Electrolux. As is the case with all cultures, the country's business behavior is a direct reflection of societal values. If you know that Swedes value equality, efficiency and modesty, for example, it helps you anticipate what will happen across the bargaining table in Stockholm or Göteborg. Here are some clues to Swedish business behavior.

Egalitarianism and Informal Business Interaction. A continuum with egalitarian cultures on one side and hierarchical cultures on the other would show Sweden located at the extreme end of the egalitarian side, where it is joined only by the other Nordic cultures, Australia, New Zealand, and North America. That means that almost all of the world's other 5500 cultures interact in business in a more hierarchical, formal way than Swedes do.

Swedes have been equality-minded for a very long time. As far back as the pre-Christian era, for instance, the Vikings already showed little regard for rank and status differences. Boat crews often elected their captains, and in 930 the Vikings who settled Iceland during the first millennium established the world's first democratic legislative assembly. Slavery was abolished in 1355; it took five more centuries for the British and Americans to take the same step.

When the Viking men were at sea, the women took charge back home, fully responsible for managing the family farm. Norse women even then could own and inherit property and were free to divorce their husbands. With a background like that it's no surprise to find well-educated, self-confident women making decisions as managers and executives of Swedish companies.

Egalitarian values also show up in the flat structure of the Swedish management model. Top executives do not hesitate to communicate directly with junior employees. And the informal way Swedes communicate with each other along with the simplicity of business protocol are further products of this strong belief in equality.

Since most of the world's business people are more hierarchical than Swedes, possibilities for misunderstandings exist. If visitors from more formal, hierarchical cultures are not treated with the deference they are accustomed to back home, they need to remember that in the Scandinavian countries lack of deference does *not* mean lack of respect.

Deal Focus. Here it's the Americans who are at the extreme end of the cultural spectrum, but Sweden is one of only a small handful of transaction-oriented, deal-focused business cultures. Whereas companies in relationship-focused markets do not do business with strangers, Swedish firms are quite open to approaches from companies they have never heard of. And Swedes usually respond positively to requests for meetings without a third-party introduction or recommendation, provided of course that the business proposal makes sense.

Another key difference between DF and RF business behavior: visitors from the relationship-oriented cultures of Asia, Africa, and the Middle East may be surprised when their counterparts in Stockholm are ready to talk business at the first meeting after only a very few minutes of chit-chat. The efficient Swedes like to get down to business right away. Even more so than the Germans they dislike small talk, which they refer to as *dödprat* (dead talk).

Verbal Directness. Business visitors from relationship-focused cultures such as China or Japan may also be shocked by Swedish bluntness, which may be perceived as rudeness by negotiators used to polite evasions and circumlocution. Swedes conducting business in Shanghai or Tokyo sometimes have to remind themselves to phrase things more indirectly to avoid causing offense and loss of face. In general, Swedes are as careful as Asians are to avoid conflict and confrontation at the bargaining table.

Nevertheless, Nordic bluntness does sometimes unintentionally cause offense. In our Global Management seminars we use a case involving a young Swedish engineer on his first visit to China. Engaged in a joint-venture negotiation in Shanghai, Sven realized that the head of the Chinese negotiating team didn't understand one clause of the proposed agreement. To clear up the misunderstanding the Swede turned to the 55-year old senior engineer and said brightly,

"I see you don't understand this clause. Let me explain it to you briefly ..."

Afterwards Sven was surprised when the Chinese side fell silent, and then adjourned the meeting without setting a date for the next session. That evening he had to call his home office to report that after a very promising beginning, negotiations had now suddenly broken down.

Of course, sometimes it's the direct Swedes who are confused by relationship-focused Asian indirectness. An example is what happened when an export sales representative from Stockholm attended a trade show in Guangzhou. Erik was pleased when a manager from a big Chinese company showed interest in the products displayed in his Swedish firm's booth. They discussed specs, delivery, quality and payment terms as well as price, and Erik answered numerous questions.

When the Swede suggested he visit Mr. Wang's office the next afternoon to discuss a possible sales agreement, the Chinese replied, "Well yes, but I will be quite busy tomorrow." Hearing mostly the "yes" part, Erik went to the his prospect's office the following day and was disappointed to hear that Mr. Wang was "in a meeting that will take the rest of the day." At the hotel bar that evening a Scandinavian expatriate manager explained to Erik that in China, "Yes, but ..." really means "No."

Emotionally Reserved Communication Style

Emotionally reserved communication is another source of cross-cultural confusion, though this time the Swedes have plenty of company. Most northern Europeans, including Scandinavians, as well as East and Southeast Asians, prefer to avoid open displays of emotion. That contrasts with the emotionally expressive southern Europeans, Latin Americans and Middle Easterners, who show emotion freely when they communicate. This difference can cause trouble when reserved and expressive negotiators are trying to reach agreement at face-to-face business meetings.

Paraverbal Language. Swedes are relatively soft-spoken compared to expressive Italians, Greeks and Spaniards. They may be startled or upset if a negotiator from an expressive culture shouts or pounds the table during a meeting. On the other hand, visitors from the Middle

East or southern Europe are often confused by Scandinavian reserve. They wonder what's going on.

Then there's the problem of conversational overlap. Some years ago researchers recorded many hours of negotiations between Swedish and Spanish companies meeting in Stockholm. Playing back the tapes they found that the Spaniards interrupted their Nordic counterparts five times as often as the Swedes interrupted the Spaniards. Here the problem is that for people raised in a reserve culture, frequent interruptions are irritating, even insulting.

Personally I understand how the Swedish negotiators reacted to these frequent interruptions. As an American of mostly Scandinavian extraction, I was taught that people should take turns when conversing, like the players in a table-tennis match. But as a manager in Florence, when I had four Italians in my office for a meeting, sometimes all four would be talking at the same time.

Nonverbal Language. The reserved Swedes maintain an arms-length distance at business meetings, while expressive counterparts like to move in close. Swedes also smile less than Americans and Latins. Touch behavior is limited to the handshake. Eye contact is less intense than that employed by Arabs, for example, but stronger than many East and Southeast Asians are comfortable with.

Expect to see few gestures; Swedes do not talk with their hands. A toss of the head is body language for "come here."

Related to the Swedish reserved manner of communicating is their famous sense of modesty and moderation. The word *lagom* is difficult to translate, but has to do with "moderation in everything." Boasting and self-promotion are regarded very negatively. So the recent explosion of interest in "elevator speeches" in the U.S.B learning how to "sell yourself" to your boss or a senior executive in 30 seconds – would be regarded as a vulgar display. Modesty, humility and a lack of assertiveness are very positive traits in Sweden.

Time Behavior. Swedes pride themselves on being punctual and on adhering to schedule, and expect their business partners to do the same. Business visitors from polychronic cultures, where people are more relaxed about clocks and calendars, should take note.

Business Protocol and Social Etiquette

Dress Code. Conservative. Suit and tie for men, at least at the first meeting. Suit or dress for women.

Meeting and Greeting. Expect a firm handshake. Address people by Mr., Miss or Mrs. plus their family name until invited to move to first names. With younger people this is likely to happen sooner. Address professionals with the appropriate title plus family name, e.g. Doctor Johansson, Engineer Ericsson.

Business Entertainment. Business lunches and dinners are held at formal restaurants. Spouses are invited to business dinners but usually not to lunches. Unlike in many parts of southern Europe, it is common to see businesswomen pick up the check. Although Swedish etiquette is generally informal, toasting is an exception. Usually the host is the first to propose a toast, followed by the senior people present. Wait until you hear your host say "skoal" before taking a sip of your drink.

Business Gifts. Despite recent reforms, alcohol is still expensive in Sweden, so good wine, cognac, or whiskey make fine gifts.

Social Etiquette. Bring a bouquet of flowers and candy for the children when invited to a Swedish home. If you are seated next to the hostess as the guest of honor, get ready to make a speech.

The Swedish Negotiating Style

Your Presentation. If you normally employ "hard sell" tactics, think again. Swedes consider themselves intelligent enough to understand the good and bad points in your proposal.

Bargaining Range. Your initial quote should be realistic. Opening with an inflated number to give you "bargaining room" is likely to backfire in Sweden.

The Contract. Swedish companies consider written agreements definitive, and may not take kindly to a request to renegotiate a recently-signed contract.

Danes and Swedes Through American Eyes

"The Oresund Connection: Bridging A Culture Gap?"

In his *Financial Times* piece of 28 October 2000, Nigel Andrews quotes Bille August on cultural differences: "The differences, especially between the Danes and southern Swedes, are not as strong as people say. . . There's a friendly rivalry, as between any neighbor countries, and perhaps a comical exaggeration of differences."

The famed film director's observation is spot on. All over the world people like to make fun of their neighbors on the other side of the border. My Canadian friends, for instance, take enormous delight in explaining the difference between Canadians and Americans. "A Canadian is an American *with* health insurance, but *without* a handgun." And of course Swedes take equal delight in calling Danes "Latins of the North" while the Danes gleefully dub Swedes "Prussians of the North."

You want more comical exaggeration? Here are typical examples from C.R. Svensson's *Culture Shock! Sweden* (Time Books International). The author tells us about a Swedish TV ad for Viking Lotto which purports to show the reactions of winners from Nordic countries. "The Danes are out at a restaurant, celebrating lustily with food and drink ... Meanwhile the Swede who won is sitting on the couch in his living room, surrounded by his family. As the winning numbers come on the television, he says in a moderately pleased voice, 'Well, it looks like I won.' His wife says, 'Well done' and smiles to herself, and the family settles back to watching television."

Then the author relates a joke (told by Swedes on themselves) about two Danes, two Norwegians, two Finns and two Swedes stranded on four separate islands: "By the time they are all rescued the Danes have set up a cooperative, the Norwegians are out fishing, the Finns have cut down all the trees and the Swedes are still waiting to be introduced."

We all know that comic hyperbole frequently contains a kernel of truth. Many Swedes see Danes as "relaxed, casual, cheerful and fun-loving." Perhaps that stereotype is simply the flip side of the way Danes see Swedes, describing them as "boring, humorless, gloomy, uptight party-poopers."

But watch out! My Italian and Greek friends wickedly characterize both Danes and Swedes as boring and uptight – anything but relaxed and fun-loving.

Which is just one more proof that cultural differences are largely a matter of perception. And perception changes according to one's angle of vision, doesn't it?

So when Swedes chide Danes for being "sloppy, undisciplined, often late for meetings and disdainful of rules," that might be the obverse of how some Swedes see themselves: as over-regulated, clock-obsessed citizens of a land where everything is forbidden.

For years I used to wonder why Swedes label (should I say 'libel'?) Danes as greedy merchants: shrewd business negotiators who never see a contract as final – "an agreement in Denmark is always open to renegotiation" – and who "are able to lie to Swedes twice as well as Swedes can lie to Danes."

Then at a recent meeting in Scandinavia a perceptive Swedish woman suggested an answer. She believes that old stereotype reflects Swedish companies' lack of careful preparation for business negotiations with their Danish cousins. The Swedes think, "Why bother? We speak practically the same language, share the same basic values." Then when Swedes get the short end of the deal they blame the unsatisfactory outcome on Danish shrewdness and sharp practices.

Of course, if those disappointed negotiators had bothered to prepare properly, the way they would have for a session with Japanese, say, or Chinese, the result would have been more favorable. That explanation makes sense to me. Over the years I've observed a similar attitude on the part of many U.S. business people when they sit down at a conference table with British counterparts. Some Yanks are easily lulled into complacency, thinking "Hey guys, this will be a snap – just like at home."

I've also been intrigued about why many Swedes characterize Danes as 'better liars'. Makes me think of that old saying in my country, "diplomats are people sent abroad to lie for their country." But it also reminds me of another old saying I've heard many times in Copenhagen: "It takes two Danes to outwit one Dutchman at the bargaining table."

We know that stereotypes and humorous exaggerations generally grow from a speck of truth, something like pearls growing around a grain of sand. As a long-time observer of the Nordic scene I would agree that a certain cultural distance separates Swedes and Danes. But just how big and important are the differences? Consider for a moment how outsiders view these two Scandinavian cultures.

Southern Europeans and most Americans for example are always impressed with the modesty and moderation of Nordic peoples. Americans are famous all over the world for boasting and blowing their own horn. Mark Twain had a lot to say about that in the 1900s; it's still very true today.

In fact, on this cultural trait Americans and Scandinavians are positioned at opposite ends of a continuum. Many Danes and Swedes are so modest they have trouble getting promoted in U.S. companies, where hot air often provides the tailwind needed to boost you up the corporate ladder. The human resources manager of one New York company once told me that most of her firm's Danish and Swedish employees need "assertiveness training."

Now, in a moment of weakness I might be persuaded that some Swedes take moderation to the extreme, given their quiet obsession with *lagom*. But seen from outside Norden the differences between Danes and Swedes are almost imperceptible.

How about punctuality? People in both these Nordic lands are sticklers for being on time, the Swedes perhaps a bit more so. But I disagree with those who say Swedes are even more-clock obsessed than the Germans or the German-Swiss.

At a Copenhagen seminar I was conducting in early 2001 a Danish export marketer related an experience he had with German *Pünktlichkeit* after a trade show in Hannover. He and a colleague had agreed to met two German counterparts at a hotel at 14:00. Because of unusually heavy traffic that afternoon the Danes arrived in the hotel lobby at 14:05, to be told the Germans had already left. Seems that since the Danes hadn't used their mobile to report the five-minute delay, their German customers assumed they weren't coming.

In contrast, while the Swedes are known for valuing punctuality I've never heard of a Swede walking out because they were kept waiting for a few minutes. Like most people I try hard to be on time for a meeting anywhere in the world: it shows respect for the people we are dealing with. But both Danes and Swedes belong with the group of cultures anthropologist Edward T. Hall calls very monochronic (time-conscious): primarily northern Europeans, North Americans, Australians and New Zealanders.

Any slight variation in time-consciousness between Swedes and Danes shrinks to nothing when compared to the time behavior of polychronic cultures – societies where people and relationships are far more important than clocks. Having lived twice in India and having done business in places like Egypt, Pakistan and Thailand, I'm quite used to waiting 45 minutes or an hour for my local counterparts to show up for a meeting.

One time in Brazil I was invited to dinner at 8:00 pm.. Arriving around 8:30 I found my hostess still in the shower. Why? Because in that polychronic culture, a dinner invitation for eight o'clock in the evening really means "please come at 9:30."

Now THAT experience, dear reader, represents a serious difference in cross-cultural time behavior. So please don't talk to me about intra-Nordic variations. Maybe some Swedes are marginally more punctual than some Danes. But viewed from Mumbai or Mexico City, the people of both cultures definitely qualify as clock-worshipers.

The similarities loom even larger when we look at the really important issues. Both Scandinavian peoples are world-renowned for their broad and deep democratic values, their concern for the environment and for their international humanitarian activities. Both are havens for refugees and both are experiencing anti-refugee backlash from some of their citizens.

The people of both societies are nominally Lutheran but rarely attend church, proudly display their respective national flags, go to great lengths to avoid conflict and confrontation, espouse the Scandinavian model of management and are relentlessly egalitarian. With similarities like that, how important can a few subtle cultural differences be? So what if Swedes talk a lot about 'lagom' while Danes emphasize *hygge*?

For me, you see, it's like the question of whether the glass is half-full or half-empty. And when it's snaps, make mine a full glass please!

The Finnish Negotiator

This small Nordic country is an increasingly attractive market despite its meager population of just over five million inhabitants. One reason is Finland's high per capita income, making it a good market for quality consumer goods. But the country's trading contacts with Russia and the Baltic countries also make Finland a good base for marketing to these growth markets.

Language of Business. Some business people are concerned about dealing with Finland because they anticipate communication problems, knowing that the Finnish language is unrelated to the Western European languages. However, while Finnish belongs to the Finno-Ugric rather than the Indo-European language family, today Finns learn Swedish, German and English in school, and many speak French or Spanish, and other languages as well.

Of course when communicating with non-native speakers of English it is always wise to speak slowly and clearly and to check for understanding. However, the Finns' linguistic skills have largely erased the communication barrier. And in case an interpreter is needed your local counterpart will have no difficulty providing one.

Initial Contact. Send a letter or fax in English with information about your company and your product or service, follow up with a phone call. If your potential customer, supplier or partner is interested, agree on a date and time for a visit and then confirm these arrangements in writing.

Traveling to Helsinki is easy. No vaccination is required and the water is safe to drink. And though the winters can be bitterly cold, Finnish hospitality is always warm and gracious.

Meeting Protocol. At first acquaintance Finns tend to be somewhat reserved and formal by the standards of more emotionally expressive cultures. However, they lose some of this reserve after you get to know them. The dress code for men is suit and tie, for women a suit or dress. Use last names plus any academic or professional title until your local counterpart suggests moving to a first-name basis.

Punctuality is very important for social encounters as well as for business meetings. As for small talk, conversational topics to avoid include politics, jobs and money – and be wary of too many negative comments about the weather.

Shake hands with both men, women and older children when meeting and departing, but avoid further physical contact. Finns do not appreciate arm-grabbing and back-slapping. They also tend to be relatively taciturn and soft-spoken, and avoid showing emotion in public. Interrupting another person during a conversation is considered rude.

Nonverbal Communication. It is polite to maintain eye contact with the person you are speaking to. When seated, men should avoid crossing their legs in such a way that an ankle rests on the other leg. When standing it is impolite to talk with hands in one's pockets or with arms folded; the former posture is too casual, the latter indicates arrogance.

Wining and Dining. "Power breakfasts" have not caught on in this northern outpost. For lunch and dinner, Finnish formality extends to table manners. Be as prompt as you are for a business meeting. Men keep their jackets on throughout the meal unless the host removes his.

Do not start eating until your host or hostess has begun, and remember not to touch your wine glass until the host offers a toast. Speaking of which, in contrast to some other European cultures you do not propose a toast to the host or hostess.

Be sure to avoid picking up food with your fingers. This taboo extends even to fresh fruit. For example, spear an apple with a fork and peel it elegantly with your knife. Among the special local dishes worth trying are reindeer steak and fresh wild berries. Don't miss the cloudberries, for example.

Be prepared for plenty of liquid accompaniment to the food. Finns especially enjoy vodka and beer, but wine is becoming more popular as import duties have been reduced.

You will find that just because Finns tend to be somewhat formal at table does not mean they are stiff or unfriendly. They are gracious and generous hosts. Spouses (and children) are usually included in meal invitations. You are encouraged to take seconds, but do finish whatever is on your plate. And when the check arrives, remember there are no 'Dutch treats' in Finland: the person who invites pays the whole check.

Buffet Behavior. If you are invited to a smorgasbord or buffet meal it may be a good idea to let your host or hostess lead the way. In any case, here is the correct way to attack the buffet table:

- Start with the potatoes and cold fish, often herring. This may be washed down with a small glass or two of 'snaps', the local firewater.
- Then you take a fresh plate and dig into the salads and the cold roasted and smoked meats.
- Next another clean plate for whatever hot dish may be on offer.
- After that come the cheese and fruit courses. Coffee is served after the meal, and only after the coffee do you start talking business.

Tipping. Here the rules are simple. Restaurant checks normally include the tip in a 15% service charge, but you may wish to leave the small change. In taxis it is enough to let the driver keep the small change. However, do tip porters, doormen and coat checkers.

Gift Giving. Imported liquor is expensive in Finland so consider bringing a bottle or two in with you to give as gifts. If invited home for dinner, cut flowers in an uneven number make a fine hostess gift. Avoid white and yellow flowers as too funereal, and a huge bouquet as too ostentatious.

Your Presentation. Since Finns avoid displays of emotion in public, don't expect them to wax enthusiastic when you present your product or project. Prepare a methodical, well-organized presentation with plenty of facts, figures and documentation. Be careful of hype and exaggerated claims. Use handouts and slides or overheads for numbers and the most important points.

Negotiating Style. It would be unwise to build a wide bargaining margin into your initial offer. Finns do not appreciate bazaar haggling. Open with a realisitic bid and be prepared to adjust price or terms in response to proposals from your counterpart. Decision-making in

Finland is a methodical, deliberate process. Expect your local partners to take a bit more time than you would find normal back home.

Business Ethics. This is one of the reasons doing business in Finland is such a pleasure. You are most unlikely to run into demands for bribes or 'facilitation' payments.

Business Hours. Offices are open Monday through Friday from 8:00 or 8:30 am to 4:00 or 4:30 pm. Banks open for business at 9:30 am and close at 4:00 pm Monday through Friday. You can shop the stores starting at 9:00 am Monday through Saturday and until 5:00 pm Tuesday through Thursday, 8:00 pm on Mondays and Fridays and 2:00 pm Saturdays. Remember that most businesses close at 1:00 pm on workdays before a holiday.

Major Holidays and Festivals. Don't expect to do business on the following dates:

January 1	New Year's Day
Shrove Tuesday	Seven weeks before Easter
Easter	Two days
April 30	May Day Eve
May 1	*Vappu* or May Day
November 2	All Saints Day
December 6	Independence Day
December 24/25	Christmas Eve and Christmas Day
December 26	St. Stephen's Day
December 31	New Year's Eve.

Finns take their summer vacation any time from mid-June until late August.

The German Negotiator

There are north/south and east/west differences in German business customs, not to mention individual variations. Keeping this in mind, the following profile describes the important general tendencies in business behavior you are likely to encounter whether your meeting takes place in Hamburg or Munich, Leipzig or Cologne.

Language of Business. Many German business people are comfortable conducting business in English. Larger companies normally have competent English speakers on staff. However, since the language of business is the language of the customer, a professional export sales team should include a fluent speaker of German.

Deal-Focus. Germans tend to be deal-focused in business, generally ready to negotiate based on the perceived merits of the deal. They do not usually feel the need to develop a close personal relationship before talking business. Rapport-building takes place while the two sides are discussing the deal. Visiting negotiators can usually expect to get down to business after a few minutes of general conversation.

Orientation to Time. Germans feel very strongly about punctuality. Being on time may actually mean arriving a few minutes early, because tardiness signals unreliability. If you are half an hour late for a meeting, your company may be half a month late with your delivery! Therefore, should you be unavoidably detained, be sure to phone your counterpart as soon as possible to reschedule the meeting. Schedules and meeting agendas are rigidly adhered to, and business meetings are rarely interrupted.

Expect to follow a prepared meeting agenda. Your meeting will seldom if ever be interrupted by phone calls or unscheduled visitors. In fact, in over a hundred meetings with Germans since 1963 I cannot recall a single instance of a serious interruption during a business discussion.

Formality, Hierarchy and Status. German society retains a level of social formality which is reflected in business protocol. Formal behavior is a way to show appropriate respect to people with high rank, professional titles and higher academic qualifications. This is important since more German managers have doctorates than anywhere else in the world. About 40% of the board members of the 100 largest corporations have a doctor's degree.

Address Dr. Wilhelm Schmidt as "Dr. Schmidt" or "Herr Doktor." His female colleague with a doctorate would be "Frau Doktor." It is polite to address less exalted business contacts with 'Herr', 'Frau' or 'Fräulein' followed by their last name, including secretaries. While U.S. secretaries for example are usually addressed by their first name, in Germany it is always 'Frau Braun,' not 'Waltraudt.' Women about 20 or older should be addressed as *Frau* whether married or single.

German formality is also expressed in meeting and greeting protocol. Handshakes are expected whenever you meet or leave someone. This greeting may not be accompanied with a smile: many Germans save their smiles for friends and family, regarding smiling at strangers as a silly mannerism.

Business Communication Style. Germans are relatively reserved, not given to enthusiastic public displays of emotion, although some southern Germans are a bit more expressive. As opposed to Latin Europeans and Latin Americans, Germans use few gestures or animated facial expressions, and avoid interrupting another speaker.

Verbal Communication. Clarity of understanding being the prime goal of communication for Germans, they pride themselves on speaking their mind. Whereas relationship-focused people often use indirect communication, Germans value direct, frank, even blunt language. Visitors from high-context cultures should realize that Teutonic bluntness and abruptness are not meant to offend them.

Nonverbal Communication

The Handshake. Expect a firm handshake (one or two vigorous pumps) with direct eye contact when meeting as well as when departing.

Gestures. Hand and arm gestures are restrained. It is rude (as well as against the law) to tap one's forehead while looking at another person.

Your Business Presentation

Content. Germans respond best to detailed presentations supported by copious facts. They look for plenty of history and background information rather than fancy visuals. Include thorough documentation.

Humor. Be wary of including jokes in your presentation. Humor rarely translates well and business presentations are a serious matter in Germany.

Negotiating Style

Bargaining Range. Most Germans respond better to realistic initial quotations than to the classic 'high-low' tactic. They may react negatively to what they perceive as bazaar haggling. Consider building a small margin into your opening bid to cover unexpected developments, but take care to avoid over-inflating your initial offer.

Negotiating Style. Like the Japanese, German negotiators are known for thorough preparation. They are also well known for sticking steadfastly to their negotiating positions in the face of persuasion and pressure tactics.

Decision-Making. Germans take time to deliberate and confer with responsible colleagues before making an important decision. Expect them to take more time than Americans but perhaps less than the Japanese and most other Asians.

Business Protocol

Dress Code. Suit and tie for men at least for the initial meeting, suit or dress for women. Germans tend to judge men by the condition of their footwear, so shoes should be clean and well polished.

Business Gifts. This is not a gift-giving culture. German negotiators are likely to feel uncomfortable if presented with an expensive gift. If you do wish to bring something small, choose a tasteful, quality logo gift or an item your country or region is famous for.

Wining and Dining. Germans tend to maintain a clear separation between their professional and private lives. Although they are excellent hosts, Germans may place less emphasis on business entertainment than visitors from relationship-focused cultures. Your German counterpart may not feel comfortable talking business over *Frühstück:* the "power breakfast" has yet to make an impact in the Federal Republic. When you go out to lunch or dinner, expect to talk business before or after rather than during the meal, unless your local counterpart takes the initiative.

Social Etiquette

Dinner Invitation. If invited to a German home for dinner, be sure to accept. Avoid arriving early but do show up within ten or 15 minutes of the time given.

Hostess Gifts. Avoid bringing wine unless it is a good vintage from a top wine-producing area. Flowers make a good *Mitbringsel,* but avoid red roses (for lovers only) and canna lilies or chrysanthemums (for funerals only). Bring an uneven number (except for 6 or 12) but never 13, and remember to unwrap the bouquet before presenting it to your hostess. If those floral taboos have you confused, a box of high quality chocolates is always an excellent alternative.

Good Manners. A man precedes a woman when entering a bar, restaurant or other public place and walks to the lady's left when outdoors. It is polite to stand when a woman, older person or an individual of high rank enters the room.

Compliments. Germans tend to be uncomfortable with the effusive compliments that are common in some cultures, such as the U.S. Similarly, visiting foreigners are unlikely to be overwhelmed with flattery, with one major exception: Germans are quick to show appreciation for a visitor's efforts to speak their language.

Germans take business seriously. They expect their counterparts to do the same.

The Dutch Negotiator

The Netherlands is an attractive market for three main reasons. First, its 15 million inhabitants enjoy a high per capita income. Second, its central location within Europe makes the country a good entry point to the Continent and an excellent distribution center for the European Union. Third, the Dutch have been world traders for centuries – they really know how to do business

Let's take a look at the way the Dutch do business, highlighting those aspects most likely to trouble for visiting negotiators.

Language of Business. Even though most Dutch business people speak English fluently it is polite to offer to bring an interpreter to the first meeting, just in case. Nine times out of ten you will be told no interpreter will be needed.

Making Contact. Like other deal-focused people, the Dutch are quite open to doing business with strangers, including foreigners. Which means that once you have a name you can make direct contact with a potential customer or partner rather than arranging for someone to introduce you.

You may phone for an appointment and then confirm the arrangements in writing. Address the letter to the person you wish to see and include all the information your counterpart will need to prepare for the meeting. The letter should be formal, using the addressee's correct title. Give your counterpart several weeks' notice: impromptu meetings are not popular with the well-organized Dutch. Avoid July and August as well as the Christmas holiday season.

Business Protocol

Dress Code. Men should wear a suit or blazer and slacks, women neat business attire.

Punctuality. Perhaps the most important single rule of Dutch business protocol is to be on time for meetings. If you find that you are going to arrive late, phone the person you are scheduled to meet and explain the problem.

Meeting and Greeting. When introduced, repeat your name clearly while shaking hands. At gatherings where you introduce yourself, just give your last name. It's unnecessary to say "Hello" or "How are you?" Your handshake should be firm and accompanied with strong eye contact. Be sure to shake hands again when you leave. Men wait for women to offer their hand. At a social gathering, it is polite to shake hands with the children as well as the adults you meet.

Names and Titles. Visitors from informal cultures such as Denmark, Australia and the U.S. should remember to avoid using first names until their Dutch counterpart suggests it.

Small Talk. Remember that Holland refers to only a part of the country; the correct name is The Netherlands.

Women in Business. Although few local women have reached senior positions in Dutch companies, women business visitors should encounter no particular problems doing business in the Low Countries.

Communication Style

Expect a sober, somewhat reserved approach rather than an expressive manner until you get to know them. The Dutch sometimes accuse Americans for example of superficial friendliness. They also may not smile at people they have just met, preferring to maintain a certain polite reserve while they size you up.

Verbal Language. The Dutch value direct, straightforward language. They like to get right to the point, avoiding polite circumlocution. Their priority when communicating is always to be clearly understood.

This trait should not be a problem for negotiators from deal-focused, low-context cultures such as northern Europe and North America. However, when the Netherlanders mix directness with assertiveness it can be misunderstood. I have attended meetings in

Europe at which the legendary Dutch bluntness managed to offend one or two of the Yanks present.

The people of The Netherlands distrust flowery language and empty rhetoric. They want you to say what you mean and mean what you say. In sharp contrast with some other cultures, a Dutch 'yes' can be taken as a firm commitment. And when they mean 'no' they will say it quite plainly, rather than mincing words to spare your feelings.

Despite their facility with English the Dutch occasionally get their numbers turned around. For example, they may quote you $53,000 but really mean $35,000, or vice versa. All discussions involving numbers and quantities should be carefully confirmed in writing to avoid confusion, but of course this is a good idea when doing business in any culture.

Nonverbal Communication

Interpersonal Distance. Expect your counterparts to stand and sit about an arm's length apart from each other.

Touch Behavior. This is a low-contact culture. Until you become good friends avoid slapping a Dutchman on the back or seizing his upper arm to display friendliness. In fact, it's a good idea to avoid any physical contact beyond the handshake.

Gaze Behavior. Maintain steady, moderate eye contact across the conference table. Some visitors from East Asia may find Dutch eye contact more intense than they are accustomed to.

Gestures. Body language in the Low Countries is less expressive than that of southern Europe and Latin America. It is also less casual than in some more informal cultures such as the U.S. and Australia. American men need to remember to keep their hands out of their pockets when talking to Dutch people, even in a relaxed social situation.

If you have done business in France or Italy you have probably learned that tapping your head while looking at someone means you think they are crazy or stupid. (In Germany in fact this rude gesture is actually illegal: if the police catch you doing it you will be socked with a heavy fine.)

So it's important to understand that if your Dutch counterpart taps the right side of his head while looking your way it actually has the opposite meaning: he is complimenting you on your intelligence. (Had your contact wanted to impugn your sanity he would have pointed his forefinger at the middle of his forehead. Or perhaps grabbed at an imaginary fly in front of his face!)

The Dutch Negotiating Style

Your Presentation. Like many other business people, the Dutch are put off by hard sell tactics and hype. Prepare a straightforward presentation, making sure that every claim you make is fully supported by the facts. On the other hand, there is no need to understate or to downplay the benefits of your proposal. Just be as factual as possible, even at the risk of being slightly boring. To your Dutch counterpart, business is inherently interesting. There is no need to put on an American-style "dog and pony show" to hold your audience's attention.

Bargaining Behavior. Expect your counterparts to be shrewd negotiators. Don't insult their intelligence by heavily padding your opening offer in the expectation of granting generous concessions later. Just as most Dutch negotiators want to get down to business quickly and avoid lengthy preliminaries, they also value a realistic bargaining range. Within Europe the Dutch are know to be tenacious and persistent, at times perhaps even a wee bit stubborn at times. When things get tense at the negotiating table take care not to raise your voice: this would definitely be counter-productive.

Decision-Making. Dutch negotiators rarely make snap judgments but neither do they agonize unnecessarily over business decisions. Allow a little more time than you would expect in New York or Chicago.

Business Gifts. The Netherlands is not a gift-giving business culture. If you do wish to bring something small, choose a tasteful logo gift or an inexpensive item your country or region is famous for and present it at the end of the meeting.

Wining and Dining. Remember that the expression "going Dutch" reflects an important local custom. Unless you have been unambiguously invited as a guest, be prepared to pay for your share of any restaurant meal. If your counterpart has treated you to lunch or dinner, be sure to reciprocate as soon as it is practical.

A female business visitor entertaining her local male counterparts normally encounters little serious resistance when she insists on picking up the check, especially if she pays with a credit card.

The Dutch normally drink wine with lunch or dinner unless eating Chinese, Indian or Indonesian food, when beer is usually the beverage of choice.

Social Etiquette

Manners. When outdoors it is polite for men to walk on the street side. This custom arose as a way of protecting the lady from the mud splashed up by passing carriages. In today's Amsterdam it is a good way of preventing a thief on a motorbike from grabbing the woman's handbag.

As a Dinner Guest. Since business entertainment in the Netherlands normally takes place at restaurants, an invitation to dinner at home is a very friendly gesture. Do send or bring flowers for the hostess, remembering that red roses are for lovers and white lilies are for funerals.

Avoid bringing a bottle of wine for the host: some hosts would take it as a comment on the inadequacy of their cellar.

If your host picks you up at your hotel, it is acceptable to ask him to stop at a florist shop on the way. Do unwrap the bouquet before handing it to your hostess.

Men stand until the ladies are seated, and everyone waits for the hostess to start eating. Keep both hands above the table. Plan to stay for an hour and a half or so after dinner.

The Czech Negotiator

The Czech Republic is the western-most Slavic country, bordering both Germany and Austria. So it's hardly a surprise that the Czechs are the most westernized of the Slavic peoples, often dubbed "the Germans of East Central Europe." The latter comparison however is one not all Czechs find flattering: the Nazi occupation left enduring wounds in this country.

Nevertheless, Czech values, attitudes and beliefs have been influenced by German culture in various ways. First of all there were the centuries of Austro-German Habsburg rule. Second, the presence of German-speaking people living in Bohemia (*Böhmen*), the western-most province of the Czech lands. And then, between the wars and especially again after 1989, came the flood of German trade, tourism, and investment.

Thus, geography and history have combined to make the Czechs the most transaction-oriented business people among East Central Europeans. They are relatively willing to talk business with strangers and usually quick to get down to business. Their communication style tends to be more reserved than that of their more outgoing, expressive Polish and Hungarian neighbors.

Today the Czechs, along with the Poles and Hungarians, are leading East Central Europe back into the modern world. Investment and knowhow from Western Europe and other sources is a key factor in stimulating the recovery.

Language of Business. While the national language is Czech, younger business people are likely to speak English or German, frequently both. Still, wise visitors ask their local counterparts whether an interpreter will be needed, because older managers may not speak foreign languages. French is not as popular as it was between the wars, and Russian is definitely passé.

Deal-Focused Business Behavior. Most Czech companies today are relatively open to contact from foreigners. As noted above, they tend to get down to business without the elaborate preliminaries expected in relationship-oriented cultures. In fact, some Czechs note that even Americans, so famous for their "Let's get down to business!" approach, at times engage in too much small talk.

Verbal Directness. Visiting negotiators can usually expect to encounter the same frank verbal communication characteristic of northern Europe. Urban Czechs are almost as direct as the Germans, Dutch and Swiss-Germans.

Formality, Status and Hierarchies. Czechs are likely to be more formal than North Americans, Scandinavians, or Australians. Business behavior is more akin to that of the French, Germans and British than that of the informal Danes, for instance. Formality is expressed in meeting-and-greeting rituals as well as in the way business people dress. Hierarchical values are evident in the top-down approach to management and in the scarcity of women executives.

Visiting businesswomen will encounter rather traditional attitudes towards gender roles. But once a business woman has established her professional credentials, she will be taken as seriously as she would be in most of Europe.

Time Behavior. Visitors are expected to be on time for meetings and can expect the same of their local counterparts. Business meetings usually run without serious interruptions. On the other hand, negotiations often last longer than they would in markets such as the U.S. or Germany. Wary after decades of semi-isolation from the global marketplace, many Czechs take their time in sizing up potential foreign business partners before coming to a decision.

Reserved Communication. Business visitors from expressive cultures must be prepared for a more restrained manner than they may be used to. Czechs tend to avoid open displays of emotion. Negotiators accustomed to dealing with northern Europeans will find few surprises in this regard.

Paraverbal and Nonverbal Behavior

If your local counterparts suddenly become very quiet or avoid eye contact at the negotiating table, you know you have stepped on their toes. To get back on track, make a light-hearted remark, perhaps a self-deprecatory one.

Other tips:
- Keep your voice down. Czechs are put off by loud voices; avoid histrionics and table-pounding.
- Maintain an interpersonal distance of between 15 to 25 inches (25 to 40 cm).
- Use little touch behavior. Czechs avoid physical touching except for the handshake.
- Expect moderate eye contact. You will encounter a direct gaze across the negotiating table, perhaps less intense than in the Middle East and southern Europe, but more direct than is considered polite in East and Southeast Asia.

Business Protocol and Etiquette

Making Contact. Make appointments by telephone, fax or email about two weeks in advance. Corresponding in English is quite acceptable, although taking the trouble to have your letter translated into Czech will really impress your prospective customer or business partner. Best times for business meetings: between 9:00 am and noon and from 1:00 to 3:00 pm.

Dress Code. Dark suits and ties for men, conservative dresses or suits for women.

Meeting and Greeting. In a business situation, say "dobry den'" ("hello"), shake hands, make direct eye contact and state your full name. Formulas such as "How are you?" are unnecessary. Shake hands again when leaving the meeting. In social settings the verbal greeting often suffices; handshakes are unnecessary. Note: Whereas in many cultures men wait for women to extend their hand, in the Czech Republic the man often offers his hand to a woman first.

Forms of Address. When introduced, address your counterparts by their professional or academic title plus family name. Only relatives and close friends address each other by first names.

Exchanging Cards. Your cards should show your organizational title and any advanced degrees.

Topics of Conversation. Remember that Czechs consider their country part of Central Europe rather than of Eastern Europe. Referring to the Czech Republic as part of East-Central Europe is acceptable. Avoid references to politics in general and to the Communist era in particular. Good topics are football (soccer), ice hockey, hiking, biking and all kinds of music.

Gift Giving. While not expected, gifts of moderate value are welcome. Bring a bottle of good scotch or cognac, or small items such a quality pen or cigarette lighter. A bottle of imported wine or liquor is the best choice when invited to someone's home for a meal. In some circles, a bouquet of flowers may be considered inappropriate: flowers tend to carry a romantic connotation.

Negotiating Behavior

Expect slow, methodical progress. Your opening offer should be realistic: the 'high-low' tactic common in many business cultures will backfire with the Czechs. Patience and a soft-sell approach will get you the best results.

Group H

Deal-Focused – Informal – Monochronic – Variably Expressive

The Australian Negotiator

Making Contact. As in the deal-focused cultures of North America and northern Europe, Australian business people are usually quite willing to make appointments with people they know little about. Introductions and intermediaries are normally unnecessary; you can make direct contact. Send a letter, fax or e-mail with relevant information about your company and product, follow up with a phone call requesting a meeting. Another good way to make contact is at international trade shows.

Deal Focus. Australians are usually ready to get down to business shortly after meeting a prospective business partner for the first time. The elaborate preliminaries and extensive small talk expected throughout most of the Pacific Rim are out of place in Sydney or Perth. A few beers at a pub smooths the way to getting to know each other.

Communication Style

Verbal Language. Australian men tend to be less talkative and less demonstrative than their U.S. counterparts. Whereas American salespeople may be proud of their silver tongues, the Australians in contrast regard silence as golden. Aussies often employ understatement, and their dry humor features irony and sardonic wit.

One cultural characteristic which can cause problems for some visitors is the Australian penchant for vigorous argument. Negotiators who seek to downplay areas of disagreement and differences of opinion should prepare themselves for spirited verbal confrontation. Some first-time Asian visitors misinterpret this style of communication as provocative, even hostile. Those who have negotiated with the French are less likely to misunderstand this confrontational behavior.

Aussies can at times be even more direct than the Germans and the Dutch, not to mention Americans. Valuing frank and straightforward speech, they may be unaware that East and Southeast Asians visitors might find such directness offensive.

Informality and Egalitarianism. This may be the only culture in the world where business people interact even more informally than in Scandinavia, the Midwestern United States, or Western Canada. Australians perceive many Americans as overly concerned with status distinctions based on academic degrees, wealth and position in the corporate hierarchy.

Business visitors should avoid trying to impress Aussies with titles and accomplishments. Anything smacking of boastfulness or showing off gives a negative impression. While Americans for example are taught to "blow your own horn" and "don't hide your light under a bushel," Australians learn that "the tall poppy gets cut down." People who boast or flaunt their success are considered obnoxious.

A good example of Australian egalitarianism is provided by seating etiquette in taxis. As is sometimes the case in Denmark, male passengers traveling alone are expected to sit next to the (male) driver as a sign that they do not regard themselves as above the taxi driver in social status. Women are exempt from the front-seat rule unless the driver is also female.

Speaking of gender: in contrast to Scandinavia, Australian egalitarianism does not necessarily extend to women in business. Female visitors should be prepared for behavior which they may perceive as chauvinistic or patronizing.

Orientation to Time. While definitely more time-conscious than most South and Southeast Asians, Australians tend to be less obsessed with time and schedules than Germans, Swiss, Americans, and Japanese. This somewhat relaxed attitude towards time is especially noticeable outside of Sydney. Sure, visitors are expected to be roughly on time for meetings, but few Aussies will get upset if you are a few minutes late.

The work pace in this part of the world is slower than that of New York, Hong Kong, Tokyo or Singapore. Local business people are likely to resent foreigners who try to hurry things along.

Paraverbal and Nonverbal Communication. Individual Australians vary from very expressive to quite reserved, depending partly on their particular ethnic background. For example, an Aussie of Greek or Italian ancestry is likely to use more and larger gestures, speak louder and interrupt others more often than their fellow countrymen whose forefathers came from Britain, Ireland, or Northern Europe.

Interpersonal Distance. As with northern Europeans, North Americans and East Asians, Aussies generally stand or sit about an arm's apart in a business situation. The normal interpersonal distance tends to be larger than it is with Arabs, southern Europeans and Latin Americans.

Touch Behavior. Expect less physical contact than is the case with Latin and Mediterranean cultures, but more than those of East and Southeast Asia.

Eye Contact. Maintain steady eye contact when conversing with your counterparts across the bargaining table. Good eye contact indicates interest and sincerity.

Gestures. Australians typically use fewer and smaller gestures than most Americans and southern Europeans.

Taboo Gestures. The 'thumbs-up' sign is considered obscene. Also rude is extending one's first and middle fingers with the palm facing in. It is impolite to point at someone with the index finger: use the whole hand instead. When you have a cold, avoid blowing your nose loudly. It is also impolite to sniffle repeatedly. The solution is to leave the room and blow your nose in privacy.

Queue Behavior. The Australians have inherited the British custom of forming lines and politely waiting one's turn.

Business Protocol and Etiquette

As one might expect in an informal culture, Australian protocol rituals are not elaborate. For business, men wear a suit or blazer and tie, often removing the jacket in the summer. Business women wear a dress or skirt and blouse.

Meeting and Greeting. Expect a firm handshake and direct eye contact. Some Australians believe a soft handshake reflects weakness, and that lack of a direct gaze indicates unreliability or dishonesty. A man should wait for a woman to offer her hand rather than holding out his hand.

Forms of Address. Use full names when you first meet but expect to move quickly to first names. Wait for your local counterpart to suggest switching to given names.

Business Cards. While it is customary to exchange cards, do not expect the two-handed ritual of the *meishi* commonly encountered in Japan and the rest of East Asia.

Topics of Conversation. The best choice is sports, especially water sports, Australian football, golf and tennis. Positive comments on local food, beer and wine are always welcome. Visitors should avoid invidious comparisons with elements of their own cultures. Also to be avoided are comments about hard one works; workaholics are pitied in this delightfully laid-back society.

Gift Giving. Australia is not a gift-giving business culture. If invited to dinner at home consider bringing either an item for which your city or region is famous or wine, flowers or chocolates.

Wining and Dining. "Tea" is the evening meal and "supper" a late-night snack. Don't expect to be invited to someone's home until you know them fairly well. After a big meal, avoid saying you are "stuffed"; this word has a vulgar connotation in Australia.

Pub Etiquette. You are expected to pay for a round for the group you are drinking with when it's your turn. Don't pay for a round out of turn. People who do this are regarded as show-offs.

Negotiating Style

Your Presentation. The general advice that "modesty is the best policy" applies especially to making sales presentations. Marketers find that the soft sell works better. Veterans of the Australian market have also learned not to over-praise their company's product. Here it's better to show the benefits and superiority of your product or service to the customer rather than talking about them. Whenever possible, let your documentation, testimonials and third-party reports speak for you.

Bargaining Range. Since Australians tend to dislike bazaar haggling, visiting negotiators will get better results by opening discussions with a realistic bid. The negotiating process may take more time than it would in the U.S., though less than in strongly relationship-focused markets such as China, Japan or Saudi Arabia.

The Canadian Negotiator

Canada's mosaic of cultures can complicate things just a bit for business visitors. You need to be aware of the cultural background of the business people you will be dealing with, be it Anglophone, Francophone, New Canadian, or other. New Canadians are recent immigrants from Hong Kong, Eastern Europe, and many other parts of the world. Due to space limitations this profile focuses on the negotiating behavior of the two major business cultures, those of English and French Canada.

Anglophone Canadian negotiators tend to be deal-focused, direct, moderately informal, very egalitarian, reserved and relatively time-conscious. Most French Canadians are a little more formal, moderately relationship-focused, hierarchical, emotionally expressive, and somewhat polychronic.

Mainstream U.S. negotiators are likely to find the business culture of English Canada similar to their own. The most obvious differences are that Anglophone Canadians are usually less expressive, less assertive, and a bit more formal and conservative than U.S. Americans.

On the other hand, Yanks may encounter larger cultural differences when doing business with French Canadians. The latter often come across as reluctant to deal with people they don't know, likely to go off on a tangent during meetings rather than getting straight to the point, overly formal, quick to argue, and sometimes quite emotional.

Languages of Business. English-speaking visitors from overseas find it easy to communicate with Anglophone Canadians. Fluency in French is an asset for those doing business in Quebec. However, good interpreters are easy to find in major business centers such as Montreal, Toronto and Vancouver.

Making Contact. In French Canada it's important to have connections. Cold calls do not usually get good results, so arrange to be introduced or meet potential business partners at trade shows.

In English Canada business people are more open to a direct approach, though of course a referral is useful. When contacting Anglophones, send a letter, fax or e-mail in English with basic information about your company and your product, indicating you will be in touch soon regarding a meeting. Then follow up with a phone call suggesting possible dates and ask your counterpart to suggest a time and place.

First Meeting. Whereas the deal-focused English Canadians are usually ready to get down to business quickly with a potential new business partner, Francophones normally prefer lengthier preliminaries. They want to know more about a prospective supplier or partner before talking specifics.

Orientation to Time. In both of Canada's mainstream business cultures visitors are expected to be on time for appointments. However, in most other respects French Canadians are less monochronic than their Anglo neighbors. Meeting agendas in Quebec tend to be flexible and schedules somewhat fluid.

Formality and Informality. Egalitarianism is a key value for English Canadians, many of whom are uncomfortable in the face of status distinctions and class differences. In this respect they differ noticeably from their British cousins.

Francophone Canadians in contrast tend to be somewhat more hierarchical, more in tune with the values of their mother country. Nevertheless, one's social class and family background are usually less important than in France. Visiting women executives are unlikely to face big obstacles to doing business anywhere in Canada.

Anglophones usually want to get on a first-name basis fairly quickly, even with people they have just met. This informality is a sign of friendliness and warmth. Visitors to French Canada will encounter a slightly greater degree of formality.

Communication Style. Low-context English Canadians tend to be more direct than high-context Francophones. Valuing a frank, straightforward exchange of information, Anglophones may be unaware that East and Southeast Asians for example can be offended by such directness.

Canadians may be confused by Asian and Middle Eastern negotiators who employ indirect, roundabout, ambiguous communication as a form of politeness.

French Canadians also often speak less directly than Anglophones. The Quebecois are also more emotionally expressive and extroverted than English Canadians, their expressiveness showing up in both paraverbal and nonverbal behavior. For example, Francophones tend to interrupt each other frequently, stand closer together, touch each other more often during conversations, and use more gestures and livelier facial expressions than their Anglophone neighbors.

English Canadians are more reserved. In the Western and Atlantic provinces the normal interpersonal distance in a business context is about an arm's length. People tend to stand and sit further apart than Arabs, southern Europeans and Latin Americans. Touch behavior tends to be moderate. That is, less physical contact than in Latin and Mediterranean cultures but much more than in East and Southeast Asia. Gestures and facial expression are more restrained than in Quebec, and people try to avoid interrupting each other in mid-sentence.

Negotiating Style

Your Presentation. Export salespeople used to the U.S. market should note that Canadians of both major business cultures prefer the soft-sell approach. They are likely to resent an overly-aggressive, pushy sales presentation. Avoid hype and overblown product claims.

Bargaining Range. Take care not to over-inflate your initial offer: Many Canadian buyers are turned off by the classic 'high-low' tactic. Instead, build a certain safety margin into your opening bid to cover unexpected developments, but avoid overdoing it.

Business Protocol and Etiquette

Dress Code. Male visitors should wear a suit or blazer with tie. Women may wear a suit, dress or skirt and blouse.

Forms of Address. In English Canada start out with Dr, Mr, Mrs, Miss or Ms. but be prepared for your counterpart to suggest switching to a first name basis soon after meeting you. Most Anglos are uncomfortable using honorifics and titles. Expect more formality in Quebec, though less than in France.

Meeting and Greeting. Visitors should expect a firm handshake and direct eye contact. Some Canadians believe that a soft handshake reflects weakness and that lack of direct eye contact signifies shiftiness or dishonesty. English Canadians shake hands less often than most Europeans. Their handshakes are quite brief compared to those of Latin Americans but firmer than East and Southeast Asians. French Canadians shake hands more often than Anglophones: when being introduced, when saying hello, and again when saying goodbye.

Gift Giving. Business gifts are given after a deal has been closed. But remember that expensive, ostentatious gifts are out of place in Canada. Better choices are tasteful logo gifts or an item your city, country or region is famous for. Asians should not be surprised if your counterpart unwraps the gift in your presence: that is the North American custom. Good hostess gifts are flowers, candy, wine, and special items from your country or region.

Wining and Dining. According to North American custom it is considered rude and aggressive to repeatedly insist that a guest eat and drink. This can be a problem for visitors from the Middle East and other parts of the world where the custom is to say "no thank you" two or three times before 'reluctantly' accepting the proffered food or drink. You should respond in the affirmative if you wish to have something that is offered. Do not assume you will be asked twice!

Americans, Anglophone Canadians, and Francophone Canadians. Our son Reed Gesteland, a software consultant based in Chicago, had an interesting experience in 2001 which allowed him to compare business and social behavior in Chicago, Toronto, and Montreal. He attended a series of meetings in the three cities which IBM hosted to promote networking among their business partners.

In Chicago and Toronto most of the attendees went to the buffet tables as soon as the event started, and almost all of them sipped soft drinks, although beer and wine were freely available. When the "open mike" session began, only a few participants volunteered to take the microphone and spent three to five minutes talking about their companies. The rest of them had to be coaxed to the mike. By 7:30 pm everyone had left.

What a difference in Montreal! The attendees stood around chatting amiably and drinking red wine; no soft drinks were in evidence. (Reed learned later that soft drinks could be requested.) As soon as the open mike session began, the participants volunteered to speak right away, one after the other. No one needed to be coaxed, and each one rattled on at great length until gently cut off by the emcee. When people sat down to listen to the speakers, they all crowded together instead of leaving every other chair vacant, as the attendees had done in Chicago and Toronto. And the group stayed around drinking red wine until the room was closed at about 9:15 pm.

Reed's observations clearly illustrate some of the cultural differences between the expressive French Canadians and their more reserved U.S. and Anglophone Canadian counterparts. The former loved to talk at great length, stood and sat close to each other, drank wine rather than soft drinks, and networked until 9:15 instead of slipping away by 7:30.

For business visitors from outside North America, I suppose the basic point is that in certain respects English Canadians may have more in common with U.S. Americans than with their French Canadian compatriots. But watch out! One of our Canadian friends recently assured me there are two major differences between Canadians and Americans. "Well, what are they?" I asked innocently.

"Oh," replied my Canuck buddy with a grin, "A Canadian is an American *with* health insurance, but *without* a handgun."

The U.S. Negotiator

Properly speaking, all citizens of North and South American countries are Americans. However, since there is no other convenient way of referring to U.S. citizens we use 'American' to refer to people from the United States.

The USA is a multi-ethnic, multiracial, multi-cultural society. Despite this diversity, there is a mainstream U.S. business culture. For example, you can expect most American negotiators to be reasonably time-conscious ("Time is money"), deal-focused ("Let's get down to business"), and informal ("What's your first name?").

The language of business is American English. Very few Americans speak a foreign language well enough to handle a complex business negotiation. If your English is not adequate, consider hiring an interpreter or asking your U.S. counterpart to do so.

Making Contact. Perhaps because the USA is an immigrant society with a high degree of geographical mobility, most urban Americans are used to doing business with strangers. If you can't easily obtain a referral or introduction, you can usually approach your prospective counterpart directly, without going through an intermediary. The more well-known is your company or organization, the easier it is to make direct contact.

Send a letter, fax or e-mail in English with basic information about your company and your product, stating that you will be in touch regarding an appointment. Follow this with a phone call requesting a meeting two or three weeks hence. Your counterpart will suggest a time and place.

Deal Focus. Americans are usually ready to "get down to brass tacks" shortly after meeting a potential business partner for the first time. It's not that U.S. negotiators are unaware of the importance of getting to know their counterpart, of building a relationship. It's just that task-focused Yanks prefer to build trust and rapport while business discussions are proceeding.

Orientation to Time. Coming from a monochronic culture, Americans treat time as a tangible asset which can be saved, spent, lost, found, invested and wasted. Northerners tend to be more concerned about punctuality and schedules than Southerners, but few Americans are as time-conscious as Germans and German-Swiss.

Informality. Because a key U.S. value is egalitarianism, Americans tend to feel uncomfortable in the face of overt status distinctions except those based on individual achievement. However, formality does vary by corporate culture. In large companies such as IBM and GM, lower-ranking employees defer noticeably to high-ranking executives.

The relative lack of status distinctions is reflected in the breezy informality for which Americans are famous. They want to get on a first-name basis quickly, even with people they have just met. Informality is meant to show friendliness and warmth. Business visitors from more formal cultures should realize that easy familiarity is not intended to show disrespect.

Communication Style

Depending on ethnic and regional background as well as individual personality, U.S. negotiators vary in the way they communicate. But in general, Americans may appear more expressive and extroverted compared to East Asians and northern Europeans, while at the same time they are perceived as distant and introverted by Latin Europeans and Latin Americans.

Verbal Communication. Most Americans speak much more directly than Arabs or people from East and Southeast Asia, but less directly than Germans and German-Swiss. They tend to be suspicious of negotiators who prefer indirect, ambiguous communication. On the other hand, Americans may also be offended by the direct, blunt language favored by Germans and Dutch.

Paraverbal Communication. Many U.S. negotiators speak louder at the bargaining table than people from more reserved cultures. Uncomfortable with silence, they may also feel compelled to quickly fill in any gaps in the conversation – behavior which Japanese for example find offensive. Americans know it is rude to interrupt others in mid-sentence; if they do this anyway in the course of a lively discussion, no offense is intended.

Nonverbal Communication

Meeting and Greeting. Expect a firm handshake and direct eye contact. Some Americans believe a soft handshake reflects weakness and that lack of a direct gaze indicates unreliability or dishonesty. In the U.S. people shake hands less often than most Europeans. Their handshakes are quite brief compared to those of Latin Americans but firmer than East and Southeast Asians.

The normal interpersonal distance in a business context is about an arm's length, similar to the norm in northern Europe.

Touch behavior varies from moderate to relatively high-contact : Less physical contact than is the case with Latins and Mediterranean cultures but more than East and Southeast Asians. American business men may slap each other on the back and grab one another by the elbow or upper arm to express friendliness.

Business Protocol

Dress Code. While the proper attire varies according to location and type of business, visitors are well advised to wear a suit and tie to the first meeting with most new contacts.

Meeting and Greeting. Expect a firm handshake and a direct gaze. Americans sometimes offer their card at the end of the meeting rather than at the beginning.

Forms of Address. Follow the lead of the people you are meeting. A general rule is to start out with Mr, Mrs., Miss or Ms. but to be prepared for your counterpart to switch immediately to first names. If such informality makes you uncomfortable, make it quite clear how you wish to be addressed. Titles are likely to be ignored except in formal meetings unless you are a medical doctor or high government official. With those exceptions, most Americans are uncomfortable with honorifics and titles.

Gift Giving. The U.S. business world is not a gift-giving culture. Many American negotiators feel uncomfortable if presented with an expensive gift. If you do wish to bring something small, choose a tasteful logo gift or an item your country or region is famous for. A hostess gift of flowers, candy or wine is appreciated, but not expected, when invited to someone's home for dinner.

Wining and Dining: If invited to that American specialty, the cocktail party, expect to mix informally with a large number of complete strangers, often without introductions by host or hostess. It is appropriate to approach individuals and groups with a smile and introduce yourself.

Negotiating Style

Your Presentation. Americans respond best to brisk, factual presentations delivered by a competent speaker of English and enlivened by visual aids where appropriate. They may interrupt with questions rather than hold their questions until the end.

Bargaining Range. U.S. negotiators experienced in international business are used to a wide variation in bargaining ranges. Expect them to test your opening offer for flexibility. They may respond better to realistic quotations than to the overused high-low tactic. Build a safety margin into your opening bid to cover unexpected developments, but avoid over-inflating your offer.

Concession Behavior. Be prepared for some hard bargaining. Take care to make each concession with great reluctance, and then only on a strict "if ... then," conditional basis. Always demand something of equivalent value in return.

Ploys and Counter-ploys. A favorite American bargaining tactic is time pressure: "Next week our prices are going up seven percent ..." The best way to counter this ploy is to simply ignore it.

Another favorite ploy is to ask for quotations on a sliding scale by quantity. For example, say you quote prices based on 1000, 10,000 and 50,000 units. Your U.S. counterpart is then likely to ask for 12,500 units, but at the low price you quoted for 50,000. Counter this ploy by smiling and repeating that the lower price is valid only for orders of the indicated quantity.

You may also encounter the Trial Order gambit in which your potential customer demands your lowest price even for a small 'test' order. If you are tempted to buy this customer's business with a low 'introductory' offer, you can expect to have trouble later when you try to move him up to the normal price.

Decision-Making. American negotiators are probably the fastest decision makers in the world, and proud of it. Some U.S. executives live by the motto, "Right or wrong, but never in doubt." Expect expressions of impatience if your decision-making process seems to be taking too much time.

The Contract. Expect heavy emphasis on the legal aspects and the fine points of the written agreement. Many U.S. negotiators include lawyers in the discussions from the start until the signing ceremony. They often bring a draft agreement to the bargaining table and proceed to negotiate clause by clause. Should a dispute or disagreement arise later, the American side may rely strictly on the terms of the contract and become suspicious if their counterpart invokes non-contract issues such as the importance of the long-term relationship.

Resource List

Series

The *Culture Shock!* series now covers most of the countries included
in this book. Times Books International, Singapore and Kuala
Lumpur. Especially useful for expatriate preparation, the individual volumes vary as to their usefulness for visiting businesspeople.

Ravette Publishing Limited, Horsham, West Sussex, England puts out
a series of small books that are especially appealing to readers who
like their intercultural information spiced with wit. Look for *The
Xenophobe's Guide To ...*

Global Focus
Axtell: *Do's and Taboos Around the World.* John Wiley & Sons, 3rd ed.
1993.
Do's and Taboos of International Trade. Wiley, 2nd edition 1994.
Do's and Taboos of Hosting International Visitors. Wiley, 1990.
GESTURES: Do's and Taboo's of Body Language. Wiley, 1991.

Brake, Walker and Walker: *Doing Business Internationally.* Irwin, New
York, 1995.
Lewis: *When Cultures Collide.* Nicholas Brearly Publishing, London,
1996.
Morrison, Conaway, Borden: *Kiss, Bow or Shake Hands?* Adams Me-
dia Corp. (USA) 1994.

Regional Focus: ASIA and the PACIFIC RIM
Bosrock: *Put Your Best Foot Forward – ASIA.* IES, St. Paul MN, 1994.
Dunung: *Doing Business in Asia.* New York, Lexington Books 1995.

Japan
Kenna and Lacy: *Business Japan.* Passport Books, USA 1994.
Rowland: *Japanese Business Etiquette.* Warner Books, New York 1985.
Zimmerman: *How to Do Business in Japan.* Random House, New york
1985.

China

Fang: *Chinese Business Negotiating Style.* Sage Publications, Thousand Oaks CA: 1998.

Hu and Grove: *Encountering the Chinese.* Intercultural Press, Yarmouth ME, 1991.

Kenna and Lacy: *Business China.* Passport Books, USA 1994.

Schneiter: *Getting Along with the Chinese.* Asia 2000 Ltd, Hong Kong 1992.

Seligman: *Dealing with the Chinese.* Mercury Books, London.

Wang, Brislin, Wang, Williams and Chao. *Turning Bricks Into Jade.* Intercultural Press, Yarmouth ME, 2000.

South Korea

Current and Choi: *Looking At Each Other.* Seoul International Tourist Publishing, 1983.

Kohls: *Learning To Think Korean.* Intercultural Press, Yarmouth ME, 2001.

Taiwan

Kenna and Lacy: *Business Taiwan.* Passport Books, USA, 1994.

The Philippines

Andres: *Understanding Filipino Values.* New Day Publishers, Quezon City, Philippines: 1981.

Gochenour: *Considering Filipinos.* Intercultural Press, Yarmouth ME,1990.

Malaysia

Datin Noor Aini Syed Amir: *Malaysian Customs and Etiquette.* Times Books, Singapore, 1991.

Thailand

Fieg and Morelock: *A Common Core.* Intercultural Press, Yarmouth ME,1989.

Hollinger: *'Mai Pen Rai' Means Never Mind.* Asia Book Company Ltd, Bangkok 1977.

Holmes and Tangtontavy: *Working With The Thais.* White Lotus, Bangkok 1995.

Vietnam
Jamieson: *Understanding Vietnam*. University of California Press 1993.

Australia
Renwick: *A Fair Go for All*. Intercultural Press, Yarmouth ME, 1991.

Regional Focus: MIDDLE EAST and AFRICA
Devine and Braganti: *Traveler's Guide to Middle Eastern and North African Customs and Manners*. St. Martin's Press, NY 1991.
Nydell: *Understanding Arabs*. Intercultural Press, Yarmouth ME, 1987.
Patai: *The Arab Mind*. Hatherleigh Press, New York: Revised edition, 2002.

Regional Focus: EUROPE
Bosrock: *Put Your Best Foot Forward – EUROPE*. IES, St. Paul MN, 1994.
Mole: *Mind Your Manners*. Nicholas Brealey Publishing, London, 1995.

Great Britain
Smith: *Watch Your Step*. Hoest Sprog, Copenhagen, 1992.
Walmsley: *Brit-Think, Ameri-Think*. Penguin Books, 1987.

Netherlands
Bolt: *The Xenophobe's Guide to the Dutch*. Ravette, West Sussex UK 1995.
Vossestein: *Dealing With The Dutch*. Royal Tropical Institute, Amsterdam, 1997.
White and Boucke: *The UnDutchables*. White/Boucke Publishing, USA 1989.

France
Asselin and Marston: *Au Contraire!* Intercultural Press, Yarmouth ME, 2001.
Hall and Hall: *Understanding Cultural Differences*. Intercultural Press, USA 1990.
Platt: French Or Foe? Culture Crossings, Ltd., London, 2nd edition 1998.

Germany
Hall and Hall: *Understanding Cultural Differences.* Intercultural Press, USA 1990.
Nees: *Germany: Unraveling An Enigma.* Intercultural Press, Yarmouth ME, 2000.
Schmidt: *Understanding American And German Business Cultures.* Meridian World Press, Montreal, 2001.

Sweden
Robinowitz and Carr: *Modern-Day Vikings.* Intercultural Press, Yarmouth ME, 2001.

Finland
Dahlgren and Nurmelin: *Sauna, Sisu & Sibelius.* Yrityskirjat Oy, Finland, 1998.

Spain
Ames: *Spain Is Different.* Intercultural Press, Yarmouth ME, 1992.

Greece
Broome: *Exploring The Greek Mosaic.* Intercultural Press, Yarmouth ME, 1996.

Regional Focus: CENTRAL and EASTERN EUROPE
Richmond: *Understanding the Eastern Europeans.* Intercultural Press, Yarmouth ME, 1995.

Russia
Dabars: *The Russian Way.* Passport Books, Lincolnwood IL, 1997.
Richardson: *Russia: Survival Guide.* Russian Information Services Inc., 1995.
Richmond: *From Nyet to Da.* Intercultural Press, Yarmouth ME, 1992.

Poland
Chrulska: *Cultural Differences in International Business: A Comparative Analysis of the Polish Business Culture and the Business Cultures of Selected Trading Partners.* Unpublished MBA thesis at Gdansk Managers Training Foundation and Gdansk University, 2000.

Regional Focus: LATIN AMERICA

Devine and Braganti: *Latin American Customs and Manners.* St. Martin's Press, New York, 1988.

Mexico

Condon: *Good Neighbors: Communicating with the Mexicans.* Intercultural Press, Yarmouth ME, 1985.

Heusinkveld: *Inside Mexico.* John Wiley & Sons, New York 1994.

Kras: *Management in Two Cultures.* Intercultural Press, Yarmouth ME, 1989.

Moran and Abbott: *NAFTA: Managing The Cultural Differences.* Gulf Publishing Company, Houston TX, 1994.

Windsor: *The Complete Guide To Doing Business In Mexico.* AMACOM, New York, 1994.

Brazil

Harrison: *Behaving Brazilian.* Harper & Row, New York, 1983.

Oliveira: Brazil: *A Guide For Businesspeople.* Intercultural Press, Yarmouth ME, 2001.

Regional Focus: NORTH AMERICA

Lipset: *Continental Divide.* Routledge, New York, 1991.

United States of America

Althen: *American Ways.* Intercultural Press, USA 1988.

Hall and Hall: *Understanding Cultural Differences.* Intercultural Press, USA, 1990.

Lipset: *American Exceptionalism.* W.W. Norton & Company, New York, 1996.

Stewart: *American Cultural Patterns.* Intercultural Press, USA, 1972.